Barbara Swain's
COOKERY for 1 or 2

ANOTHER BEST-SELLING COOKERY VOLUME FROM H.P. BOOKS

Publisher: Helen Fisher; Editors: Judi Ellingson, Carlene Tejada; Senior Editor: Jon Latimer; Editor-in-Chief: Carl Shipman; Art Director: Don Burton; Book Design: Tom Jakeway; Book Assembly: Tom Jakeway, Laura Hardock; Typography: Cindy Coatsworth, Connie Brown; Food Stylists: Barbara Swain, Janet Pittman; Photography: George deGennaro Studios—Dennis Skinner, David Wong, Tom Miyasaki.

Published by H.P. Books, P.O. Box 5367, Tucson, AZ 85703   602/888-2150
ISBN: Softcover, 0-912656-95-6; Hardcover, 0-912656-96-4
Library of Congress Catalog Card Number, 78-60432 © 1978 Fisher Publishing, Inc.
Printed in U.S.A.

Cover Photo: Steak Diane, page 62, Potatoes Anita, page 99, and Broccoli Polonaise, page 117, with French rolls.

Just for Us!

We've finally been discovered! For years, those of us who cook for just 1 or 2 have been virtually ignored. We've struggled with recipes, equipment and packaged goods designed for families of 4 or more. But our day has come! We've become a majority strong enough to get things OUR way!

This book is just for us. It's for those who have been dining alone or alone together all along, and those just entering the world of singles and couples. This cookbook is for people who used to cook for more and now, with their children gone, find that the old recipes don't work. And it's for those who have never cooked before, like newly marrieds, singles on their own or husbands waiting for working wives to get home. It's for all of us—the people with, believe it or not, the best opportunity to enjoy fine cookery to the fullest!

This book introduces an approach to cooking for 1 or 2 that has evolved out of years of trial and error, and the input from students and friends. It considers the fact that most of us are busy people with limited time, limited storage and somewhat unpredictable schedules. In brief, the theory is simply to buy the foods that make the most sense for small-quantity cooking, store them so they stay in top condition, and combine them creatively in an infinite number of ways.

I am not a gourmet—and I suspect I never will be. But I do enjoy having a certain amount of style and ceremony in my life, as long as it doesn't inconvenience me too often or cost too much. At that point my practical side looms up. Also, I love new experiences and I'll try almost any exotic new food or recipe. Based on this combination of characteristics I have selected several types of recipes for this book.

The Mainstay Recipes—These are the basic recipes made with the meat cuts, produce items and other ingredients that work best in small-quantity cooking. Recipes like omelets, Welsh Rabbit or Baked Custard can be whipped up from staple items when it seems there is nothing in the house to eat.

Restaurant Specialties—We associate certain recipes with fine restaurant fare too complex to make at home. Not so! They are often missing from home recipe collections only because they cannot be easily prepared for more than 1 or 2 at a time.

Leftover Users—Some recipes are ideal because they can absorb all sorts of leftovers and odds and ends. Soup stocks, bread dressings and crepes are stars of this category.

The Lead-Me-From-Temptation Recipes—I have consumed untold calories in my efforts to devise small-size recipes of such tempting foods as pancakes, cream puffs and cakes. The results I happily share with all who have little freezer space and even less will power.

Except for cakes and a few other recipes where "chemistry" determines success, feel free to make these recipes your own by varying them according to your preferences and the contents of your pantry. That's a great part of the fun of cooking. Many of the recipes are here primarily to share a basic technique that's particularly useful in small-quantity cooking. Variations or similar recipes are presented to get you started on your own creations.

The favorite classic and foreign recipes here are in fairly authentic form. I have modified some to save you from buying exotic ingredients or equipment you will rarely use.

The recipes for 1 can always be doubled to serve 2. Expect to use a larger pan and extend the cooking time in some cases. The recipes for 2 can usually be cut in half to serve 1. My decision to make a recipe to serve 2 usually rested on some ingredient that could not be cut in half or on the special nature of the dish that just called for it to be shared with someone else.

The suggestions given here are just guidelines, subject to change according to your creative whims. I would be very disappointed if they were ever allowed to interfere with the fun of cooking. In my life and career, I have cooked for many different occasions and none has given me greater pleasure than cooking for just 1 or 2. I wish the same for you!

Barbara Swain

Barbara Swain became interested in small-quantity cooking soon after she graduated from UCLA with honors in Home Economics. Living as a single, Barbara discovered most foods were packaged for large families and often produced useless leftovers. She decided to do something about it. She began experimenting with recipes, storage techniques and ways to use leftovers.

In a short time Barbara realized many other people were interested, too. As Home Economist for Southern California Edison and as Director of Home Economics for Knudsen Dairy, she found more and more people asking her about small-quantity cooking. To answer these questions, Barbara developed and taught a course in cooking for 1 or 2 at UCLA. She found her students were interested in more than just recipes. They wanted to know about nutrition, selecting and buying foods, and how to make each meal special. The information Barbara developed to answer their questions is the basis for this book. Barbara's tips on buying and storing food, on equipping a kitchen and setting a table will not only make you a better cook, they will make your cooking more fun!

Why Cooking Small Is Great

"Dinner for Two" evokes an image of flickering candlelight, soft music, sparkling crystal and intimate conversation. Unfortunately, the fantasy often lasts just long enough to empty the food budget and fill up the refrigerator with aging produce, off-flavored cream and untold containers of leftovers. Well, don't let that fantasy go. Let's turn on the lights and look at the pros and cons of cooking for 1 or 2.

ADVANTAGES

• You have more time to prepare special recipes and add extra touches to your meals. "Wait a minute," you say, "I'm a very busy person and I have only 24 hours in a day like anyone else." But time is so relative. If you had to cook for 4 people in the 30 to 60 minutes you allow for meal preparation, you'd have to settle for streamlined menus. When you're cooking for just 1 or 2, you have time to work through a new recipe, remove the choke from an artichoke or give special attention to the table setting. When two are cooking together, the possibilities are doubled.

• It's easier to afford more expensive ingredients. Government reports claim single people and couples pay more per person for food than families. But the very fact you are shopping for only 1 or 2 means food takes a much smaller bite out of your total budget. So, if a basket of strawberries in January or an occasional lobster tail makes you happy, it is a luxury you can afford.

• You have more freedom to experiment. Without the special dietary requirements of a whole family to consider, you can bring home some unknown taste experience or an exotic new recipe and have a good chance it will be accepted. If you miss, it's no disaster. At the very worst you might have to throw away 1 or 2 servings of whatever it was.

• You can eat what you want when you want. With fewer schedules to accommodate, you can adjust the size, timing and content of your meals to suit yourself. You can go on a special diet, gorge on a favorite food, or skip a meal entirely.

• Cooking becomes a relaxing emotional release and a creative experience. After work, let your kitchen be a retreat where your creative juices can flow. There are no committee compromises, no executive vetoes, and not a single "I told you so." Not only that, cooking is the only job I know where the threat of having to eat your mistakes is no threat at all.

DISADVANTAGES

• Leftovers, spoilage and waste. These problems are all part of the same cycle. When we buy or cook more food than we can use, part of it stays around the refrigerator long enough to spoil and become waste. The alternative is to eat the oversupply—which leads to . . .

• Monotony. Monotony is eating the same casserole every night until the last mouthful is consumed, so it won't go to waste. Monotony is serving steak every night because at least it all gets eaten. It's easy to fall into a dull eating routine. It's hard to break the pattern because . . .

• Few foods are packaged for 1 or 2 people. The food industry has begun to recognize and cater to smaller families, so our choices are improving. But even then . . .

• Few recipes are designed to serve 1 or 2. In the pages ahead you'll find 225 recipes for 1 or 2 with many variations to lead you to your own creative choices. Problem solved!

Clearly the advantages win! So let's make that "Dinner for Two" fantasy a reality. In the following pages you will discover an approach to cooking for 1 or 2 that will reveal the benefits and adventures that have been waiting for you all along.

Starting Your Basic Stock

There's a limit to how much food 1 or 2 adults can eat. If all the ingredients in every appealing recipe are purchased, the kitchen will soon be filled with deteriorating, half-used foods of unknown age. A major solution to the problem of leftovers and waste in small households is to build meals around meat cuts, produce items, staples and condiments that are best suited to small-quantity cooking. With a stock of very basic and versatile foods that don't leave problem leftovers, foods will be used up faster and consequently be fresher.

The recipes in this book are built around such foods. Together, I call them my Basic Stock. The following guidelines and the chart on the next 2 pages are here to help you establish a Basic Stock suited to your individual needs and taste.

The foundation of your basic stock is composed of the meat cuts, produce items and bakery goods that come in portions to serve just 1 or 2. Many meat cuts are perfect for the basic stock. My favorite is a boned and skinned half chicken breast. It takes little space in the freezer, thaws quickly and cooks in minutes. It can be used in main dishes, salads or hors d'oeuvres. Besides that, it's low in fat.

The ideal fresh fruit or vegetable for the basic stock will keep well for over a week and can be served raw or cooked. It's a bonus if it also looks good as part of a centerpiece on your table. An all-purpose apple like a McIntosh ranks high. Serve it with cheese for dessert, cut it up in a Waldorf Salad or bake it. As a last resort, put it through a juice extractor and drink it!

A basic stock bakery item should not have too definite a flavor. Try individual hard rolls, English muffins and sliced white or wheat bread.

Expand your basic stock with staples and condiments that have a long storage life and can be used in any amount in a variety of ways. Consider the advantages of ketchup or chili sauce over canned tomato sauce for tomato flavoring. Or chicken stock granules over bouillon cubes or canned stock for small-quantity cooking. With a well-selected stock of staples you could buy the same meat and produce for weeks and never repeat a recipe.

Personalize your basic stock to fit your cooking habits and tastes. If you have a cooking specialty such as barbecuing, health foods or Italian cooking, add the special condiments and equipment you need. Then use them daily to add even greater variety to all your cooking.

Buy your basic stock foods in their most versatile forms. The more versatile a food is, the more occasions you'll find to use it. Generally, foods are most versatile in their whole form. Consider the orange. It can be consumed as is, be turned into juice and grated peel or used as all sorts of garnishes. Breads and rolls can become breadcrumbs, dry breadcrumbs, croutons, canapés, toast or stuffings. Whole foods often last longer, too. Whole nuts, spices, and leaf herbs, for instance, retain flavor longer than their chopped or ground counterparts. The less surface area there is to get dry, oxidized, discolored or rancid, the better.

Take advantage of appropriate convenience foods. The frozen food section of your grocery store is filled with single-serving entrees, vegetables, potato products and desserts. These foods add tremendous variety to your meals and give you an occasional night off from the kitchen. Single-serving packets and cans of soups, cereals and other foods are also available. These items can frequently be used as ingredients in other recipes.

I use cake mixes a cup or so at a time as I would biscuit mix. Gelatin and pudding mixes can be used in smaller measures, too.

Spice mixes and herb blends can provide well-rounded seasoning in an instant. They can save the waste of 6 or 7 bottles of expensive, rarely used spices and herbs on your shelves.

Once you have decided on the foods you want in your basic stock, keep an eye out for recipes that use them. Also, learn to substitute your basic stock foods for similar ingredients. The chart on the next two pages will give you some help.

BASIC STOCK STAPLES & CONDIMENTS

BASIC STOCK	AMOUNTS Amounts are for average products.	SUBSTITUTIONS & EQUIVALENTS Expect some variations in flavor & texture.
DAIRY PRODUCTS		
Milk: extra-rich, whole, lowfat or nonfat	1 quart equals 4 cups. 1 pint equals 2 cups.	Various milks are interchangeable in recipes. Differences in fat content may be noticeable.
Whipping Cream Sour Cream Vanilla Ice Cream		For baking, 1 cup buttermilk equals 1 tablespoon vinegar or lemon juice plus milk to make 1 cup. 1 tablespoon whipping cream plus 3 tablespoons milk equals 1/4 cup half-and-half.
Sharp Cheddar Cheese, well-aged Parmesan Cheese	1 cup lightly packed, shredded Cheddar cheese weighs 4 oz. 1/4 cup grated Parmesan cheese weighs 1 oz.	Use well-aged cheeses for smooth cheese sauces. Young cheeses, such as longhorn or Monterey Jack, may become stringy and not melt properly. Cheddar, Swiss, Monterey Jack and longhorn cheeses are interchangeable in sandwiches, omelets and salads.
Eggs, large	1 egg white equals 2 tablespoons.	In cakes, custards and sauces, 2 egg yolks can be substituted for 1 whole egg.
RICE & PASTA		
Converted Long-Grain Rice, not instant Wide Egg Noodles	1/2 cup uncooked long-grain rice or brown rice weighs 3-1/2 oz., or makes 1-1/2 cups cooked rice. 1 cup uncooked wide egg noodles weighs about 2 oz., or makes about 1 cup cooked noodles.	Brown rice can be substituted for white rice, but cooking time should be extended. Thinner egg noodles can be substituted for wide egg noodles, but cooking times should be reduced.
FATS		
Oil, such as corn oil or peanut oil Butter Clarified Butter, page 159	2 tablespoons butter, margarine, clarified butter or any oil weigh 1 oz. 1 stick (1/4 lb.) butter equals 1/2 cup or 8 tablespoons.	Oil, butter, regular margarine, clarified butter, shortening, bacon fat, chicken fat & lard are generally interchangeable. For baking, 1/2 cup shortening equals 1/2 cup plus 1-1/2 tablespoons butter.
FLOURS & STARCHES		
All-Purpose Flour Cornstarch	1 cup sifted all-purpose flour weighs 4 oz. If scooped from package and not sifted, may weigh up to 5-1/2 oz. 1 cup sifted cake flour weighs 3-1/2 oz.	For baking, 1 cup sifted all-purpose flour equals 1 cup plus 2 tablespoons sifted cake flour. For thickening, 2 tablespoons flour equal 1 tablespoon cornstarch, arrowroot, potato or rice starch, & will thicken 1 cup liquid to cream sauce consistency.
LEAVENING AGENTS		
Baking Powder Baking Soda		Precise measuring of these ingredients is especially important in small-quantity baking.
SWEETENERS		
Superfine or Granulated Sugar Light Brown Sugar Powdered Sugar Honey	1 cup granulated, superfine or brown sugar weighs 7 oz. 1 cup unsifted powdered sugar weighs about 1/4 lb. or 4 oz. 1 cup honey weighs 3/4 lb. or 12 oz.	Superfine sugar dissolves faster than granulated sugar. For baking, 1 cup white sugar equals 1 cup firmly packed brown sugar. 1 cup honey equals 1-1/4 cups granulated sugar plus 1/4 cup water. For surest results in baking do not replace more than half the granulated sugar with brown sugar or honey.
ACIDS		
White Wine Vinegar Lemons Oranges	1 medium lemon weighs about 1/4 lb. & yields about 3 tablespoons juice & 2 teaspoons grated peel. 1 medium orange weighs about 1/3 lb. & yields about 1/4 to 1/2 cup juice & 4 teaspoons grated peel.	Vinegars are generally less acid than lemons or limes. 1 tablesoon lemon or lime juice equals 4 teaspoons vinegar. 1 teaspoon freshly grated lemon or orange peel equals 1 teaspoon dry lemon or orange peel, or 1/2 teaspoon extract.
MEAT FLAVORINGS		
Beef Stock Granules Chicken Stock Granules		Meat stocks, whether homemade, canned, or reconstituted from canned concentrates, cubes or granules, are interchangeable.
ONION PRODUCTS		
Onions Shallots Garlic Green Onions (Scallions)	1 large onion weighs 1/2 lb. & makes 1-1/2 cups minced onion. 1 small onion weighs 1/4 lb. & makes 1/2 to 2/3 cup minced onion. 1 average shallot weighs 1/2 oz. & makes 1 tablespoon minced shallots. 1 average green onion with fresh top equals about 1 tablespoon minced or sliced green onion.	1/4 cup minced onion is interchangeable with 1 to 2 tablespoons minced shallots in cooking. 1/2 cup minced onion equals 1-1/2 teaspoons onion powder. 1 average garlic clove equals 1/8 teaspoon garlic powder or 1/2 teaspoon garlic salt but reduce salt. 1 tablespoon instant minced onion, rehydrated, equals 1/4 cup minced onion.

BASIC STOCK STAPLES & CONDIMENTS

BASIC STOCK	AMOUNTS Amounts are for average products.	SUBSTITUTIONS & EQUIVALENTS Expect some variations in flavor & texture.
TOMATO PRODUCTS Fresh Tomatoes Ketchup or Chili Sauce Tomato Juice or Tomato Paste	1 large tomato weighs 1/2 lb. 1 medium tomato weighs 1/4 to 1/3 lb. & makes about 1/2 cup finely chopped tomato. 1 small tomato weighs about 3 oz. A 14 oz. bottle of ketchup contains about 1-1/2 cups.	Ketchup, chili sauce & cocktail sauce are generally interchangeable. 1/4 cup tomato paste plus 3/4 cup water equal 1 cup canned tomatoes or juice for cooking. 1/4 cup tomato paste plus 1/4 cup water equal 1/2 cup tomato sauce or tomato puree for cooking. 1/2 cup tomato sauce plus 1/2 cup water equal 1 cup tomato juice for cooking. 1-1/3 cups peeled, chopped fresh tomatoes, cooked 10 minutes, equal 1 cup canned tomatoes for cooking.
MUSHROOM PRODUCTS Fresh Mushrooms Duxelles, page 161	10 to 15 large or 40 to 50 small, *very fresh* mushrooms equal 1 lb. 1/4 lb. fresh mushrooms makes about 1-1/4 cups sliced mushrooms.	3 tablespoons duxelles or 1 cup sliced fresh mushrooms cooked in 1 tablespoon butter, or drained sliced mushrooms from a 2- or 2-1/2-oz. can, are generally interchangeable in cooking.
CRUMBS Soft Breadcrumbs, page 164 Buttered Breadcrumbs, page 164	1 thin slice bread makes about 1/2 cup or 1 oz. lightly packed soft breadcrumbs. 1/4 cup fine dry breadcrumbs weighs almost 1 oz.	1/2 cup soft breadcrumbs equals 3 tablespoons fine dry breadcrumbs plus 2 teaspoons water in mixed dishes. Fine dry breadcrumbs & fine soda cracker crumbs are generally interchangeable.
CONDIMENTS Mayonnaise Regular Prepared Mustard or Dijon Mustard Prepared Horseradish Worcestershire Sauce Soy Sauce Tabasco Sauce Capers Sweet Pickles or Sweet Pickle Relish		1-1/2 teaspoons prepared mustard equals 1/2 teaspoon dry mustard. Regular prepared and Dijon mustard are interchangeable.
HERBS & SEASONINGS Fresh Parsley Basil Dill Oregano Tarragon Thyme Salt Seasoned Salt		1 tablespoon finely minced fresh herbs equals 1 teaspoon dry herbs. 1 teaspoon salt equals about 1-1/2 teaspoons seasoned salt. 1 tablespoon lightly packed, minced fresh parsley equals 1 teaspoon dry parsley.
SPICES & EXTRACTS Whole Black Peppercorns Ground Red Pepper (Cayenne) Curry Powder Chili Powder Ginger, Ground Paprika Cinnamon, Ground Nutmeg, Ground or Whole Vanilla Extract		1/4 teaspoon ground ginger equals 1 teaspoon chopped fresh ginger or 2 teaspoons chopped crystallized ginger. Liqueurs can be substituted for flavor extracts to taste if extra liquid does not harm texture. 1 teaspoon freshly grated lemon or orange peel equals 1/2 teaspoon lemon or orange extract.
NUTS & SEEDS Almonds, slivered or sliced Walnuts or Pecans Sesame Seeds	1/4 cup chopped or sliced nuts weighs about 1 oz.	In general, nuts are interchangeable. Consider texture as well as flavor in making substitutions.
SWEET CONDIMENTS Semisweet Chocolate Chips Coconut, flaked or shredded Raisins or Other Dried Fruits Red Currant Jelly Orange Marmalade	6 oz. semisweet chocolate chips equal 1 cup. 1/4 cup lightly packed coconut weighs about 3/4 oz. 3/4 cup jam weighs 8 oz.	1 oz. baking chocolate equals 1/2 cup semisweet chocolate chips, but reduce sugar in recipe by 1/4 cup and fat by 2 teaspoons. Dried fruits are usually interchangeable if cut into equal size pieces. Fruit jams and preserves such as peach, pineapple and apricot are interchangeable.
WINES & LIQUORS Dry White Wine or Champagne Dry Sherry Dark Rum Plain Brandy or Cognac Kirsch (Cherry Brandy) Orange-Flavored Liqueur		Dry white wine and champagne may be used interchangeably. Various flavored liqueurs can often be used interchangeably. Gold rum can be used in place of dark rum but flavor will be lighter. Plain brandy and Cognac may be used interchangeably.

Mastering The Food Market

• Keep a pad and pencil in the kitchen to note food items you're about to run out of. Nothing is more aggravating than going back to the store for that one item you knew you needed all along.

• Before you shop, take a quick survey of the pantry, refrigerator and freezer. Note anything you need to use with leftover perishable foods. Make sure you have plenty of your basic stock foods. Generally note what food items you have so you can avoid buying duplicates.

• Select one food store for most of your grocery shopping. Unless you have unlimited time and cheap transportation, select a convenient store with the services, prices and the quality and variety of food you like. When shopping for just 1 or 2, it's hard to justify standing in several check-out lines to save a few cents.

My favorite services are a meat counter where I can buy 1/4 pound of shrimp or 2 boned chicken breasts, and a fresh bakery where I can buy 2 French pastries, 6 cookies and 1 cheese Danish.

• Shop at off-peak hours when you're not hungry. It seems easiest to shop on the way home from work, but that's when markets are most crowded and you're probably famished. Hungry people often buy more on impulse than people who have eaten.

As an alternative, keep an ice chest in your car and shop at noon, picking up a bag of ice to keep perishables cold. Or stop for a bite of dinner after work, run a few errands and then shop after the rush hour. Weekend mornings or evenings are better for many people.

• Resist the temptation to buy in quantity. Even with unlimited storage space, quantity buying for 1 or 2 people is rarely an advantage. Supplies aren't used fast enough and many items aren't as non-perishable as we'd like to think.

It's smart to buy economy sizes of truly non-perishable things or products you use all the time. A large roll of aluminum foil occupies about the same space as a small roll and costs less per foot. If you eat corn flakes every morning, buy the biggest box you can accommodate.

• Buy small sizes of produce items and condiments. If you buy small tomatoes, onions and oranges, you can avoid a lot of half pieces in your refrigerator. A small tomato will be consumed in 1 salad, and a small onion will easily be used in 1 or 2 recipes. Small sizes are often less expensive and frequently better quality.

You may have to pay a little extra for small containers of condiments, but you'll save by avoiding the waste that comes from throwing out bad food—or worse yet, eating it!

• Buy only very fresh, undamaged food products. Avoid foods that are already overripe or possibly deteriorated. Don't buy canned or packaged goods that are even slightly damaged. Ice cream in misshapen containers or frozen peas that don't rattle in the package indicate these products may have been thawed and refrozen. One exception: day-old baked goods can be a bargain if you use them immediately or freeze them.

• Don't go overboard for bargains on perishable foods. Buy produce only in the amount you can use. This is one place you don't pay more for small quantities.

• Pick up your perishable foods last and rush them home. Plan your route through the market. Pick up produce, deli, dairy and meat products after non-food and packaged items. Add frozen foods last. Go straight home. An hour in the trunk of the car on a hot day can really shorten the life of a quart of milk or a bunch of watercress. Wrap your perishable foods for storage as you unload the grocery bags.

The Storage Stage

A box of crackers, a quart of milk or a head of lettuce seldom get a chance to go bad in a big household. But it happens all the time to singles and couples. When you shop for 5 dinners and only 3 are eaten, you could have a problem! Unless the food is stored properly from the start, it might spoil before the next week. The way you store may be even more important in preventing waste than what foods you choose.

The primary enemies of food are air, heat and light. By controlling these factors through proper packaging and temperature regulation, you can add days, weeks or even months to the freshness of your groceries. Storage for specific foods is discussed in the introductions to the chapters on preparing those foods.

PROPER PACKAGING

Generally, food is best stored in airtight containers. The containers should maintain the dryness of foods such as crackers, or the moistness of foods such as brown sugar. Because air is a source of oxidation and possible contamination, the less air in the package the better. There are a few exceptions. Fresh meat should be wrapped loosely. Liquids or other foods to be frozen need some air space for expansion.

Wide-mouth peanut butter or honey jars are ideal for refrigerator or freezer storage. Plastic ice cream and deli food containers are also useful and usually nest together for storage between uses. Coffee cans and other cans with snap-on lids make excellent canisters for dry ingredients. Line them with plastic bags, if you like. Foil trays from prepared frozen foods can be reused many times.

You can purchase plastic freezer containers. Square containers use space efficiently and stack well. A 6-ounce plastic container is perfect for many single servings. A 2-ounce size is great for storing egg whites or yolks, or small amounts of ingredients. Some glass containers can be put directly from the freezer into the oven. These are fine for microwave ovens, too. Heat-sealed plastic bags are handy because they are transparent, flexible and make it easy to reheat their contents in boiling water. Always keep aluminum foil, plastic bags, plastic wrap and wax paper on hand.

Collect an assortment of containers and materials for storing food. Small wide-mouth containers are very useful for freezing leftovers and single servings.

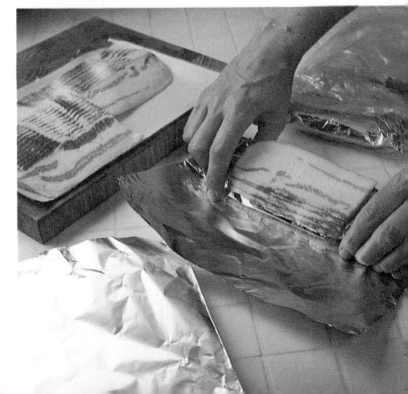

To freeze bacon, place 4 half strips on the end of a piece of foil, then fold bacon and foil over. Repeat twice. Wrap remaining foil around and fold ends in. Store in a plastic bag. Single servings can be snapped off.

IN THE FREEZER

Your freezer is the most expensive food storage space you have, based on operating costs. Save that space for foods you use frequently.

• Maintain a freezer temperature of 0°F (-20°C) or colder. If ice cream stays very firm, the temperature is about right.

• Put foods in airtight containers or wrap securely. Exclude air to prevent drying. Leave room for expansion in jars or cartons.

• Freeze foods in single-serving portions for quick thawing and cooking.

• Freeze foods you seldom use, such as shredded coconut, marshmallows, nuts and fresh ginger. Also freeze leftover egg whites, bread crumbs, grated cheese and butter. Chicken stock or lemon juice can be frozen in ice cube trays.

• Excess produce or dairy foods can be frozen. Freezing causes texture changes, so only use these foods in cooking. Chop onions, green pepper or other produce, freeze on a baking sheet, then store in plastic bags. Use thawed milks, creams, sour cream, yogurt, cottage cheese and cream cheese in baking.

IN THE REFRIGERATOR

• Maintain a refrigerator temperature of 35° to 40°F (2° to 5°C). Store meat, fish and dairy foods in the coldest parts—the meat keeper, the area around the cold air outlets or the space just under the freezer compartment. Store soft drinks, pickled items and other condiments in the door section.

• Cover or wrap all refrigerated food to prevent drying or flavor transfer.

• To retain freshness, refrigerate various opened staples. Items that benefit include pancake syrup, jams, peanut butter, ground coffee, olive oil, nuts and dried fruits.

• After serving cottage cheese, sour cream or mayonnaise in a separate dish, do not return the product to its original container. It may have deteriorated in quality at room temperature.

• If a fresh food threatens to spoil, cook it and refrigerate or freeze it for later use. Milk or cream can be made into cream soup, custard or hot chocolate. Or simply bring it to a boil and store it in an airtight jar for cooking later. Asparagus can be cooked, refrigerated and served later, hot or cold. Ground beef can be sautéed and refrigerated or frozen for use in skillet dishes.

Storing Fresh Fruits & Vegetables

COLDEST PART OF REFRIGERATOR
35° to 40°F (2° to 5°C)

Less Than One Week	One Week or More
Strawberries	Romaine Lettuce
Raspberries	Parsley
Sweet Corn	Beets
Soft Leafy Lettuce	Radishes
Spinach	Leeks
Asparagus	Cabbage
Mushrooms	Carrots
Watercress	Celery
Brussels Sprouts	Celery Root
Iceberg Lettuce	Artichokes
Cauliflower	Turnips
Broccoli	Apples
Green Onions	Blueberries
Summer Fruits, ripe	

WARMEST PART OF REFRIGERATOR
45° to 55°F (5° to 15°C)

Less Than One Week	One Week or More
Tomatoes, ripe	Cucumbers
Green Beans	Zucchini
Avocados, ripe	Summer Squash
	Green Peppers
	Melons, ripe
	Oranges

COOL ROOM TEMPERATURE
50° to 60°F (10° to 15°C)

One Week or More
Grapefruit
Lemons
Limes
Potatoes
Sweet Potatoes
Winter Squash, uncut

ROOM TEMPERATURE
65° to 70°F (20°C)

Less Than One Week	One Week or More
Bananas	Dry Onions
	Garlic

AT ROOM TEMPERATURE

• Some foods keep best at room temperature. Store them in the coolest and driest parts of the kitchen, not on top shelves, on top of the refrigerator or under the sink.

• Enclose dry foods in airtight canisters or containers. Screw-top jars are effective.

• Organize cupboard storage so canned and packaged goods don't get lost. Finding a box of rice after you've replaced it is regrettable.

• Don't display glass jars of herbs and spices outside the cupboard. Light is detrimental to their flavor and color. A cool dark place is best.

Storing Fresh Fruits & Vegetables

● Most fresh fruits and vegetables keep best in a cold, humid atmosphere.

● Generally, do not wash or trim produce before storing. Remove only tops and damaged or rotting parts. Tops draw moisture from the vegetables.

● Rinse leafy vegetables to restore crispness. Drain and wrap in slightly damp paper towels. Vegetables such as sweet corn, asparagus and mushrooms benefit from being wrapped in damp towels, also.

● Store each type of produce, with or without paper towel wrap, in separate plastic bags to prevent drying and flavor exchanges.

● Store fruits, including tomatoes and avocados, separately from vegetables to prevent ethylene gas reactions between produce items.

● To prevent darkening of cut fruit, coat cut surfaces of avocados, peaches, apples, pears and bananas with lemon or other citrus juice.

RIPENING FRUITS

Many fruits, such as avocados, peaches, pears and bananas, are not fully ripened when purchased. A few days at room temperature out of the sun-light will usually ripen them, but there's a quicker way! Place all the fruits in a paper bag and enclose an apple, which will speed the ripening process. Loosely close the bag and put it in a cool dark place. The collected ethylene gases from the fruits will ripen them quickly and evenly. Check the bag frequently and remove ripened fruit.

Avocados—An avocado is ripe when it yields to light pressure when held between the palms or when a toothpick pushed into the stem end slides easily to the seed.

Bananas—To slow ripening, refrigerate bananas or wrap in a damp cloth and put them in a loosely closed paper bag in a dark area. Keep the cloth damp. The skin will darken in the refrigerator.

Onions and Potatoes—Do not overstock in spring when sprouting is a problem. Store in a cool dry place out of sunlight. Sun causes potatoes to turn green. Cut off green areas before cooking.

Tomatoes—Keep tomatoes at room temperature until color develops. They will not ripen once they have been refrigerated.

Cooking & Serving Small

● Use small bowls, pans and appliances for small-quantity cooking. Don't chase a tiny amount of batter around a large bowl. Too much of it will just end up in the dishwasher.

When a little food is cooked in a large pan, the juices spread out and evaporate or burn. You end up with dried-out food and no sauce.

Cooking and cleaning are easier when the amount of food and the size of the appliance are compatible. Smaller appliances also use less energy than large appliances. A microwave oven is ideal: the less you cook, the less time and energy it takes.

● Use your basic stock ingredients to add variety to your cooking. Add flavor and decoration with seasonings, nuts, condiments, dairy products, cheeses, jams and jellies, liqueurs, tomato products, mushrooms and flavor bases.

● Use leftovers and odds and ends to make cooking more interesting. Why make a plain omelet when there is leftover creamed spinach in the refrigerator? Leftovers, bits of produce and dairy products are great flavors just waiting for a recipe.

● Don't forget what's cooking! If the phone rings while you are sautéing minced shallots, turn off the heat or move the pan. When several items on the range need attention, handle them one at a time and turn the heat off under the others.

● To speed up cooking time, cut foods in smaller pieces and bake in smaller pans. Grated carrots cook faster than whole carrots, thin steaks broil faster than thick ones. Small casseroles or shallow au gratin dishes shorten cooking times slightly.

● Prepare your favorite long-cooking and convenience food recipes in quantity. Freeze in serving portions. Be sure all ingredients are freezable.

● While waiting for recipes to cook, prepare ingredients for future use. Grate cheese for the freezer or make breadcrumbs, Clarified Butter, page 159, or other items.

● Serve food on warmed or chilled plates whenever appropriate. Small amounts of food cool off or warm up faster than larger quantities. Candle warmers and icers help maintain the desired serving temperatures.

Breakfast & Brunch

There isn't any meal I associate more with singles and couples than breakfast or brunch. Colorful table linens, everyday dishes and a potted plant can create a delightful, informal table for your morning meal. Set your table by a window or on a terrace to enjoy the sun and the outdoors. If you are breakfasting in bed, open the windows and listen to the sounds of nature.

THE MENU

You're probably already familiar with the great variety of breakfast menus. Brunch, the combination of breakfast and lunch, is usually served between 10:00 and noon. It can include a wide range of interesting egg, cheese, meat and fish dishes, and even a vegetable. The basic menu pattern includes a juice or brunch cocktail, fruit, entree, breakfast bread and a hot beverage.

Simple Brunch
Cranberry Juice
Gourmet Grapefruit, page 14
Sausage
Extra Special Pancakes and Syrup, page 26
Coffee, Tea or Hot Chocolate, page 31

Sumptuous Brunch
Ramos Fizz, page 23
Cantaloupe Wedges and Raspberries
Eggs Benedict, page 17
Asparagus Polonaise, page 117
Sour Cream Coffeecake, page 31
Coffee or Tea

FRUITS

The color, cut and arrangement of the fruit on your menu may be a major part of your table or bed tray decoration. Just 1 or 2 fruits plus a garnish can give spectacular effects. Choose a fruit to contrast with the color and flavor of the main dish. A warm, syrupy baked apple is not best with pancakes; try tangy fruits instead.

Any fruit or juice can be served, but the vitamin C in these fruits can add special nutrition to your breakfast or brunch:

Oranges	Strawberries
Grapefruits	Gooseberries
Tangerines	Red Raspberries
Cantaloupes	Black Raspberries
Honeydew melons	Blackberries
Papayas	Blueberries
Strawberry Guavas	Boysenberries
Kiwi	Tomatoes

MEATS

My favorite basic stock breakfast meats are bacon and brown-and-serve sausages. The brown-and-serve sausages are already fully cooked and frozen. Package and freeze bacon, see page 9, to have a few slices available in minutes.

Other delicious and appropriate meats for the morning menu include:

Ham	Ground beef patties
Canadian bacon	Chicken livers
Deviled ham	Creamed chicken
Bologna	Creamed shellfish
Wieners	Smoked salmon
Small steaks	

CHEESES

Cheese dishes are a great way to get important dairy foods into the diet—and a lot of protein at the same time. Cheese can even be served as is for brunch. A Scandinavian breakfast of hard rolls or bread with cheese, boiled ham and a soft-cooked egg is hard to beat for simplicity, balance and great taste. Complete the menu with butter, jam and coffee, tea or hot chocolate. The cheese dishes here are also ideal for a light supper.

BREADS

Buying just 1 or 2 bakery pastries at a time may save you from many tempting leftovers. When you feel like baking your own sweet breads, try the two small coffeecakes included in this chapter.

For most breakfast and brunch menus, basic stock breads serve the purpose. Individual French rolls and sliced bread are already in single-serving portions, and English muffins can be split before freezing for faster toasting later.

Ambrosia *Photo on page 28.*

Feel free to add other fruits.

2 navel oranges or other oranges
2 to 4 tablespoons flaked coconut

With a sharp knife, peel oranges by cutting just under the membrane beneath the peel. Cut out orange sections by slicing along both sides of each section membrane. Put sections and any juice in a small bowl. Add juice squeezed from remaining membranes. Spoon into 2 stemmed dessert glasses and sprinkle with coconut. Or slice peeled oranges, arrange slices in a spiral on 2 small plates and sprinkle with coconut. Makes 2 servings.

Variations

Substitute 1 or more of the following fruits, cut in bite-size pieces, for part of the orange: banana, kiwi, pineapple, strawberries, apple, raspberries, seedless grapes. Coat banana and apple pieces with orange juice to prevent darkening.

Ambrosia Dessert: Prepare recipe with desired fruits. Add sugar and orange-flavored liqueur to taste. Serve with cookies or pound cake.

How To Make Ambrosia

Use a very sharp thin-bladed knife to peel oranges or grapefruit. Peel just under the membrane beneath the peel, exposing the juice cells.

To release orange or grapefruit sections, slice along both sides of each section membrane. Or slice down one side of each section membrane, gently twist the knife blade and draw it up the side of the next membrane.

Gourmet Grapefruit

Now you can please all of the people all of the time!

1 large grapefruit
Topping & Garnish, see below

Cut grapefruit in half and remove seeds. Trim a small slice from bottom of each half if necessary so grapefruit sits flat. With a grapefruit knife or paring knife, cut around edge just inside outer membrane and on both sides of each section membrane. Cut out the white core. Drizzle 1 tablespoon selected topping over each half. Refrigerate 15 minutes to blend flavors if time permits. If desired, broil until bubbly and browned on edges. Add garnish. Makes 2 servings.

Toppings & Garnishes

Maple syrup, molasses, honey or brown sugar sprinkled with cinnamon. Garnish with maraschino cherry or fresh strawberry.

Sherry, rum, grenadine or flavored liqueur. Garnish with plain or toasted flaked coconut.

Baked Apple

A warm baked apple is a wonderful way to start a winter brunch. Or serve it for dessert.

1 to 2 tablespoons light brown sugar,
  firmly packed, or honey
1/4 teaspoon cinnamon
1 tablespoon butter, cut in small pieces
1 tablespoon Soft Breadcrumbs, page 164,
  if desired

1 large baking apple, such as Rome Beauty,
  Golden Delicious, McIntosh or Pippin
2 tablespoons water
Half-and-half or whipping cream, if desired

Preheat oven to 350°F (175°C). Combine brown sugar or honey, cinnamon, butter and soft breadcrumbs, if desired. Remove core from apple and remove peel from top third of apple. Place apple in a 10-ounce soufflé pot or custard cup. Fill center with brown sugar mixture. Pour water over. Bake 40 to 60 minutes, basting occasionally, until apple is tender. Serve warm or at room temperature with half-and-half or whipping cream, if desired. Makes 1 serving.

Variations

Rum & Raisin Baked Apple: Chop about 10 raisins and add to brown sugar mixture. Substitute 1 tablespoon dark rum for 1 tablespoon of the water.

Pecan-Orange Baked Apple: Add 1 tablespoon chopped toasted pecans and 1/4 teaspoon grated orange peel to brown sugar mixture. Substitute 1 tablespoon orange-flavored liqueur for 1 tablespoon of the water.

Dessert Baked Apple: Add spices such as nutmeg, cloves or allspice. Or add dry fruits such as chopped prunes or dates. Top with toasted walnuts or almonds. Serve with Sweetened Whipped Cream, page 149, Whipped Crème Fraîche, page 149, or ice cream.

French Omelet

As easy as scrambled eggs, once you get the knack of it.

Filling, see below
1 to 2 tablespoons Clarified Butter, page 159, or butter

2 eggs
Dash salt
Salt and pepper to taste

Prepare selected filling; set aside. Heat butter in an 8-inch skillet or omelet pan over medium-high heat. In a small bowl, beat eggs and a dash of salt until frothy. When butter is hot, pour in eggs. As soon as underside of eggs is set, quickly stir with the underside of a fork until eggs are half-cooked but still very soft and slightly runny. Working quickly, distribute eggs evenly in pan and spread filling over one half. As soon as underside is set again, use a pancake turner to fold in half. Cook briefly to warm filling and brown omelet. For best flavor, omelet should be moist in center. Loosen omelet with pancake turner. Place a serving plate upside-down over pan and invert omelet onto plate. Sprinkle with salt and pepper. Makes 1 serving.

Fillings

Cheese: 2 tablespoons grated Parmesan cheese or up to 1/4 cup lightly packed, shredded Cheddar, Swiss or Monterey Jack cheese. Add diced green chilies or minced black olives, if desired.
Jam: About 2 tablespoons jam or preserves such as strawberry, apricot, peach, orange marmalade or apple butter. Omit salt and pepper. Sprinkle powdered sugar over omelet and top with sour cream.
Ham: 2 to 3 tablespoons minced ham or 2 tablespoons deviled ham.
Spinach: 2 to 3 tablespoons buttered cooked spinach or leftover creamed spinach. Warm before using. Top with sour cream.
Mushroom: 2 tablespoons Duxelles, page 161, or 2 to 4 tablespoons sautéed sliced mushrooms. Top with sour cream.
Miscellaneous: 2 to 3 tablespoons guacamole, warmed creamed chicken, diced chicken livers, cold cuts or hot dogs, crumbled crisp bacon, cocktail shrimp, flaked crab, flaked tuna or cottage cheese.

Eggs Rosinsky

Even when you think the cupboard is bare, you'll be able to fix this special dish.

Clarified Butter, page 159, or butter
2 eggs
1 to 2 tablespoons dry sherry

Salt and pepper to taste
1 to 2 tablespoons shredded Parmesan cheese

Preheat broiler. Heat about 1 tablespoon butter in an 8-inch broiler-proof skillet. Break eggs into hot butter. As soon as undersides of eggs are set, pour in sherry; quickly boil until syrupy. Before eggs are fully cooked, sprinkle with salt and pepper and Parmesan cheese. Immediately put under broiler and broil until cheese is lightly browned. Makes 1 serving.

Poached Eggs

If ever you needed fresh eggs, you need them here!

Water
2 teaspoons salt, if desired
1 tablespoon white vinegar, if desired

4 fresh eggs
Salt and pepper to taste

Put water 1-1/2-inch-deep in a large skillet and bring to a boil. Add salt and vinegar for a firmer but less shiny egg. Reduce heat to a slow simmer. One at a time, break eggs into a saucer and slip into barely simmering water, keeping eggs as separate as possible. Cover skillet until egg whites coat over yolks. Remove cover. Cook 3 to 5 minutes until whites are firm but yolks are still soft when touched with the back of a spoon. With a slotted pancake turner, lift each egg from the water and rest on a folded paper towel to absorb excess water. Trim away the loose thin white. Place on serving plate. Sprinkle with salt and pepper. Makes 2 servings.

How To Make Poached Eggs

Eggs for poaching should have round yolks, generous thick whites and a minimum of thin white. If eggs are flattened and liquid, salt and vinegar added to water will firm them.

For perfect poached eggs, as for Eggs Benedict, quickly clean the surface of each egg and trim away the thin edges of egg white.

Eggs Benedict

Make this famous brunch dish just once—you'll be hooked on it.

2 recipes Hollandaise Sauce, page 120
Butter
4 English muffin halves

4 (1-oz.) slices ham or Canadian bacon
4 Poached Eggs, page 16
Salt to taste

Prepare Hollandaise Sauce and cool pan in cold water as soon as last butter is blended in. Set aside. Lightly butter English muffin halves and toast under broiler or in toaster-oven. Preheat oven to 200°F (95°C). Place ham or Canadian bacon slices on toasted muffin halves. Heat in oven until warm. Prepare poached eggs. While eggs are cooking, carefully warm Hollandaise Sauce. Put 2 warm muffin halves on each plate. Place a drained, trimmed poached egg on each muffin half. Sprinkle with salt. Pour Hollandaise Sauce over each. Makes 2 servings.

Baked Eggs in Red Sauce

Eggs and tomatoes make an appetizing dish.

Red Sauce, see below
2 eggs
Salt and pepper to taste

1 tablespoon minced parsley
1 to 2 tablespoons shredded Parmesan cheese

Red Sauce:
1 tablespoon oil
1 medium tomato, peeled and seeded
1 (1/4-inch) slice medium onion
1 garlic clove
1/2 teaspoon sugar

1/2 teaspoon Worcestershire sauce
1/8 to 1/4 teaspoon salt
1/4 teaspoon basil
1 to 2 tablespoons Duxelles, page 161,
   if desired

Preheat oven to 400°F (205°C). Place an individual shallow au gratin dish or similar baking dish in preheating oven. Prepare Red Sauce and pour into heated baking dish. Break eggs onto sauce. Sprinkle with salt and pepper, parsley and Parmesan cheese. Bake about 7 minutes until egg whites are nearly set. Baking time will vary with ovens, baking dishes and temperature of eggs. If egg whites are cooked until firm, yolks will be hard. Makes 1 serving.

Red Sauce:
Put all ingredients except basil and duxelles into a blender. Cover and blend until smooth. Put into an 8-inch skillet and stir in basil. Sauce will be pink and frothy. Simmer uncovered, stirring often, until sauce is slightly thickened and red color returns. Stir in duxelles, if desired.

Variation

Poached Eggs in Red Sauce: Omit Parmesan cheese. Break eggs into gently simmering sauce in skillet. Cover and cook until egg whites are set but yolks have not coated over.

Eggs Rancheros

If you have corn tortillas on hand, place 1 on each plate and top with eggs and sauce.

Ranchero Sauce, see below
4 eggs
Salt and pepper to taste

About 1/4 cup shredded Cheddar, longhorn
    or Monterey Jack cheese, lightly packed

Ranchero Sauce:
1 tablespoon oil
1/4 cup minced onion
1 clove garlic, pressed or minced
2 tablespoons minced green pepper
2 tablespoons minced celery with leaves
1/2 teaspoon chili powder

1 (8-oz.) can whole tomatoes
About 2 tablespoons diced green chilies,
    if desired
1/2 teaspoon oregano
1/4 teaspoon salt
1/2 teaspoon sugar

Prepare Ranchero Sauce. Spread simmering sauce over bottom of skillet. Break 1 egg into each quarter of the skillet. Cover and cook until egg whites are set but yolks have not coated over. Sprinkle with salt, pepper and shredded cheese. Replace lid until cheese is melted. Makes 2 servings.

Ranchero Sauce:
Heat oil in a large skillet. Add onion, garlic, green pepper and celery. Sauté over medium-low heat until tender. If necessary, add a little water, cover and gently simmer vegetables until fully cooked. Stir in chili powder. Cook about 30 seconds. Drain juice from tomatoes into skillet. Chop drained tomatoes by hand or in blender. Add to mixture. Add diced green chilies, if desired. Stir in oregano, salt and sugar. Simmer 3 to 5 minutes, uncovered, to slightly thicken.

Baked Eggs in Hash Cups

A great flavor blend makes an easy brunch dish.

1 (8-oz.) can hash
2 tablespoons ketchup
2 eggs
Salt and pepper to taste

Buttered Breadcrumbs, page 164, or
    grated Parmesan cheese
1 to 2 teaspoons butter

Preheat oven or toaster-oven to 400°F (205°C). Butter two 10-ounce soufflé pots, custard cups or casseroles. Put half of hash in each and press evenly onto bottom and sides. Spread 1 tablespoon ketchup over bottom of each hash cup. Bake until hash is bubbling. Remove from oven, break egg into each hash cup. Sprinkle with salt and pepper. Lightly sprinkle with buttered breadcrumbs or grated Parmesan cheese. Place a small chunk of butter on each egg yolk. Bake about 7 minutes until egg whites are nearly set. Baking time will vary with ovens, baking dishes and temperature of eggs. If egg whites are cooked until firm, yolks will be hard. Makes 2 servings.

Hangtown Fry

Hangtown Fry is part of our legacy from the California Gold Rush.

2 slices bacon
2 tablespoons chopped or slivered onion
2 tablespoons chopped or slivered
  green pepper
2 eggs

1 tablespoon milk or cream
2 tablespoons flour
Butter, if necessary
2 large or 3 medium oysters
Salt and pepper to taste

Fry bacon in an 8-inch skillet over medium heat until crisp. Drain on paper towels and keep warm. Sauté onion and green pepper in bacon drippings until tender; remove from skillet and set aside. Beat eggs and milk or cream in a small bowl. Put flour on a saucer. If bacon drippings do not coat skillet, add butter. Dip oysters into egg mixture, sprinkle with salt and pepper and dip in flour to coat well. Sauté over medium-low heat until lightly browned on each side. Pour remaining egg mixture over oysters in hot skillet. Cook gently, pulling edges to center as they set, until eggs are cooked but still moist. Season with salt and pepper. Garnish with bacon slices and onion and green pepper. Makes 1 serving.

Shirred Eggs Elegante

This is my favorite easy brunch dish.

Butter
1 to 2 tablespoons filling such as deviled
  ham, leftover creamed spinach, Duxelles,
  page 161, minced ham or crumbled
  bacon

2 tablespoons whipping cream
2 eggs
Salt and pepper to taste
Shredded Parmesan cheese or Buttered
    Breadcrumbs, page 164

Preheat oven or toaster-oven to 400°F (205°C). Butter an individual au gratin dish, 10-ounce soufflé pot or similar baking dish. Spread filling over bottom. Pour whipping cream over filling. Place in oven. As soon as cream boils, remove dish from oven and break eggs into center. Spoon hot cream over top of eggs. Sprinkle with salt and pepper and Parmesan cheese or buttered breadcrumbs. Bake about 8 minutes until egg whites are nearly set. Baking time will vary with ovens, baking dishes and temperature of eggs. If egg whites are cooked until firm, yolks will be hard. Makes 1 serving.

To make 1 cup of half-and-half, mix 3/4 cup milk and 1/4 cup whipping cream.

Ham & Egg Under a Blanket

Here's an informal dish to do for yourself on a Saturday morning.

1 egg
1 slice bread
Butter
1 slice packaged boiled ham or baked ham

About 1/4 cup shredded Havarti, Monterey
  Jack, Cheddar or Swiss cheese,
  lightly packed

Preheat oven or toaster-oven to 400°F (205°C). Poach egg in egg poacher or in simmering water, see page 16. While egg is cooking, toast and butter bread. Put ham slice on toast and warm in oven. When egg is cooked, place on ham and sprinkle with cheese to cover. Put in oven to melt cheese. Makes 1 serving.

Cheese Strata Deluxe

For a special luncheon or late evening supper.

2 tablespoons butter
1/4 cup minced onion
2 tablespoons minced green pepper
1/2 cup chopped mushrooms
1 tablespoon minced parsley
1/4 teaspoon mixed herbs such as basil,
  thyme, chervil and oregano
1 cup Soft Breadcrumbs, page 164,
  lightly packed

1 cup shredded sharp Cheddar cheese,
  lightly packed
2 eggs
2/3 cup milk or half-and-half
1/4 teaspoon Worcestershire sauce
1/4 teaspoon salt
Dash ground red pepper
1/8 teaspoon dry mustard

Preheat oven to 325°F (165°C). Melt butter in a small skillet over medium heat. Add onion, green pepper and mushrooms. Sauté until all are tender. Stir in parsley and herbs. Lightly mix breadcrumbs into mixture. Spread 1/4 of the crumb mixture in each of two 2-cup soufflé pots or similar baking dishes. Top each with 1/4 of the cheese. Repeat layers. Beat eggs in a medium bowl. Blend in remaining ingredients. Gradually pour half the egg mixture over cheese in each dish. With a fork, pierce mixture at 1/2-inch intervals to help moisten breadcrumbs. Bake about 40 minutes until a knife inserted in the center comes out clean. Cheese Strata Deluxe will puff over top of casserole but will collapse within minutes when removed from oven. To delay serving a few minutes, leave in oven and turn oven off. Makes 2 servings.

Variations

Hearty Cheese Strata: Add 1/4 cup minced ham, 2 slices cooked and crumbled bacon, 2 diced brown-and-serve sausages and 1 diced wiener to sautéed vegetables.

Make-Ahead Cheese Strata Deluxe: Assemble up to 24 hours before baking and refrigerate. Bake about 50 minutes.

Basic Cheese Strata: Omit butter, onion, green pepper, mushrooms, parsley and mixed herbs. Reduce baking time to 35 or 40 minutes.

Individual Quiches

Enjoy these classic cheese-and-bacon pies hot out of the oven or cooled for a picnic brunch.

Buttery Tart Shells, see below, or
  2 (4-inch) unbaked pastry tart shells
1/4 lb. bacon (4 thick slices or 6 thin slices)
1 egg
1 egg yolk
3/4 cup half-and-half

1/4 teaspoon salt
Dash pepper
Dash dry mustard
3/4 cup shredded Swiss cheese,
  lightly packed

Buttery Tart Shells:
1/2 cup sifted flour
1/8 teaspoon salt

3 tablespoons butter
1 tablespoon ice water

Prepare tart shells; refrigerate. Place a small baking sheet in oven and preheat to 450°F (230°C). Cut bacon crosswise into 1/4-inch pieces. Fry until crisp. Drain on paper towels. Beat egg and egg yolk in a medium bowl. Blend in half-and-half. Add salt, pepper and dry mustard. Blend well. Sprinkle bacon pieces evenly over bottoms of unbaked shells. Sprinkle cheese evenly over bacon. Pour half of egg mixture in each shell. Place tart pans on preheated baking sheet. Bake 15 minutes until crusts begin to brown. Reduce temperature to 325°F (165°C). Bake 15 more minutes until a knife inserted in center comes out clean. A milky residue on knife indicates underbaking. A watery residue indicates overbaking. Quiches should be puffed and lightly browned. Let stand 5 minutes then slide out of pans onto plates. Makes 2 servings.

Buttery Tart Shells:
Blend flour and salt in a medium bowl. With a pastry blender or 2 knives, cut butter into flour until texture resembles cornmeal. Sprinkle with ice water and quickly mix with a fork until dough lumps together. Press together and divide in half. Shape each half into a ball, pat out on a floured surface and roll out to a 7-inch circle. Fit each circle into a 4-inch tart pan. Trim pastry 1/2 inch from rim. Moisten underside of overhanging pastry and fold under to make double thickness. Crimp edge of crust with fork tines or fingers. Makes 2 tart shells.

Variations

Mushroom Quiche: Spread 1 to 2 tablespoons Duxelles, page 161, over bottom of each tart shell.
Spinach Quiche: Spread 2 tablespoons well-drained, chopped, cooked and seasoned spinach or left-over creamed spinach in bottom of each tart shell.
Onion Quiche: Sauté 1/4 cup minced onion in bacon drippings, drain well and stir into egg mixture.
Ham Quiche: Omit bacon. Substitute 1/4 cup minced ham.
Tomato Quiche: Peel, seed and dice 1 small or medium tomato. Sprinkle evenly over cheese.
Chili Quiche: Omit bacon and dry mustard. Substitute Cheddar cheese for Swiss cheese. Add about 1 tablespoon diced green chilies and 2 tablespoons minced or sliced black olives to egg mixture.
Crustless Quiche: Omit Buttery Tart Shells. Pour egg mixture over bacon and cheese in 2 buttered 10-ounce soufflé pots or custard cups. Bake in preheated 325° F (165°C) oven 25 to 30 minutes until quiche tests done. Serve in baking dishes.

Sunday Brunch Fizz

Some basic ingredients blend for a delightful drink—at home.

1/3 cup gin
Juice of 1 lemon (about 3 tablespoons)
1 egg yolk or egg white
1 tablespoon superfine or granulated sugar,
   more if desired

2 tablespoons whipping cream or
   half-and-half, or 1/4 cup milk
1/4 to 1/2 cup soda water
Ice

Combine gin, lemon juice, egg yolk or white and sugar in a blender. Cover and blend about 10 seconds. Add more sugar, if desired. Add whipping cream or half-and-half or milk. Blend on slow speed 1 or 2 seconds. Pour into two 8- to 10-ounce glasses. Add soda water and ice to fill. Stir. Makes 2 servings.

Variations

Ramos Fizz: Use egg white. Add juice of 1 lime, 6 dashes of orange-flower water and additional sugar to taste. Orange-flower water, made from distilled orange blossoms, is available at liquor departments or gourmet stores.

Substitute vodka for gin, lime juice for lemon juice, honey for sugar.

Substitute 1/4 to 1/3 cup orange, pineapple or grapefruit juice for lemon juice. Reduce sugar to taste.

Add any of the following before adding sugar: cassis, grenadine, maraschino cherry juice, orgeat syrup, coconut syrup, orange-flavored liqueur or almond-flavored liqueur. Add sugar to taste.

How To Make Individual Quiches

Pour egg mixture over selected filling ingredients in unbaked tart shells. Depending on the crust size and amount of filling ingredients, there may be extra egg mixture.

To test doneness of a quiche or any custard, insert a knife into the center. If the blade comes out clean and dry, except for particles of filling ingredients, the custard is done.

Welsh Rabbit

When the Welsh hunter came home without a rabbit for dinner, his wife cooked this one.

Welsh Rabbit Sauce, see below
4 slices bacon
4 (3/8-inch) slices tomato

Salt and pepper to taste
Flour
4 English muffin halves

Welsh Rabbit Sauce:
1 egg yolk
1/4 cup beer, fresh or flat
1/8 teaspoon dry mustard
1/4 teaspoon Worcestershire sauce

Dash paprika
Dash ground red pepper
1 cup shredded, aged sharp Cheddar cheese,
  lightly packed

Prepare Welsh Rabbit Sauce to point where Cheddar cheese is stirred in. Set aside. Preheat oven to 250°F (120°C). Cut bacon slices in half, fry until crisp and drain on paper towels. Sprinkle tomato slices with salt and pepper. Lightly coat with flour. Sauté in bacon drippings until golden on both sides. Toast English muffin halves and place a tomato slice on each. Place muffin halves and bacon on a baking sheet and keep warm in oven. Complete Welsh Rabbit Sauce. Arrange 2 muffin halves on each plate. Pour Welsh Rabbit Sauce over and garnish with bacon. Makes 2 servings.

Welsh Rabbit Sauce:

Beat egg yolk in stainless steel, enamel or nonstick saucepan or double boiler until smooth. Beat in beer and seasonings. Stir in Cheddar cheese. Warm over low heat or simmering water, stirring constantly, just until cheese melts and sauce thickens. Do not boil. Serve immediately.

Variations

Welsh Rabbit for One: Reduce by half all ingredients except egg yolk.
Golden Buck: Omit tomato, if desired. Top each English muffin half with a poached or fried egg.
Basic Welsh Rabbit: Pour Welsh Rabbit Sauce over toast, large Plain Croutons, page 162, or toasted English muffin halves. Garnish with fresh tomato slices, sautéed mushrooms or bacon bits.

To make uniform 3-inch pancakes, use a 1-ounce coffee measure to ladle pancake batter onto the hot skillet.

Sherried Chicken Livers

If you use canned mushrooms, replace part of the water with the drained juice.

2 slices bacon, diced
1 to 2 tablespoons minced shallots
1 to 2 tablespoons minced green pepper
1 garlic clove, pressed or minced
2 tablespoons flour
1/4 teaspoon salt
Pepper to taste
Paprika to taste
1/2 lb. chicken livers (about 1 cup)

1 tablespoon butter
1 tablespoon flour
3/4 cup water
1 teaspoon beef stock granules
1/4 teaspoon thyme
1/4 cup Duxelles, page 161, or
    1 (2-oz.) can sliced mushrooms
2 tablespoons dry sherry
1 tablespoon minced parsley

Sauté diced bacon in an 8-inch skillet over medium-low heat. As soon as bacon drippings coat the skillet, add shallots, green pepper and garlic. Sauté until bacon is cooked and onion is tender. Place on a plate, leaving drippings in skillet. Combine 2 tablespoons flour, salt and desired amount of pepper and paprika in a small paper bag. Rinse chicken livers, drain on paper towels and shake in flour mixture to coat. Shake off excess flour. Sauté chicken livers on all sides in bacon drippings about 5 minutes until golden. Place on a plate. Melt butter in skillet, stir in 1 tablespoon flour. Cook until frothy. Blend in water, beef stock and thyme. Cook and stir 2 to 3 minutes until thickened and smooth. Return bacon, vegetables and chicken livers to skillet. Add sherry and duxelles or drained canned mushrooms. Cook slowly, stirring gently, until chicken livers are cooked through and no longer pink in center. Garnish with minced parsley. Makes 2 servings.

Cottage Cheese Pancakes

A light and tender high-protein pancake to fit almost anyone's diet.

1 egg
1/4 cup cottage cheese
2 tablespoons flour

1 teaspoon oil
Pinch salt
Oil

Separate egg into 2 small bowls. Beat egg white until it forms soft peaks. Set aside. Add remaining ingredients to egg yolk. Beat with an electric mixer until smooth. Stir about 1/3 of the beaten egg white into yolk mixture to soften batter. Fold in remaining egg white until blended. Heat a large oiled skillet over medium heat, about 375°F (190°C). Drop batter by spoonfuls onto hot skillet and spread with back of spoon to form 3-inch circles. When underside is golden brown and edges begin to dry, turn and brown other side. Makes four or five 3-inch pancakes.

Extra Special Pancakes

If you're out of buttermilk, substitute 1/4 cup plain yogurt and 1/4 cup water.

1/2 cup sifted flour	1/2 cup buttermilk
1/4 teaspoon baking soda	1 teaspoon sugar
1 egg	1/4 teaspoon salt
1 tablespoon oil	Oil

Sift flour and baking soda together; set aside. Beat egg in a medium bowl until light and fluffy. Add remaining ingredients and beat until blended. Stir in flour mixture until moistened. Beat until smooth. Heat a large oiled skillet over medium-high heat, about 390°F (200°C). Pour about 2 tablespoons batter for each pancake onto hot skillet. When underside is golden brown and bubbles on top are breaking, turn and brown other side. Makes ten 3-inch pancakes.

Baking Mix Pancakes

If you double the recipe, use a whole egg instead of 2 egg whites.

1 egg white	1 teaspoon sugar
1/4 cup milk	1/2 cup buttermilk biscuit mix
1 teaspoon oil	Oil

Beat egg white in a small bowl. Blend in milk, oil and sugar. Stir in buttermilk biscuit mix until moistened. Beat until almost smooth. Heat a large oiled skillet over medium-high heat, about 390°F (200°C). Pour about 2 tablespoons batter for each pancake onto hot skillet. When underside is golden brown and bubbles on top are breaking, turn and brown other side. Makes six 3-inch pancakes.

Emergency Syrup

You may prefer it to your favorite bottled syrup!

1/4 cup granulated sugar	1/4 cup water
1/4 cup brown sugar, firmly packed	Dash salt

Combine ingredients in a small saucepan and bring to a boil. Stir constantly until sugar is dissolved. Makes 1/2 cup, enough for 2 servings.

Variations

Honey Syrup: Blend a spoonful of honey into finished syrup.
Fruited Syrup: Blend a spoonful of fruit preserves into finished syrup.

Monte Cristo Sandwiches

Sliced sourdough bread also makes French Toast Supreme, see below, or garlic toast.

4 slices round loaf sourdough bread
Butter, room temperature
2 long, thin slices cooked ham
2 long, thin slices natural or processed
    Swiss cheese
2 long, thin slices cooked turkey, if desired

Monte Cristo Batter, see below
2 tablespoons Clarified Butter, page 159,
    or butter
Powdered sugar
Red currant jelly

Monte Cristo Batter:
2 eggs
1/2 cup whipping cream or half-and-half

Pinch salt

Butter bread slices on 1 side. Assemble each sandwich using 1 slice ham, 1 slice cheese and 1 slice turkey, if desired. Trim off overhanging ham, cheese or turkey. Trim crusts, if desired. Cut each sandwich into 3 pieces. At this point sandwiches may be wrapped and refrigerated or frozen. Before serving, prepare Monte Cristo Batter. Dip sandwiches into batter, coating edges and both sides until nearly all batter is absorbed. Heat butter in a large skillet over medium heat. Fry sandwiches on edges and on each side until lightly browned, adding butter as necessary. Arrange sandwiches on plates. Sprinkle with powdered sugar. Top with a spoonful of jelly. Makes 2 servings.

Monte Cristo Batter:
Beat eggs in a pie plate or shallow dish. Blend in whipping cream or half-and-half and salt.

French Toast Supreme

A round loaf sliced sourdough bread makes this recipe the very best!

1 egg
2 tablespoons whipping cream or
    half-and-half
1 tablespoon dry sherry
1/8 teaspoon grated orange or lemon peel,
    if desired

Dash salt
1 center slice or 2 end slices round loaf
    sourdough bread
About 1 tablespoon Clarified Butter,
    page 159, or butter
Powdered sugar

Beat egg in a pie plate or shallow dish. Blend in whipping cream or half-and-half, sherry, orange or lemon peel, if desired, and salt. Cut center slice bread into triangles or cut end slices into halves. Dip bread into egg mixture to coat all sides and soak until egg mixture is absorbed. Heat butter in a large skillet over medium heat. Fry bread 3 to 4 minutes until lightly browned on both sides. Sprinkle with powdered sugar. Makes 1 serving.

Toad-in-the-Hole

This whimsical-looking brunch or supper treat was created by the English to use leftover meats.

Toad-in-the-Hole Batter, see below	Butter
4 to 6 brown-and-serve sausage links, thawed	Jam

Toad-in-the-Hole Batter:

1 egg	1/2 cup sifted flour
1 egg white, if desired	1/4 teaspoon salt
1/2 cup milk or half-and-half	

Preheat oven to 425°F (220°C). Prepare Toad-in-the-Hole Batter. Arrange 2 or 3 sausage links in each of 2 glass or ceramic 10-ounce soufflé pots, custard cups or similar baking dishes. Place in preheated oven 5 minutes, remove and immediately pour half the batter into each baking dish. Bake 20 minutes. Reduce oven temperature to 350°F (175°C) and bake 15 to 20 minutes. Toad-in-the-Hole crust should be very crisp and browned. The sides should rise well above rim of baking dish and center may be either full or collapsed. To delay serving, turn off oven and leave door closed. Serve Toad-in-the-Hole in baking dishes or lift from baking dishes onto plates. Serve with butter and jam. Makes 2 servings.

Toad-in-the-Hole Batter:

In a medium bowl, beat egg and extra egg white, if desired for additional volume. Blend in milk or half-and-half. Stir in flour and salt until moistened. Beat about 1 minute until no lumps remain. Or combine all ingredients in a blender, cover and blend until completely smooth. Batter may be prepared up to 24 hours in advance and refrigerated until ready to use.

Variations

Toad For One & Popovers: Make Toad-in-the-Hole Batter. Prepare half of batter in a baking dish according to directions above. Divide remaining half between 2 preheated 6-ounce custard cups to make popovers. Bake as above except remove popovers after 10 to 15 minutes at 350°F (175°C).

Large Toad-in-the-Hole: Bake entire recipe in one 3-cup soufflé pot or casserole. Bake 20 minutes at 425°F (175°C), then 20 to 25 minutes at 350°F (175°C).

Substitute pieces of wieners, fully cooked ham, steak, roast beef or lamb for brown-and-serve sausage links.

For a quick cup of hot chocolate, stir about 2 tablespoons Hot Fudge Sauce, page 155, into 3/4 cup hot milk.

Toad-in-the-Hole with jam and butter, and Ambrosia with kiwi, page 13

Cinnamon Coffeecake

Give your Sunday a nice start!

1 egg
1 tablespoon oil
1/4 cup milk
1/2 teaspoon vanilla extract

1/4 cup sugar
3/4 cup buttermilk biscuit mix
Cinnamon-Sugar Topping, see below
Honey Glaze, see below

Cinnamon-Sugar Topping:
1 teaspoon sugar
1/4 teaspoon cinnamon

2 to 3 tablespoons coarsely chopped walnuts
   or pecans

Honey Glaze:
1/4 cup powdered sugar
1 teaspoon honey

1/2 to 1 teaspoon water or milk

Preheat oven to 350°F (175°C). Line a 9" x 5" loaf pan with wax paper, see page 134. Beat egg in a medium bowl. Beat in oil. Blend in milk, vanilla and sugar. Stir in buttermilk biscuit mix to moisten. Beat vigorously about 1 to 1-1/2 minutes until smooth. Prepare Cinnamon-Sugar Topping. Pour batter into prepared pan and sprinkle topping evenly over surface. Bake about 20 minutes until cake springs back when lightly touched. Cool in pan on rack 5 to 10 minutes. Remove from pan by lifting ends of wax paper liner. Prepare Honey Glaze. Drizzle glaze over top. Serve warm. Makes 3 to 4 servings.

Cinnamon-Sugar Topping:
Combine ingredients in a custard cup and mix well.

Honey Glaze:
Blend powdered sugar, honey and 1/2 teaspoon water or milk in a small bowl. Mix until smooth and syrupy. Increase water or milk as desired for better consistency.

In-a-Hurry Eggnog

If you don't have time to sit and eat, enjoy this on your way out.

1 egg
1 small banana or 1/2 large banana,
   very ripe

3/4 cup milk
1 teaspoon honey
Dash nutmeg

Put all ingredients except nutmeg in a blender. Cover and blend until smooth. Pour into a large glass and sprinkle with nutmeg. Makes 1 serving.

Variations

Ice Cream Eggnog: Substitute 1 scoop any flavor ice cream for banana.
Honey Eggnog: Omit banana. Increase honey to 2 teaspoons.

Sour Cream Coffeecake

It's hard to be humble when you serve the world's best coffeecake.

1/2 cup sifted flour	1/2 teaspoon vanilla extract
1/4 teaspoon salt	1 egg
1/8 teaspoon baking soda	1/4 cup dairy sour cream
1/4 cup butter (1/2 stick), room temperature	Nutty Cinnamon Topping, see below
1/2 cup sugar	Powdered sugar

Nutty Cinnamon Topping:

2 teaspoons sugar	2 to 3 tablespoons coarsely chopped pecans
1/2 teaspoon cinnamon	or walnuts

Preheat oven to 350°F (175°C). Line a 7" x 3" loaf pan with wax paper, see page 134. Sift flour with salt and baking soda; set aside. With an electric mixer, beat butter in a medium bowl. Add sugar. Beat until light and airy. Add vanilla and egg. Beat until fluffy. Stir in half the flour mixture until moistened. Beat until smooth. Add sour cream. Beat until smooth. Stir in remaining flour mixture. Beat about 30 seconds until smooth. Prepare Nutty Cinnamon Topping. Spread half of batter evenly over bottom of prepared pan. Sprinkle with half of topping. Cover with remaining batter. Sprinkle remaining topping evenly over surface. Bake 30 to 35 minutes until cake pulls away from pan and springs back when lightly touched. Cool in pan 15 minutes. Remove from pan by lifting ends of wax paper liner. Sift powdered sugar generously over top before serving. Makes 3 or 4 servings.

Nutty Cinnamon Topping:
Combine ingredients in a small bowl. Mix well.

Hot Chocolate

Nothing tastes better on a cold morning—or a cold night!

1 rounded tablespoon chocolate chips	1 tablespoon whipping cream, if desired
1 teaspoon sugar	Few drops vanilla extract
Dash salt	Marshmallows, if desired
3/4 cup milk	

Combine chocolate chips, sugar, salt and 2 to 3 tablespoons of the milk in a small saucepan. Warm gently over low heat, stirring constantly, until chocolate melts and mixture is blended. Gradually blend in remaining milk and whipping cream, if desired. Heat to serving temperature and stir in vanilla. Pour into a cup or mug. Top with marshmallows, if desired. Makes 1 serving.

Variation

Mexican Chocolate: Add 1/8 teaspoon cinnamon and a pinch of grated orange peel to chocolate mixture before adding remaining milk. Serve with whipped cream and cinnamon stick, if desired.

Appetizers

The appetizer or first course provides those important initial taste, texture and temperature experiences that set the stage for the main course. Through balance and contrast it allows the main dish, and even the dessert, to be fully appreciated. If it is repetitive, it steals from their impact. If it is too spicy or rich, it can overshadow them.

Selecting an appetizer to show off the main course and dessert is an easy process. Suppose your dinner includes:

Salmon with Egg & Caper Sauce, page 94
Boiled Potato with Butter & Parsley, page 101
Steamed Fresh Spinach & Lemon Wedge, page 122
Rum-Glazed Cake, page 133

Because you are looking for contrast, the salmon automatically excludes a seafood cocktail. A cream soup is out because of the creamy sauce on the salmon. Green salad with spinach is redundant. What does this menu need? Because all these foods are hot and soft-textured, something cold and crunchy would be nice. My vote would go to either Gazpacho with its crisp cucumber and green pepper, or a simple Ambrosia featuring chunks of red apple. Both are cold, crunchy and colorful!

Here are some other possibilities for your menus:
Cream Soups—Great with main-dish salads or meals without other dairy foods, or as a contrast to fresh fruit desserts.
Broth Soups—These provide a hot start for a rich, complex meal, or a light supper of fruit and cheese.
Seafood Cocktails—High in protein, these will "beef-up" a main dish that is light in protein.
Fruit Cocktails—Cold, fresh and sweet. Some have great texture. Serve with almost any hot meal where fruits are not included.
Cold Soups—Perfect for a summer meal of hot foods or as a contrast to a spicy main dish. Cold fruit soups are like fruit cocktails.
Fruit and Vegetable Juices—Both simple and delicious, some can be served hot and spiced.
Salads—See the next chapter. They provide that often needed crunchy texture and icy coldness.
Miscellaneous Appetizers—Consider Celeri Remoulade or Jellied Madrilene in Avocado. Serve antipasto or prosciutto and melon with Italian dinners.

HORS D'OEUVRES

There are times when the best reason for serving an hors d'oeuvre is simply to keep your guest from starving while you finish preparing the dinner. But its real purpose is to intensify the enjoyment of the main course, especially if there is no appetizer. One light hors d'oeuvre, with perhaps some nuts or cheese, is usually enough.

Recipes for a few hors d'oeuvres are included in this chapter, but, with a few specialty items, your basic stock foods and a little imagination, you should be able to produce some original hors d'oeuvres at a moment's notice. Check your supply against the list below. Serve some items with dips made from sour cream, mayonnaise, cottage cheese, cream cheese or yogurt. Others can be served on crackers or cut up and served on toothpicks. Only a few need to be cooked. If you use crackers, choose an unflavored variety for versatility. Or, make your own by toasting thin slices of individual French rolls.

FOODS WITH HORS D'OEUVRE POTENTIAL
Produce

Apples	Celery	Onions
Artichokes	Cucumbers	Pears
Avocados	Grapes	Pineapples
Broccoli	Green Onions	Radishes
Cantaloupes	Green Peppers	Tomatoes
Carrots	Jicama	Turnips
Cauliflower	Mushrooms	Zucchini

Dairy & Deli Items

All Cheeses	Pickled	Smoked
Cold Cuts	Herring	Salmon
Eggs	Pickles	Wieners

Frozen Foods

Bacon	Chicken	Sausages
Chicken	Livers	Steaks
Breasts	Hamburger	

Canned and Packaged Foods

Caviar	Mushrooms	Sardines
Crackers	Nuts	Shellfish
Marinated	Pickled Beets	Tuna
Beans	Popcorn	Vienna Sausages

From back: Angels on Horseback, page 34, Stuffed Mushrooms, page 34, and Blue Cheese Crisps, page 35

Angels on Horseback *Photo on page 33.*

When you want something a little unusual to start your meal.

1 or 2 individual French rolls
4 slices bacon, cut in half
8 small fresh oysters
Salt and pepper to taste

Paprika to taste
1 tablespoon minced parsley, if desired
2 lemon wedges

Cut rolls into eight 1/3-inch slices. Toast slices until golden brown. Place bacon on a small broiler pan. Broil until limp and translucent. Sprinkle oysters with salt, pepper, paprika and parsley, if desired. Wrap a half slice bacon around each oyster and secure with a toothpick. Broil about 4 minutes until bacon is crisp. Turn and broil until other side is crisp. Remove toothpicks, place oysters on toasted slices and serve immediately. Garnish with lemon wedges. Makes 8 appetizers.

Variation

Substitute 8 melba toast rounds for French roll slices.

Stuffed Mushrooms *Photo on page 33.*

A special treat for just the two of you.

8 to 10 fresh medium-small mushrooms
  (about 1/4 lb.)
1 tablespoon butter
1 tablespoon minced shallots or
  2 tablespoons minced onion
1/4 teaspoon Worcestershire sauce

1/4 cup Soft Breadcrumbs, page 164,
  lightly packed
1/4 cup shredded sharp Cheddar cheese,
  lightly packed
Salt and pepper to taste
2 tablespoons water

Preheat oven to 350°F (175°C). Select well-shaped mushrooms with closed caps. Wash quickly under running water and drain on paper towels. Pull stems from mushrooms and finely chop. Melt butter in a small skillet over medium-low heat. Add chopped mushroom stems and shallots or onion. Sauté until tender and translucent. Stir in Worcestershire sauce, soft breadcrumbs, cheese and salt and pepper. Salt insides of mushroom caps and fill with sautéed mixture, mounding over the top. At this point, mushrooms may be refrigerated up to 24 hours. Before serving, put 2 tablespoons water in a shallow dish and arrange stuffed mushrooms in dish. Bake about 20 minutes. Serve hot. Makes 8 to 10 appetizers.

Blue Cheese Crisps *Photo on page 33.*

Make this spread in quantity and be ready for impromptu get-togethers.

1/2 cup butter (1 stick), room temperature
1 (4-oz.) pkg. blue cheese, room temperature

1/2 cup minced pecans or walnuts
Individual French rolls

Combine butter and blue cheese in a small bowl. Blend well. Stir in pecans or walnuts. Cut rolls in 1/3-inch slices. Toast desired number of slices on one side. Spread blue cheese mixture on untoasted sides. Broil until bubbling. Store remaining spread in an airtight jar in refrigerator or freezer. Makes about 1-1/4 cups spread, enough for about 48 appetizers.

Broiled Cheese Puffs

Here's an appetizer you can put together at a moment's notice.

2 tablespoons mayonnaise
1 tablespoon shredded Parmesan cheese,
  or 2 tablespoons Cheddar cheese
1/8 teaspoon Worcestershire sauce

1 tablespoon minced onion, shallots or
  green onion
1 or 2 individual French rolls

Combine mayonnaise, cheese, Worcestershire sauce and onion. Blend well. Cut rolls into ten 1/3-inch slices. Toast slices on one side. Spread mayonnaise mixture on untoasted sides, mounding slightly. Broil until golden and bubbling. Makes 10 appetizers.

Curried Mayonnaise Dip

Perfect for fresh vegetable dippers.

1/4 cup mayonnaise
1/2 teaspoon curry powder
1/2 teaspoon soy sauce

1/2 teaspoon lemon juice
1/4 teaspoon grated onion, if desired

Combine all ingredients and refrigerate 1 hour to blend flavors. Serve with fresh vegetable dippers such as cauliflower flowerets, cherry tomatoes, cucumber slices, celery sticks, radishes, whole or sliced mushrooms and turnip slices. Or serve with chilled, partially cooked broccoli flowerets or Brussels sprouts, or cooked artichokes. Makes about 1/4 cup dip.

Steak Tartare

Serve this when you find someone who loves rare meat!

1/3 lb. boneless round steak or sirloin tip,
   or 1/4 lb. freshly ground lean beef
1 egg yolk
Salt to taste
Freshly ground black pepper to taste
Few drops Worcestershire sauce

2 tablespoons minced onion
Lettuce leaves
1 tablespoon capers
1 tablespoon minced parsley
Pumpernickel or rye bread, thinly sliced
   and buttered

If using round steak or sirloin tip, use the bowl of a spoon to scrape bits of red meat away from white connective tissue. Discard connective tissue and fat. In a small bowl, combine scraped beef or ground beef with egg yolk, salt and pepper to taste, Worcestershire sauce and 1 tablespoon of the minced onion. Shape into a flat oval patty and place on a lettuce-lined salad plate. Sprinkle capers, parsley and remaining onion over beef. Surround beef with small squares of buttered bread. Makes 2 servings.

Variation

Steak Tartare Entree: Do not mix egg yolk into beef. Form an indentation in the center of the beef patty and insert raw yolk. Surround with small onion ring, if desired. Sprinkle condiments over. The guest mixes the yolk into the meat. Makes 1 serving.

How To Make Steak Tartare

For classic Steak Tartare, beef is scraped rather than ground. Trim all visible fat from beef and use an inverted spoon to scrape muscle fibers from connective tissue.

An elegant hors d'oeuvre for two! Garnish the flavored raw beef patty with capers, parsley and onion. Spread on squares of buttered pumpernickel or rye bread.

Seviche

A delicate raw fish marinated in lime juice and highlighted with spicy ingredients.

1/3 lb. fresh scallops or white fish such as
   red snapper or sea bass
About 1/4 cup lime juice
2 tablespoons finely minced onion
1/2 small tomato, peeled, seeded and diced

1 to 2 teaspoons diced green chilies or
   hot sauce to taste
1/4 teaspoon salt
1/8 teaspoon oregano
2 lettuce leaves, if desired

If using scallops, cut into 1/4-inch dice. If using fish, remove skin and bones and, with knife at an angle, thinly slice fish. The slices should fall apart into small pieces. Put fish into a medium glass, ceramic or enamel bowl. Gradually add lime juice, stirring gently with a fork. The acid in the lime juice will cause the fish to turn white. Continue adding juice and stirring until all the fish is white and juicy. Fold in remaining ingredients except lettuce leaves. Cover and refrigerate at least 3 hours. Seviche will keep in refrigerator several days. Remove from bowl with a slotted spoon. Serve in shells or icers or on lettuce-lined salad plates. Makes 2 servings.

Variations

Peruvian Seviche: Substitute red onion rings for minced onion. Serve with corn on the cob and baked sweet potato. Makes 1 main dish serving.

Add 1 tablespoon oil and minced cilantro (fresh coriander).

Add 1/4 avocado, diced.

Seafood Cocktail Supreme

Freshly cooked seafood deserves a fresh sauce.

Cocktail Sauce Supreme, see below
1/4 lb. cooked cocktail shrimp or
   flaked crabmeat

1/2 cup minced celery
2 lemon wedges
2 parsley sprigs, if desired

Cocktail Sauce Supreme:
2 teaspoons grated onion
1 tablespoon lemon juice
1/4 cup ketchup or chili sauce
1 to 2 teaspoons prepared horseradish

1/2 teaspoon Worcestershire sauce
Dash Tabasco sauce
Salt to taste

Prepare Cocktail Sauce Supreme. Mix shrimp or crabmeat with celery. Spoon into 2 icers, shells or other small chilled dishes. Spoon Cocktail Sauce Supreme over. Garnish with lemon wedges and parsley sprigs, if desired. Makes 2 servings.

Cocktail Sauce Supreme:
Combine all ingredients in a small bowl. Refrigerate to blend flavors.

Jellied Madrilene in Avocado

Heat leftover jellied consommé madrilene and serve as a hot consommé.

1/2 (13-oz.) can jellied consommé madrilene
Lemony Sour Cream Sauce, see below
1 large ripe avocado

Lemon juice, if necessary
Lettuce leaves or parsley sprigs
1/8 teaspoon freshly grated lemon peel

Lemony Sour Cream Sauce:
1/4 cup dairy sour cream
2 teaspoons lemon juice

1/8 teaspoon freshly grated lemon peel
Salt to taste

Refrigerate can of jellied consommé madrilene overnight. Prepare Lemony Sour Cream Sauce. Cut avocado in half and remove seed. Cut a small slice from bottom of each half if necessary so avocados sit flat. If preparing avocados before serving time, moisten all cut surfaces with lemon juice to prevent discoloration. Place avocado halves on lettuce-lined salad plates or in small bowls of crushed ice garnished with parsley sprigs. Spoon jellied madrilene into each avocado half until overflowing. Spoon Lemony Sour Cream Sauce over and garnish with grated lemon peel. Makes 2 servings.

Lemony Sour Cream Sauce:
Combine all ingredients. Refrigerate to blend flavors.

Variation

Seafood Madrilene: Omit avocado. Spoon jellied consommé madrilene into icers. Top each serving with about an ounce of cocktail shrimp or flaked crabmeat. Spoon Lemony Sour Cream Sauce over and garnish with parsley sprigs.

Iced Borscht

Keep the bright pink color of this special soup in mind when you select a tablecloth or placemats.

1 (8-oz.) can beets, not pickled
1 (1/4-inch) slice medium onion
1 tablespoon lemon juice or
   white wine vinegar
1/4 teaspoon sugar
1/4 teaspoon salt or garlic salt

1/4 teaspoon dill weed
1/2 cup dairy sour cream
Salt to taste
Additional dairy sour cream, if desired
Minced chives, green onions or parsley

Put beets with juice into a blender. Add lemon juice or vinegar, sugar, salt or garlic salt and dill weed. Cover and blend until smooth. Add 1/2 cup sour cream. Blend on slow speed. Refrigerate several hours or overnight to blend flavors. Add salt to taste. Serve in icers, chilled mugs or bowls. Garnish with a dollop of sour cream, if desired. Sprinkle with minced chives, green onions or parsley. Makes 2 servings.

Gazpacho

Spain gives us this refreshing variation of the tomato.

1 to 2 tablespoons oil or olive oil
1 tablespoon freshly squeezed lemon juice or
   wine vinegar
1 cup tomato juice or vegetable juice cocktail
2 tablespoons minced onion
1/2 small garlic clove, finely minced
1/2 teaspoon salt
Pepper to taste

1/4 teaspoon chervil, marjoram or oregano
Dash ground cumin, if desired
Dash Tabasco sauce
1 large tomato, peeled, seeded and diced,
   see page 49
1/3 cup peeled, seeded and diced cucumber
2 to 3 tablespoons minced green pepper
1/4 cup Plain Croutons, page 162

Whip oil and lemon juice or vinegar together in a medium bowl. Blend in remaining ingredients except cucumber, green pepper and croutons. Cover and refrigerate several hours or overnight. Serve in bowls or mugs with an ice cube in each serving, or serve in icers. Sprinkle with cucumber, green pepper and croutons. Makes 2 servings.

Variation

Add minced celery, diced avocado, minced cilantro or chopped green onions or chives.

Cream of Vegetable Soup

Make a variety of cream soups from leftover cooked vegetables.

1/2 cup chicken stock or broth from cooked
   vegetables
Small wedge onion
1 cup coarsely chopped cooked vegetables such
   as broccoli, cauliflower, celery, corn,
   asparagus, cabbage, mushrooms, peas,
   spinach, carrots or green beans
2 tablespoons butter
2 tablespoons flour

1 cup milk or half-and-half
1/4 teaspoon herbs such as chervil, thyme,
   marjoram, basil and tarragon
1/8 teaspoon Worcestershire sauce
Milk, chicken stock or vegetable broth,
   if necessary
Seasoned salt to taste
Freshly ground black pepper to taste
2 tablespoons dry sherry

Combine chicken stock or vegetable broth, onion and half the vegetables in a blender. Cover and blend until completely smooth. Add remaining vegetables. Switch blender on and off once or twice to finely chop but not liquefy vegetables. Melt butter in a medium saucepan over medium heat until frothy. Stir in flour. Cook gently, stirring constantly, until frothy. Do not let flour brown. Add milk or half-and-half, herbs and Worcestershire sauce. Simmer and stir until thickened and smooth. Blend in vegetable mixture. Cook over low heat about 5 minutes, stirring frequently. If soup is too thick, stir in additional milk, chicken stock or vegetable broth. Add seasoned salt and pepper to taste. Just before serving, stir in sherry. Makes 2 servings.

Celeri Remoulade

Celery root, also called celeriac, *is a lesser-known relative of celery.*

2 small celery roots (about 1 lb.)
2 cups water
1 teaspoon salt
2 tablespoons lemon juice

1/4 cup mayonnaise
1 tablespoon Dijon mustard
2 lettuce leaves

Scrub celery roots, dry and slice 1/8-inch thick. Cut thick fibrous peel from each slice. Stack peeled slices and cut into 1/8-inch julienne strips. Combine water, salt and lemon juice in a small saucepan. Bring to a boil. Drop celery root strips into boiling water. Cover and simmer 5 minutes. Drain immediately in a colander and cool slightly. While warm, mix with mayonnaise and mustard. Marinate several hours or overnight. Spoon onto lettuce-lined plates. Makes 2 servings.

How To Make Celeri Remoulade

Beneath the unattractive exterior of a celery root is a delicately flavored interior. Select small, uniformly shaped celery roots for best texture. Cut away thick woody skins.

Celeri Remoulade is a wonderful dish to start a fall or winter dinner. Make it even more appetizing with a garnish of cherry tomatoes and minced parsley.

Strawberry Soup Glacé

So refreshing! And easy, too.

1 pint fresh strawberries	Honey to taste
2 tablespoons orange-flavored liqueur	Sour Cream Sauce, see below

Sour Cream Sauce:

2 to 4 tablespoons dairy sour cream	Freshly grated lemon peel to taste
1 teaspoon honey	Dash salt

Wash strawberries and reserve 2 prettiest ones for garnish. Hull remaining strawberries. In a blender, puree hulled strawberries with orange-flavored liqueur. Add honey to taste. Refrigerate until serving time. Prepare Sour Cream Sauce. Pour strawberry mixture into chilled bowls or icers and top with Sour Cream Sauce. Garnish with reserved strawberries. Serve with chilled spoons. Makes 2 servings.

Sour Cream Sauce:
Combine ingredients in a small bowl and blend. Refrigerate.

Peach Soup à la Crème

This soup could pass for a dessert!

1 large ripe peach, peeled and seeded (about 1/2 lb.)	1/4 cup half-and-half or whipping cream
2 teaspoons lemon juice	Up to 1 tablespoon honey, to taste
2 tablespoons almond-flavored liqueur	Toasted Almonds, page 165, sliced or slivered

Combine peeled and seeded peach, lemon juice and almond-flavored liqueur in a blender. Cover and blend until smooth. Add half-and-half or whipping cream. Blend on slow speed. Add honey to taste. Place plastic wrap on surface of soup; chill. Serve in icers or chilled bowls. Garnish with toasted almonds. Makes 2 servings.

Variations

Nectarine Soup à la Crème: Substitute 1 unpeeled nectarine for peach.
All-Season Peach Soup: Omit honey. Substitute 1 (8-ounce) can sliced peaches with syrup for fresh peach.

Salads

It's clear to me that salad is an extremely important part of today's cuisine! We make salads out of everything—vegetables, fruits, macaroni, rice, cheese, eggs, beans, fish, meat—you name it! We serve them hot, cold, cooked, raw, pickled, frozen, gelled, tossed or arranged. And we serve them all the time. We LOVE salads!

Most of all we love the green salad, almost to the exclusion of all others. One of the reasons we hesitate to give up our green salad is we think of it as our major source of vitamin A each day. That's good, but many other foods provide even more vitamin A than a green salad. Besides liver and greens like kale, dandelion and spinach, there are carrots, yams, sweet potatoes, winter squash, mangoes, cantaloupes and even broccoli, papayas and apricots. Whenever one of these foods already appears in your day's menu, why not try a different kind of salad, or even a different kind of first course all together? There are so many possibilities. It's a shame not to try them all.

WHEN TO SERVE THE SALAD

Salads can be properly served before, with or after the main course. The choice depends on the type of salad and the preference of the cook.

For couples and singles who enjoy preparing restaurant specialties that require last-minute attention, a salad can get in the way of the main course preparation. The French custom of serving the salad after the main dish can make such a dinner considerably more leisurely. Open the dinner wine a little early and enjoy it with a light hors d'oeuvre while you prepare the main dish. After the main course, a simple salad of fresh greens with oil & vinegar dressing is only moments away.

A green salad makes a very nice appetizer served before the main course. But fruit salads are particularly nice served with the meat as a flavor complement. Similarly, a cucumber salad is marvelous for cooling the palate while eating spicy Mexican dishes or curries.

PREPARING SALAD VEGETABLES

There are easy ways to prepare small quantities of many salad vegetables:

Minced Onion—Cut thin slices from the onion and remove peel from the slices. Stack the slices and cut through at 1/8-inch intervals. Cut the pieces again at right angles.

Sliced Green Onion or Celery—Cut green onions or celery crosswise into thirds or quarters. Stack the pieces together and slice through all at once. To mince or dice any long vegetables, cut lengthwise into strips before making cuts crosswise as shown on page 59.

Thinly Sliced Cucumbers or Zucchini—Use an adjustable manual slicer.

Peeled and Seeded Tomato—To peel a tomato, insert fork tines deep into the stem end and either submerge the tomato in boiling water 5 to 10 seconds or rotate it on a fork over a gas flame until the skin bursts, as shown on page 49. Peel the skin from the bottom back toward the stem end. Cut out the stem and refrigerate the tomato if time permits. To seed a tomato, cut it in half crosswise and push seeds from each section with your thumb, as also shown on page 49.

GREEN SALAD COMBINATIONS

Adding delicious tidbits can make your salad unique. Besides fresh vegetables and fruits, include leftover meats or cooked, unbuttered vegetables. Cold cuts, cheeses, nuts and marinated or pickled foods are also good. Try these combinations to avoid perishable leftover ingredients:

The B.L.T.—Lettuce, tomato, avocado, cucumber and green onion with sour cream dressing and crumbled crisp bacon for garnish.

Health Nut—Leaf lettuce, toasted walnuts or pecans, raisins and parsley with oil & vinegar dressing.

Gold Rush—Lettuce, grated carrot, chopped peanuts, minced celery and chopped green onion with mayonnaise and lemon juice dressing.

California Sun—Romaine lettuce, orange pieces and

onion rings with a sweetened oil & lemon juice dressing.

Oriental Blue—Butter lettuce, bean sprouts and sliced fresh mushrooms with blue cheese vinaigrette dressing.

French Basic—Leaf lettuce, minced parsley, minced green onion, tarragon and oil & vinegar dressing.

TOSSING THE GREENS

• Use a large salad bowl. A salad for 2 needs as big a bowl as a salad for 6, particularly if it is to be tossed at the table.

• Tear the greens. When leafy vegetables are cut with a knife, the delicate cells open and moisture drains out, diluting the dressing and wilting the greens. When greens are torn, the cells are left intact.

• Dry the torn greens. Dressing will not cling to wet leaves, so use a salad basket or spinner to get rid of any moisture. Or mound the greens in the center of a clean kitchen towel, bring the edges of the towel together, and shake.

• Chill the greens, serving plates and forks. Place a dry paper towel in the bottom of the salad bowl and put the greens and other vegetable ingredients in the bowl. Lay slightly damp paper towels over the leaves and refrigerate. To store over 3 hours, cover the bowl with plastic wrap. Do not prepare greens more than 24 hours in advance.

• Toss in the salad dressing just before serving. If the dressing is added too far ahead of time, the salts in the dressing will draw moisture from the vegetables, wilting the greens and diluting the dressing.

To serve homemade oil & vinegar dressing, first add oil to the greens and toss until all the leaves glisten. Then add vinegar and seasonings and toss until well-coated. This technique causes the ingredients to cling to the greens better.

Premixed or creamy dressings can simply be added to the salad and tossed until all vegetables are coated.

• Toss in any grated cheese, chopped hard-cooked egg, croutons, crumbled bacon and pepper last. If the dressing seems tart, cheese, egg and croutons help balance the flavor.

• Garnish and serve. Spoon the salad onto chilled plates. Add garnishes such as beets that might discolor the salad if tossed in earlier.

HOW TO TOSS A SALAD

Pour the oil or dressing over the salad. Lift one salad spoon straight up from the bottom of the bowl and roll the ingredients over it with a second spoon, moving from the back to the front of the bowl as shown on page 59. Repeat until all leaves are coated.

MAIN DISH SALADS

Almost any salad can be turned into a main dish by adding some high-protein ingredients. Chunks of ham added to a Waldorf Salad make it a main dish. A green salad needs only a can of tuna to create a main dish. Slivered cooked chicken turns a Russian Salad into an entree. Shrimp, crab, salmon, leftover steak, cold cuts, hard-cooked eggs, cottage cheese or almost any ripe cheese can be used in a main dish salad. Add a hot bread and you have an easy and delicious meal.

THE SALAD DRESSING

If you have a favorite bottled dressing or dressing mix, keep it on hand. But for a constant variety of fresh dressings, make your own from oil, vinegar, mayonnaise, sour cream, whipping cream, lemon juice or other basic ingredients. See Sauce Vinaigrette, page 48 and Sour Cream Dressing, page 56, for ideas about ingredients to add to your creations. If you are watching calories, consider plain yogurt, buttermilk, tomato juice, sour cream, vinegar and lemon juice and foundations for low-calorie dressings.

Fresh peaches, pears, nectarines, bananas, apples and avocados will darken after being cut. To prevent this, dip in lemon juice, orange juice, grapefruit juice, sour cream or yogurt.

Spinach Salad

Even people who think they don't like spinach love this salad!

1/4 cup oil	2 tablespoons wine vinegar
1 small garlic clove, crushed or finely minced	1/2 teaspoon Dijon mustard or
About 1/2 bunch fresh spinach	1/4 teaspoon dry mustard
1 Hard-Cooked Egg, page 160	1/4 teaspoon salt
2 to 4 slices bacon (about 3 tablespoons,	Pepper to taste
crumbled)	2 tablespoons grated Parmesan cheese

At least 1 hour before serving, measure oil into a small jar. Add garlic, close tightly and let stand at room temperature. Select freshest and most tender spinach leaves. Remove stems, wash leaves and tear into bite-size pieces to make 3 to 4 cups, lightly packed. Dry leaves by shaking in a clean kitchen towel. Put leaves into a salad bowl. Cover with slightly damp paper towels; refrigerate to crisp. Chop hard-cooked egg; refrigerate. Cut bacon strips crosswise into 1/4-inch pieces. Fry until crisp. Drain on paper towels and refrigerate. Blend vinegar, mustard, salt and pepper; set aside. To serve, remove garlic from oil. Toss oil with spinach until leaves glisten. Toss with vinegar mixture and cheese. Serve on individual plates. Garnish with bacon and chopped egg. Makes 2 servings.

Watercress & Orange Salad

Don't hesitate to buy watercress to garnish a plate. Use the rest in this salad!

Creamy Dressing, see below	1 medium orange, peeled
1 to 1-1/2 cups watercress sprigs and leaves,	2 green onions including fresh tops,
lightly packed (about 1 bunch)	thinly sliced

Creamy Dressing:

2 tablespoons oil	1/4 teaspoon Dijon mustard
2 teaspoons lemon juice	1/8 teaspoon seasoned salt

Prepare Creamy Dressing; refrigerate. Pick tender dark green sprigs and leaves from coarse watercress stems. Rinse well. Dry by shaking in a clean kitchen towel. Slice orange 1/2-inch thick. Cut slices into quarters. Combine watercress, orange pieces and green onion in a medium bowl. Pour dressing over and toss. Serve on individual salad plates or in bowls. Makes 2 servings.

Creamy Dressing:

In a tightly covered jar, combine all ingredients. Shake until creamy. Shake again before using.

Variation

Watercress & Grape Salad: Substitute 1/2 cup seedless green grapes for orange.

Caesar Salad

Because it uses only the yolk of the egg, this version of Caesar Salad tosses together faster.

1 garlic clove
1/3 cup oil or olive oil
4 to 6 cups torn Romaine leaves,
  lightly packed
About 3/4 cup (1/2-inch) bread cubes
  from sourdough or French bread
1 tablespoon shredded Parmesan cheese
1/4 teaspoon seasoned salt

1/2 to 1 teaspoon anchovy paste or
  1 mashed anchovy fillet, if desired
1/2 lemon, seeds removed
1 egg yolk, in half egg shell
3 tablespoons shredded Parmesan cheese
Salt to taste
Freshly ground black pepper to taste

The day before serving, cut garlic clove in half. Reserve half to season salad bowl. Cut other half in half again and combine with oil in a small jar. Cover tightly and refrigerate overnight. Wash lettuce and tear into large bite-size pieces. Dry by shaking in a clean kitchen towel. Wrap in a slightly damp paper towel and refrigerate in a plastic bag to crisp overnight. Before serving salad, toss bread cubes in 1 tablespoon of the garlic-flavored oil. Preheat oven to 350°F (175°C). Spread bread cubes evenly on a shallow baking sheet. Bake about 10 minutes until golden brown and crisp. While hot, toss croutons in a paper bag with 1 tablespoon Parmesan cheese and seasoned salt. Rub salad bowl with cut side of reserved garlic clove. Put lettuce into bowl. Remove garlic from oil. Blend anchovy paste or mashed anchovy into oil, if desired. To serve salad at table, place salad bowl in center of a tray. Around the bowl, arrange the oil, 1/2 lemon with fork inserted in cut side, egg yolk in half shell inside a small cup, 3 tablespoons Parmesan cheese, salt shaker, pepper grinder, croutons in a small bowl, salad spoons, 2 chilled salad plates or bowls and 2 chilled salad forks. Toss oil with lettuce until leaves glisten. Squeeze lemon over salad while twisting fork to extract juice. Immediately add egg yolk; toss until dressing is uniformly creamy. Toss with Parmesan cheese, salt and pepper. Salt lightly if anchovy is used. Toss croutons into salad or sprinkle over individual servings. Makes 2 servings.

Chopped Parsley Salad

This is my favorite way of using up lots of parsley.

3/4 cup chopped parsley, lightly packed
3/4 cup minced celery
1/4 cup minced green onions (about 4 onions)
2 to 3 tablespoons oil

2 teaspoons lemon juice or
  white wine vinegar
Salt and pepper to taste

Combine parsley, celery and green onions in a medium bowl. Toss with oil until well-coated. Toss with lemon juice of vinegar and salt and pepper. Makes 2 servings.

Variation

Chopped Salad du Jour: Substitute small amounts of finely minced radishes, mushrooms, cucumber, green pepper, cauliflower or broccoli for part of the parsley, celery or green onions.

Indiana Wilted Lettuce Salad

You'll appreciate this when you have lettuce that's less than crisp!

6 cups torn leaves of salad bowl, butter or
   red leaf lettuce, lightly packed
2 or 3 green onions, sliced
4 or 5 radishes, sliced, if desired
2 slices bacon
2 tablespoons oil

2 tablespoons vinegar
1 tablespoon water
1 teaspoon sugar
1/8 to 1/4 teaspoon garlic salt
Salt and pepper to taste

In a medium bowl, combine lettuce, onions and radishes, if desired. Set aside at room temperature. Cut bacon into 1/4-inch squares. Sauté in a large saucepan over medium heat until crisp. Reduce heat. Stir in oil, vinegar, water, sugar and garlic salt. Bring to a boil. Remove from heat. Add lettuce mixture all at once. Toss until leaves are coated with dressing and slightly wilted. Add salt and pepper. Serve immediately. Makes 2 servings.

Variation

Hot Spinach Salad: Substitute spinach leaves for lettuce.

Heart of Romaine à la Mer

Use the outer leaves for tossed salad, then enjoy the Romaine heart.

Sauce Gribiche, see below
1 Romaine lettuce heart

3 oz. cocktail shrimp (about 1/2 cup)

Sauce Gribiche:
1 Hard-Cooked Egg, page 160
1/4 cup mayonnaise
1 teaspoon sweet pickle relish or
   chopped sweet pickle

1 teaspoon chopped capers
1 teaspoon minced parsley
1/4 teaspoon tarragon

Prepare Sauce Gribiche and refrigerate. Leaving Romaine heart intact, trim stem end and cut tips from leaves so Romaine does not overlap salad plate. Cut in half lengthwise, rinse and drain well on paper towels. Place on salad plates, cut side up, and spoon Sauce Gribiche over. Sprinkle shrimp over sauce. Serve with knife and fork. Makes 2 servings.

Sauce Gribiche:
Cut hard-cooked egg in half. Separate yolk from white. Mash yolk in a small bowl. Blend in mayonnaise. Stir in remaining ingredients. Cut egg white into slivers or finely chop and fold into sauce.

Scandinavian-Style Cucumber Salad

A tart-sweet salad lightens a meal of rich foods.

1 cucumber
2 tablespoons cider vinegar or
　white wine vinegar
2 teaspoons sugar

1/2 teaspoon salt
Dash pepper
1/2 teaspoon dill weed or tarragon

Peel cucumber and slice thin enough to be translucent. Combine with remaining ingredients and refrigerate several hours if time permits. Serve in small sauce dishes or soufflé pots. Makes 2 servings.

Sunomono

Cucumbers go Japanese with a few basic ingredients.

1 cucumber
1/4 teaspoon salt
2 teaspoons granulated or brown sugar
2 tablespoons white wine vinegar

1/2 teaspoon horseradish
1/8 teaspoon ground ginger
1 tablespoon Toasted Sesame Seeds,
　page 165

Peel cucumber and slice thin enough to be translucent. Combine with remaining ingredients except toasted sesame seeds. Cover and refrigerate about 1 hour if time permits. Serve in small bowls. Garnish with toasted sesame seeds. Makes 2 servings.

Cucumbers in Sour Cream

Eastern Europeans enjoy cucumbers in sour cream.

1 cucumber
1/4 cup minced onion or 1/4 medium onion,
　sliced and ringed
1/3 cup dairy sour cream
1 teaspoon white vinegar or lemon juice

1/2 teaspoon sugar
1/4 teaspoon salt
Dash paprika
1/2 teaspoon dill

Peel cucumber and slice 1/8-inch thick. Combine with remaining ingredients in a small bowl. Refrigerate until serving time. Makes 2 servings.

Variations

Persian Yogurt Cucumber Salad: Omit vinegar or lemon juice. Substitute 1/3 cup plain yogurt for sour cream. Substitute 1/2 teaspoon dry mint for dill. Garnish with minced parsley.

Chopped Broccoli Salad

Unusual and easy to prepare the night before.

Oil & Vinegar Dressing, see below, or
   1/3 cup bottled oil & vinegar dressing
1 stalk fresh broccoli (about 1/3 lb.)
1 medium tomato, peeled, seeded and diced
1/4 cup coarsley shredded or finely diced
   sharp Cheddar cheese, lightly packed

2 tablespoons minced onion
2 to 3 tablespoons coarsely chopped
   Toasted Walnuts, page 165

Oil & Vinegar Dressing:
1 tablespoon wine vinegar
1/8 teaspon dry mustard
1/4 teaspoon garlic salt

1/2 teaspoon mixed herbs such as tarragon,
   oregano, thyme and basil
1/4 cup oil

Prepare Oil & Vinegar Dressing. Trim end and leaves from broccoli. Peel stem. Finely chop stem and flowers. Put in a medium bowl. Add tomato, cheese and onion. Toss with dressing. Cover and refrigerate at least 2 hours or overnight. Before serving, toss in toasted walnuts. Makes 2 servings.

Oil & Vinegar Dressing:
Combine all ingredients except oil in a jar. Cover tightly and shake to dissolve salt. Add oil and shake until blended. Shake again before using.

How to Peel & Seed Tomatoes

Prepare the tomato for peeling by rotating it evenly over a gas flame until the skin bursts. Or submerge it in boiling water 5 to 10 seconds. The skin should peel easily.

To remove the seeds from a tomato, cut it in half crosswise and use your thumb to push the seeds out of the sections.

Fresh Mushroom Salad

A great change from green salads.

1/4 lb. fresh small mushrooms	About 1 tablespoon white wine vinegar
2 tablespoons minced parsley	Salt to taste
2 tablespoons minced green onion	Freshly ground black pepper to taste
About 4 tablespoons oil	Butter lettuce or other leaf lettuce

Select mushrooms with completely closed caps. Wash by rolling between palms under running water. Drain and dry on paper towels. Thinly slice mushrooms. Combine mushrooms, parsley and green onion in a medium bowl. Cover with a damp paper towel; refrigerate. Before serving, toss enough oil with mushrooms to make them glisten. Mushrooms will absorb most of the oil. Add vinegar 1 teaspoon at a time for desired flavor. Add salt and pepper. Serve on lettuce-lined salad plates. Makes 2 servings.

Variation

Mushroom-Celery Salad: Replace up to 1/3 of mushrooms with thinly sliced celery. Garnish with chopped Hard-Cooked Egg, page 160.

Sauce Vinaigrette

If there is a universal salad dressing—this is it.

1 tablespoon vinegar or lemon juice	Freshly ground black pepper to taste
1/8 teaspoon salt	1/4 to 1/2 teaspoon herbs such as basil,
1/8 teaspoon dry mustard or	tarragon, dill, thyme and marjoram
1/4 teaspoon Dijon mustard	1/4 cup oil

In an airtight jar, combine vinegar or lemon juice, salt, mustard, pepper to taste and herbs. Shake to dissolve salt. Add oil. Shake to blend well. Shake again before using. Makes about 1/3 cup dressing.

Variations

Garlic Vinaigrette: Peel and halve 1 garlic clove. Store in oil in an airtight jar several hours or overnight. Remove garlic pieces before adding oil to vinegar mixture.
Creamy Vinaigrette: Add 1 to 2 tablespoons dairy sour cream, whipping cream, plain yogurt, mayonnaise or buttermilk to finished dressing.
Cheese Vinaigrette: Add crumbled blue or Roquefort cheese, shredded sharp Cheddar cheese, grated Parmesan cheese or cottage cheese to taste to finished dressing.

Add any of the following to taste: Worcestershire sauce, Tabasco sauce, ketchup, chili sauce, horseradish, chopped Hard-Cooked Egg, page 160, minced pimiento, chopped olives, crumbled bacon, sweet pickle relish, capers, Toasted Sesame Seeds, page 165, or poppy seeds.

Russian Salad

Frozen mixed vegetables come to the rescue!

1 cup frozen mixed vegetables (about 5 oz.)	1 teaspoon lemon juice
Boiling salted water	1 teaspoon capers or
1/4 cup minced celery	2 teaspoons minced sweet pickles
2 tablespoons minced green onion	1/4 teaspoon basil
1 to 2 tablespoons minced green pepper	Salt and pepper to taste
2 tablespoons mayonnaise	

Cook frozen mixed vegetables in boiling salted water according to package directions. Drain well and chill. Combine with remaining ingredients in a medium bowl. Salad can be prepared up to 24 hours in advance. Makes 2 servings.

Variations

Simplest Russian Salad: Combine chilled mixed vegetables or leftover cooked vegetables with mayonnaise. Season to taste.

Russian Salad in Tomato Cups: Cut tops from 2 medium tomatoes. Trim slice from bottoms, if necessary, so tomatoes sit flat. Scoop out seeds and pulp. Sprinkle salt in tomato cup and fill with Russian Salad.

Leeks Vinaigrette

Leeks are related to onions and garlic and add interesting flavor to salads or vegetables.

4 or 5 small leeks (about 1 bunch)	Lettuce leaves
1/2 cup chicken stock	Minced parsley
Sauce Vinaigrette, page 50,	Pimiento strips, if desired
using basil or thyme	

Use leeks with long, white, intact bulb ends. Cut off tops to make leeks 5- to 6-inches long, then cut in half lengthwise. Hold each half under running water with leafy portion down and cut side against water flow. Fan out layers and wash out all dirt. Bring chicken stock to a boil in a medium skillet. Arrange leek halves in a single layer in stock. Bring to a boil again. Cover and simmer about 5 minutes until bulb is tender when tested with a fork. Drain broth. Chill leeks. Marinate chilled leeks in Sauce Vinaigrette 1 hour before serving, if time permits. Arrange lettuce leaves on 2 salad plates. Place chilled leeks on lettuce. Pour Sauce Vinaigrette over leeks. Garnish with minced parsley and pimiento strips, if desired. Makes 2 servings.

Variation

Vegetables Vinaigrette: Omit leeks. Use 2 servings cooked, drained and chilled broccoli, asparagus, green beans, celery, cauliflower, artichoke hearts or Belgian endive. Garnish with minced green onions and capers.

Waldorf Salad

Vary the flavors and textures to suit your mood.

1/4 cup dairy sour cream
1 teaspoon brown sugar or honey
1 teaspoon lemon juice
Few gratings fresh lemon peel

1/8 teaspoon salt
1 large or 2 small red eating apples
1/3 cup diced or sliced celery
2 to 4 tablespoons coarsely chopped walnuts

Blend sour cream, brown sugar or honey, lemon juice, lemon peel and salt in a medium bowl. Wash and core apple. Cut into cubes to make 1 to 1-1/2 cups. Stir immediately into sour cream mixture to prevent discoloration. Stir in celery and walnuts. Refrigerate until serving time. Makes 2 servings.

Variations

Add any of the following to taste: raisins, chopped dates, prunes or other dried fruit, miniature marshmallows, banana slices, crushed pineapple or pineapple tidbits, seedless grapes, Mandarin orange segments or chunks of fresh orange, toasted or plain shredded coconut.

Substitute 2 tablespoons mayonaise for 1/4 cup sour cream. Substitute pecans or toasted slivered almonds for walnuts.

Avocado Grapefruit Salad

Serve it as a salad or a fruit cocktail.

Poppy Seed Dressing, see below
1 grapefruit

1 small ripe avocado
Lettuce leaves

Poppy Seed Dressing:
1 tablespoon lemon juice
1 teaspoon honey
Dash dry mustard

1/8 teaspoon salt
2 tablespoons oil
1/2 teaspoon poppy seeds

Prepare Poppy Seed Dressing. With a sharp knife, peel grapefruit by cutting just under the membrane beneath the peel. Cut out grapefruit sections by slicing along both sides of each section membrane. Put sections and any juice in a small bowl. Add juice squeezed from remaining membranes. Peel avocado, cut in half and remove seed. Cut each half into 6 to 8 slices and add to grapefruit, coating each slice completely with juice. Arrange lettuce leaves on 2 salad plates. Alternate slices of avocado and grapefruit sections in a spiral or row on lettuce. Pour Poppy Seed Dressing over. Makes 2 servings.

Poppy Seed Dressing:
Combine lemon juice, honey, dry mustard and salt in a small airtight jar. Shake until blended. Add oil and poppy seeds. Shake until blended. Refrigerate. Shake again before serving.

Seafood Louis

Why leave home to eat a salad you can make so easily yourself?

Louis Dressing, see below
2 large lettuce leaves
About 3 cups torn salad greens, lightly packed
1 large or 2 small tomatoes, cut in wedges
2 Hard-Cooked Eggs, page 160,
    peeled and quartered

1/2 cucumber, peeled and sliced 1/4-inch thick
1 cup cooked crab, shrimp or lobster,
    or a combination (about 6 oz.)
2 lemon wedges

Louis Dressing:
1/4 cup mayonnaise
1/4 cup dairy sour cream
2 tablespoons ketchup or chili sauce
1/2 teaspoon grated onion

1/4 teaspoon Worcestershire sauce
1 tablespoon minced green pepper, if desired
Salt to taste

Prepare Louis Dressing and refrigerate. Arrange lettuce leaves on 2 dinner plates or in large individual salad bowls. Top with a mound of torn salad greens. Arrange tomato wedges, hard-cooked egg quarters and cucumber slices around greens. Mound seafood in center and top with Louis Dressing. Garnish with lemon wedges. Makes 2 servings.

Louis Dressing:
Blend all ingredients in a small bowl.

Green Goddess Dressing

Especially good for green salads containing shellfish.

2 tablespoons mayonnaise
2 tablespoons dairy sour cream
1 teaspoon white wine vinegar or
    tarragon vinegar
1 teaspoon anchovy paste
1/8 teaspoon garlic salt

1/8 to 1/4 teaspoon crushed tarragon
Dash salt
1 green onion, finely minced, or
    1 teaspoon minced fresh chives
1 tablespoon finely minced parsley

Combine all ingredients in a small bowl. Stir to blend. Makes about 1/3 cup dressing.

Variations

Omit sour cream and increase mayonnaise to 1/4 cup.

Omit mayonnaise and increase sour cream to 1/4 cup.

Salade Niçoise

This delicious salad can be prepared almost entirely the night before.

Dressing Vinaigrette, see below
1/2 lb. fresh green beans or
   1 cup frozen green beans (about 5 oz.)
1 medium-large boiling potato
2 tablespoons dry white wine
Lettuce leaves
1 tomato

1 Hard-Cooked Egg, page 160
1 (6-1/2-oz.) can solid white tuna, drained
8 to 10 ripe olives
1 tablespoon capers
1 tablespoon minced parsley
1 tablespoon minced green onions or chives
2 to 4 anchovy fillets, if desired

Dressing Vinaigrette:
1-1/2 tablespoons white wine vinegar or
   fresh lemon juice
1/4 teaspoon garlic salt
1/8 teaspoon dry mustard or
   1/4 teaspoon Dijon mustard

1/2 teaspoon herbs such as tarragon, chervil,
   basil and marjoram
1/3 cup oil or olive oil

Prepare Dressing Vinaigrette. Cook green beans until tender. Drain and refrigerate. Cook potato until tender. Peel hot potato, slice 1/4-inch thick and gently combine with white wine in a medium bowl. As soon as wine is completely absorbed, mix about half the Dressing Vinaigrette into the potato. Cover and refrigerate. Stir remaining Dressing Vinaigrette into *cooled* green beans. Cover and refrigerate. Before serving, arrange lettuce leaves on 2 dinner plates or in a large salad bowl. Mound marinated potatoes and green beans in center. Cut tomato in wedges. Peel and quarter hard-cooked egg. Arrange tomato wedges, drained tuna chunks, hard-cooked egg quarters and olives around potato and green beans. Sprinkle with capers, minced parsley and minced green onions or chives. Top with anchovy fillets, if desired. Makes 2 servings.

Dressing Vinaigrette:
Combine vinegar or lemon juice, garlic salt, mustard and herbs in an airtight jar. Close and shake to dissolve salt. Add oil, close and shake to blend. Shake again before using.

Variation

Quick Salade Niçoise: Substitute 1 (8-ounce) can green beans, drained, for fresh or frozen green beans. Substitute 1 cup cubed canned or leftover cooked potatoes for fresh potato. Marinate in Dressing Vinaigrette 1 hour if time permits.

To avoid confusing hard-cooked and raw eggs, mark hard-cooked eggs with a grease pencil. Or spin an egg on a saucer: hard cooked eggs will spin, but raw eggs won't.

Shrimp-Stuffed Artichokes

When you want a showy summer picnic dish, try this!

1 recipe Artichokes & Lemon Dip,
    page 122
Shrimp Salad, see below
Lettuce leaves

10 cherry tomatoes or 2 medium tomatoes,
    cut in wedges
1/2 cucumber, peeled and sliced
2 lemon wedges

Shrimp Salad:
1/4 cup mayonnaise
1/4 teaspoon Dijon mustard
2 tablespoons well-drained pickle relish or
    finely minced sweet pickles

2 green onions, minced
1/2 cup finely minced celery
4 to 6 oz. cooked cocktail shrimp
Seasoned salt to taste

Prepare Artichokes & Lemon Dip, removing chokes. Refrigerate. Prepare Shrimp Salad. Fill artichokes with Shrimp Salad. Place on 2 lettuce-lined plates. Arrange cucumber slices, cherry tomatoes or tomato wedges, lemon wedges and a small container of Lemon Dip around each artichoke. Makes 2 servings.

Shrimp Salad:
Blend mayonnaise and Dijon mustard in a medium bowl. Fold in remaining ingredients.

Sour Cream Dressing

Actually, just sour cream and salt will do, but you may as well be creative.

1/4 cup dairy sour cream
1 teaspoon lemon juice or
    white wine vinegar
1/8 teaspoon salt
Dash sugar

Freshly ground black pepper to taste
1/4 teaspoon herbs such as basil, tarragon,
    chervil, parsley, dill and oregano
Few drops Worcestershire sauce

Combine all ingredients in a small bowl. Stir to blend. Refrigerate several hours to blend flavors if time permits. Makes about 1/4 cup dressing.

Variations

Roquefort or Blue Cheese Dressing: Add 1 to 2 tablespoons crumbled Roquefort or blue cheese.
Thousand Island Dressing: Add 1 tablespoon ketchup or chili sauce, 1 tablespoon pickle relish or finely minced sweet pickles and chopped hard-cooked egg, if available.

Add small quantities of horseradish, capers, soy sauce, Tabasco sauce, mustard or anchovy paste.

Tossed Tostada Salad

This Southern California luncheon favorite is a complete meal.

1/2 small head iceberg lettuce, torn, or
   3 to 4 cups torn mixed greens
1 (8-3/4-oz.) can kidney beans or pinto beans,
   rinsed and well-drained
1 medium tomato, cut in wedges
1 (2-1/4-oz.) can sliced ripe olives or
   about 10 whole ripe olives, well-drained
1/2 cup shredded sharp Cheddar cheese,
   lightly packed

Tostada Beef, see below
1 cup coarsely crushed corn chips
   (about 3 oz.)
1/4 cup oil
2 to 3 tablespoons fresh lemon juice
Salt to taste
Dairy sour cream
1/2 avocado, peeled and sliced

Tostada Beef:

1/3 to 1/2 lb. lean ground beef
1/4 cup minced onion
1/4 cup minced green pepper, if desired
1 garlic clove, pressed or minced

1 to 2 teaspoons chili powder
1/2 teaspoon salt
1 teaspoon flour
1/4 cup water

Place lettuce or mixed greens into a large salad bowl. Top with drained beans, tomato wedges, olives and cheese. Cover with damp paper towels and refrigerate. Prepare Tostada Beef. Before serving, sprinkle crushed corn chips over salad. Stir oil into warm Tostada Beef. Toss with salad. When all ingredients are coated with oil, toss in lemon juice and salt to taste. Serve on dinner plates or in large individual salad bowls. Top with a spoonful of sour cream and garnish with avocado slices. Makes 2 servings.

Tostada Beef:

Sauté ground beef in a medium skillet over medium heat, breaking meat into small chunks. Add onion, green pepper, if desired, and garlic. Sauté until vegetables are tender and ground beef is cooked through. Drain excess drippings. Stir in chili powder. Simmer 30 seconds. Add salt and flour. Stir to mix well. Stir in water. Simmer and stir until water is absorbed or evaporated and mixture is moist but crumbly.

Variations

Easy Tostada Beef: Cook ground beef with 1/2 package taco seasoning mix according to package directions. Omit all other Tostada Beef ingredients.
Extra Spicy Tossed Tostada Salad: Add Tabasco sauce, diced green chilies, taco sauce or other hot pepper flavor as desired.

For a simple fruit salad, arrange cut fresh or canned fruit on a lettuce-lined salad plate and top with a scoop of cottage cheese. Garnish with chopped nuts, shredded coconut or a maraschino cherry.

Cobb Salad

This chopped salad is modeled after the one made famous by the Original Brown Derby Restaurant.

3 to 4 cups finely chopped iceberg and
 Romaine lettuce (about 1/2 lb.)
1/2 to 3/4 cup finely chopped, skinned and
 boned cooked chicken breast
3 green onions, minced
1 Hard-Cooked Egg, page 160,
 finely chopped
1 medium tomato, peeled, seeded and
 minced, see page 49

4 slices bacon, fried crisp and crumbled
1 (1-1/4-oz.) pkg. blue cheese, crumbled
1 small ripe avocado, peeled, seeded and
 minced
1 teaspoon lemon juice, if necessary
Oil & Vinegar Dressing, page 49, or
 1/3 cup bottled oil & vinegar dressing
Freshly ground black pepper to taste
Lettuce leaves

Spread chopped lettuce evenly over bottom of a shallow, medium-large salad bowl. Arrange ingredients in rows over lettuce with minced chicken in a narrow strip down center, tomato, blue cheese and avocado on one side, and green onion, hard-cooked egg and bacon on other side. To delay serving, toss minced avocado in lemon juice to prevent darkening. Cover salad with a damp paper towel and refrigerate. Before serving, add oil and vinegar dressing and pepper to taste. Toss at table. Serve on chilled lettuce-lined plates. Makes 2 servings.

Variation

Cobb Salad à la Mer: Substitute 1 (3-1/2-ounce) can solid white tuna, drained and flaked, for chicken breast. Substitute lemon juice for vinegar in Oil & Vinegar Dressing.

To eliminate occasional bitterness in cucumbers, cut about 3/4 inch off the stem end of the cucumber. Rub the two cut surfaces together in a brisk circular motion several seconds. Wash off any froth that forms, cut a thin slice from the end of the cucumber and use as desired.

To mince green onions, cut first in lengthwise strips. Then cut crosswise into thirds or quarters, stack together and cut all at once.

How To Make Cobb Salad

The beautiful Cobb Salad should definitely be displayed at the table before it is tossed.

To neatly toss a salad, lift one salad server straight up from the bottom of the bowl while using other server to tumble ingredients over from back to front.

Main Dishes

Contrary to many opinions, I think markets are bursting with exciting, protein-rich foods perfect for main dishes to serve 1 or 2. In addition to the smaller cuts of beef, pork, veal and lamb, there are poultry items, a huge variety of seafood, a delicatessen case full of possibilities, plus eggs, cheese and a growing number of canned, frozen and packaged items just made for singles and couples.

This chapter is a potpourri of main dish ideas that only begins to explore the possibilities. Many of these recipes are built around meat items that you may already use. But there are a few designed to lure you into using cuts you haven't tried before. From here you can move on to Fish & Seafood, pages 88 to 97, for more food adventures. But don't stop there! You can build terrific suppers around breakfast and brunch recipes and main dish salads. Even appetizers like Seviche and Steak Tartare, and side dishes like Fettucine Alfredo can be outstanding main dishes. Taken together, this adds up to about 2 months of leftover-free main dishes for 1 or 2.

SERVING SIZES

How big is a serving? There's a bit of risk in deciding the amount of an individual serving because people's needs and wants vary so much. My fairly simple rule is to include about 1/3 to 1/2 of the recommended daily protein allowance for an adult in each main dish serving. If you would like more or less protein in your main dish servings, there is room in these recipes for the meat portion to be increased or decreased to some extent without hurting the results. For those who want considerably smaller servings, many of the single servings can be divided to serve 2.

TIPS FOR COOKING MEATS

Know which meat cuts are tender and which are not. This is the most important information you need about the meat you buy. It will determine how the meat should be cooked.

Tender cuts include the steaks from the loin and tenderloin of beef, veal, lamb and pork. Young broiler-fryer chickens, ground meat and fully-cooked ham are also tender. Less tender cuts come from the legs, shoulders and undersides of meat animals and also include stewing hens.

Choose the correct cooking technique. Meat cooking techniques are designed to preserve or develop tenderness. If a tender cut of meat is cooked by a technique for less-tender cuts, or vice versa, the results can be very disappointing.

Tender cuts are best cooked with dry-heat methods such as broiling, barbecuing, frying, pan broiling or open-pan roasting or baking. These fast techniques preserve moisture, flavor and tenderness.

The best techniques for less tender cuts are stewing, braising, covered-pan roasting, slow-cooker cooking and pressure cooking. These longer, moist methods tenderize tough connective tissue.

Protect the moisture in the meats you cook.
- Do not overcook meat, particularly tender cuts.
- Use tongs, a spatula or pancake turner to handle meats. Forks and knives release the juices.
- Generally, salt meat *after* it is browned. Salt will draw the juices from the meat surfaces and prevent proper browning. Skin and fatty surfaces may be salted before cooking.
- Do not tightly cover hot, cooked meat to keep it warm. This causes greater loss of juices. Loosely cover meat with a square of foil until ready to serve. If possible, include any juices in the sauce for the meat.

Learn to judge when meat is done. The quality of meat can be damaged by either undercooking or overcooking. I wish I could put a cooking temperature and time in each recipe that would give beautiful results every time, but there are just too many variables in meat cooking for specific instructions to work consistently. These recipes include a temperature, a reasonable range of cooking time and a reliable test for doneness. Here are some of the variables to consider:
- No two pieces of meat are the same in composition, weight, shape or temperature. Imagine the possible difference in cooking times between a leg from a fresh 2-pound broiler-fryer chicken and one from a barely thawed 3-1/2-pound fryer. The larger, colder leg could take twice as long to cook.
- The accuracy and fluctuation of oven temperatures vary greatly, as do heat distribution patterns. Heat is lost and baking times are slowed when the oven door is opened repeatedly. Even the position of the pan in the oven and its relationship to any

other pans affect cooking time and results.

• Glass, ceramic, iron and other dark metal pans absorb heat, causing foods to cook faster. Aluminum foil pans reflect heat so well they may lengthen cooking time unless placed on a small baking sheet in the oven to attract heat. Pans with high sides reduce top browning. Those with large surface areas allow juices to spread, causing them to evaporate faster or possibly burn.

WHY FRY STEAK?

Because fried meat has become synonymous with tough, dry, leathery steak, many people have made broiling their mode for cooking tender steaks. But frying techniques from France offer a superb and practical way to cook tender steaks. Here are some of the advantages:

• Better flavor—The intense and direct heat of the pan sears the meat, giving more flavor and sealing in the juices. When a sauce is made, the pan brownings are dissolved and incorporated, bringing all the flavor back to the steak.

• Minimal cleanup—There's only one pan to clean—and the sauce helps clean it for you.

• Speed—Frying is faster than either broiling or barbecuing.

• Consumes less energy—The direct transfer of heat from the pan to the meat is more efficient than broiling or barbecuing.

I think it will take only one experience with Tenderloin Sauté, Steak Diane or Pepper Steak Flambé to make you a believer.

A PLUG FOR BUYING THE WHOLE CHICKEN

I usually recommend buying foods in single- or double-serving portions, but a whole chicken is really a collection of single portions held together by some skin, bones and flesh. A whole chicken offers 2 whole chicken legs, 2 half breast portions, 2 wings, a liver and a bundle of miscellaneous parts that can end up as chicken stock, soup, crepes, omelets, sandwiches, salad or creamed chicken. From 1 chicken you can get at least 3 meals for 2 plus a few hors d'oeuvres.

If you are handy with a knife, cut up your own chicken. Bone and skin the breast portions as shown on page 163. Wrap the pieces separately in foil for freezing. Freeze the whole legs or separate the thighs and drumsticks into single-serving portions. Freeze the wings after cutting off the tips, or put the entire wing in the stock pot. Freeze the liver or sauté it immediately for use in an omelet or pâté. Use the neck, back, wing tips or whole wings, bones and skin from the breast portions and the rest of the giblets to make Chicken Stock, page 162.

STORING MEATS

To take a piece of good meat and cook it badly is disappointing, but to let it spoil before you get a chance to cook it at all is heartbreaking. Good meat deserves a little extra care to keep it in prime condition until you are ready to use it. Learn how long specific cuts of meat stay fresh in the refrigerator, and plan your meals accordingly. Freeze items you cannot use soon enough.

Meat should be stored in the coldest part of the refrigerator and should not sit in moisture. Prepackaged meats can be kept in their heat-sealed wrapping, but meats wrapped in butcher paper should be rewrapped loosely in wax paper or aluminum foil. Allow for air space between packages of meat.

Meat to be frozen should be divided into single-serving portions and wrapped in aluminum foil or heavy plastic bags. Exclude all air from packages and freeze in the coldest part of the freezer. Don't freeze too many meats at the same time because slower formation of the ice crystals will damage meat. Smaller cuts of meat have a shorter freezer life than larger cuts.

MEAT STORAGE TIMES		
	Refrigerator (35°F, 2°C)	Freezer (0°F, −20°C)
Ground Beef or Lamb	1 to 2 days	3 months
Liver	1 to 2 days	3 months
Fresh Cut Meats	2 to 4 days	6 months
Ham Slices	3 to 4 days	2 months
Wieners	4 to 5 days	1 month
Bacon	5 to 7 days	1 month
Luncheon Meats	7 days	Not advised
Cooked Meats	4 to 5 days	3 months

Reduce storing time by half for freezer sections within refrigerators.

Steak Diane

Here is the classic version of this elegant cook-at-the-table steak.

4 (3- to 4-oz.) tenderloin steaks, 1/2-inch thick
Salt to taste
Freshly ground black pepper
2 tablespoons butter
1/2 teaspoon dry mustard
2 tablespoons minced shallots, if desired

2 tablespoons butter
1-1/2 teaspoons Worcestershire sauce
1 tablespoon fresh lemon juice
1 tablespoon minced parsley
1 tablespoon minced fresh chives or
 green onions

With a rolling pin, pound steaks to 1/4-inch thickness. Sprinkle salt and pepper on both sides. At table if desired, combine 2 tablespoons butter and mustard in an electric skillet. Cook over medium heat, about 325°F (165°C), until sizzling. Add steaks and shallots, if desired. Fry steaks about 1 minute on each side, long enough to cook the surface and brown slightly. Cook longer for thicker steaks or well-done steaks. Place on dinner plates. Quickly add 2 more tablespoons butter, Worcestershire sauce and lemon juice to pan juices in skillet. Cook over high heat until syrupy. Stir in parsley and chives or green onions. Pour over steaks. Serve immediately. Makes 2 servings.

Pepper Steak Flambé

Steak becomes extraordinary with a few basic but spicy ingredients.

1-1/2 teaspoons whole black peppercorns
2 (6- to 8-oz.) boneless tender steaks,
 about 3/4-inch thick
Salt to taste
1 tablespoon Clarified Butter, page 159,
 or butter

2 tablespoons dry red wine,
 beef stock or water
1/2 teaspoon Worcestershire sauce
2 tablespoons brandy or Cognac
1 tablespoon minced parsley

Crush peppercorns with a mortar and pestle. Or place between sheets of wax paper and crush with a rolling pin or bottom of a heavy pan. Trim excess fat from steaks and slash remaining fat around edges to prevent curling. About 1 hour before serving, sprinkle crushed peppercorns evenly over both sides of each steak. Place steaks on wax paper and, using heel of hand, press peppercorns into meat on both sides. Cover steaks with wax paper and let stand at room temperature. About 10 minutes before serving, heat butter in a large heavy skillet over medium heat. Use higher heat for thin steaks, lower heat for thicker steaks. Sprinkle steaks with salt. Place in hot pan to sear. Turn steaks when browned and brown other sides. To test doneness, cut a small slit in center of steak or press finger into steak. Medium-rare steak is pink in center and gives under pressure but springs back. Place on dinner plates; cover loosely to keep warm. Reduce heat and quickly add wine, stock or water to skillet. Stir to dissolve pan brownings. Add Worcestershire sauce. Boil until syrupy. Remove skillet from heat to cool slightly. Add brandy or Cognac and carefully ignite with a long match. Shake pan until flames subside. Pour sauce over steaks. Garnish with minced parsley. Makes 2 servings.

Tenderloin Sauté

If you thought you couldn't fry a good steak, this French technique will change your mind.

2 (6- to 8-oz.) tenderloin steaks or other
    tender boneless steak, 1/2- to 1-inch thick
1 to 2 tablespoons Clarified Butter,
    page 159, or butter

Salt and pepper to taste
1/4 cup dry red or white wine
1 tablespoon butter
Minced parsley

Trim excess fat from steaks. Slash remaining fat around edge to prevent curling. Dry steaks on paper towels. In a medium, heavy skillet, heat 1 to 2 tablespoons butter over medium-high heat until almost smoking. Immediately add steaks. Sauté 3 to 4 minutes until well-browned. Turn and sauté 3 to 5 minutes, reducing heat for thicker steaks. To test doneness, cut a small slit in center of steak or press finger into steak. Medium-rare steak is pink in center, and gives under pressure but springs back. Do not cook past medium doneness. Place steaks on serving plates, sprinkle with salt and pepper and keep warm. Working quickly, add wine and 1 tablespoon butter to pan. Raise heat and quickly boil down, stirring constantly to loosen and dissolve any pan brownings. When concentrated and syrupy, pour sauce over steaks. Garnish with minced parsley. Makes 2 servings.

Sauce Bearnaise

This beautifully flavored variation of Hollandaise Sauce requires care and skill to make.

1 tablespoon white wine vinegar
1 tablespoon dry white wine
1 tablespoon minced shallots or
    green onion
1/2 teaspoon tarragon
1/4 teaspoon chervil, if desired

Dash salt and pepper
1 egg yolk
1/4 cup cold butter (1/2 stick)
Salt to taste
1 tablespoon finely minced fresh parsley

In a small stainless steel, enamel or nonstick saucepan, combine vinegar, wine, shallots or green onion, tarragon, chervil, if desired, and salt and pepper. Cover and simmer about 5 minutes. Remove cover and boil until liquid without solids measures 1 tablespoon. Strain liquid. Before serving, beat egg yolk in same saucepan. Blend in strained liquid. Half-fill a large bowl with cold water and place near range. Cut butter into 8 to 10 small chunks. Add 2 chunks of butter to egg yolk mixture. Whip constantly over very low heat, raising pan from heat as needed to keep egg yolk from overcooking. If sauce begins to granulate or curdle, immediately immerse bottom of saucepan in bowl of cold water, whipping briskly. When butter melts and blends into egg yolk mixture, add another chunk, whipping constantly. Repeat until all butter is added and sauce is thickened and smooth. Stir in salt to taste and minced parsley. Serve immediately. To delay serving, immerse bottom of saucepan in cold water to stop cooking. Before serving, warm over low heat, whipping constantly. Serve with broiled or pan-broiled steak, broiled fish or chicken. Makes 2 servings.

Variation

For heartier flavor and more texture, do not strain vinegar and shallot mixture.

Basic Beef & Sauce

Prepare this long-cooking recipe and freeze it so you can enjoy 4 different dinners later.

1 large onion, minced
1 garlic clove, pressed or minced
2 tablespoons oil
1 (10-oz.) can beef consommé
1/2 cup dry red wine or water
2 teaspoons Worcestershire sauce
1/3 to 1/2 cup flour

1 teaspoon salt
1/4 teaspoon pepper
2 lbs. boneless trimmed chuck, rump,
    sirloin tip or stewing beef
Oil for frying
Salt to taste

In a heavy 3-quart saucepan or slow cooker, sauté onion and garlic in 2 tablespoons oil until tender but not browned. Add consommé, wine or water and Worcestershire sauce. Slowly bring to a simmer. In a paper bag, mix flour, 1 teaspoon salt and the pepper; set aside. Cut meat into 1/2- to 3/4-inch cubes; dry on paper towels. Heat 3/4-inch-deep oil in a small deep saucepan over medium-high heat. When oil is hot but not smoking, shake a handful of meat cubes in flour mixture in paper bag. Shake off excess flour and drop meat into oil. Do not overcrowd and do not let oil cool. Stir meat occasionally to brown all sides. With a slotted spoon, place meat in hot broth. Repeat until all meat cubes are browned and added to broth. Adjust heat so broth steams but does not bubble. Cook 4 to 5 hours until meat is tender. Remove from heat. Skim excess fat from sauce. Add salt to taste. Cool and put into 3 or 4 airtight wide-mouth jars, plastic cartons or other freezer containers. Label and freeze. Use within 6 months. Makes 6 to 8 servings.

BASIC BEEF & SAUCE makes: Beef Stew, page 66; Quick Beef Stroganoff, page 66; Hungarian Goulash, page 66; and Beef Curry, page 67.

How To Make Basic Beef & Sauce

Brown the floured meat cubes in a small saucepan or mini deep-fryer. Add browned cubes to the simmering stock.

Various wide-mouth containers are suitable for freezing 1 or 2 servings. Leave 1/2-inch space at the top for expansion during freezing.

Beef Stew

Infinitely variable! This beef stew reflects the contents of your refrigerator and pantry.

2 servings Basic Beef & Sauce, page 65
1/2 teaspoon herbs such as chervil, oregano,
  parsley and rosemary
About 1/2 cup diced cooked potato

1 cup frozen or fully cooked mixed vegetables
  such as carrots, peas, corn, green beans,
  boiling onions, turnips and zucchini
Salt to taste

Thaw Basic Beef & Sauce. Carefully mix with herbs, potatoes and frozen vegetables in a medium saucepan. Heat gently to a simmer and cook 5 minutes. Stir in any cooked vegetables and heat through. Season with salt. Makes 2 servings.

Quick Beef Stroganoff

Even Count Stroganoff would enjoy this version of his famous dish.

2 servings Basic Beef & Sauce, page 65
1 tablespoon butter
1/2 cup sliced fresh mushrooms

1 tablespoon ketchup or chili sauce
1/4 to 1/2 cup dairy sour cream
Salt to taste

Thaw Basic Beef & Sauce. Melt butter in a small saucepan over medium heat. Add mushrooms and sauté until limp. Carefully stir beef and sauce into mushrooms. Blend in ketchup or chili sauce. Heat to serving temperature. Remove pan from heat. Blend in sour cream all at once. Add salt. Warm slowly to serving temperature. Do not boil. Makes 2 servings.

Hungarian Goulash

A recipe to cater to your gypsy spirit. It's ready in minutes so you can eat and run!

2 servings Basic Beef & Sauce, page 65
1 tablespoon butter
1/8 medium green pepper, slivered
1 teaspoon paprika

2 tablespoons ketchup or chili sauce
1/4 to 1/2 cup dairy sour cream
Salt to taste

Thaw Basic Beef & Sauce. Melt butter in a small saucepan over medium-low heat. Add green pepper and sauté until tender. Stir in paprika. Cook 30 seconds. Carefully stir in beef and sauce. Blend in ketchup or chili sauce. Heat to serving temperature. Remove from heat. Blend in sour cream all at once. Add salt. Warm slowly to serving temperature. Do not boil. Makes 2 servings.

Beef Curry

Here's Basic Beef & Sauce all curried up and sprinkled with colorful condiments.

2 servings Basic Beef & Sauce, page 65
1 to 2 tablespoons butter
1 to 2 teaspoons curry powder
1/4 cup dairy sour cream, or 2 tablespoons
 plain yogurt or 1 teaspoon lemon juice
Salt to taste
Steamed Rice, page 105

Chutney
Assorted condiments such as chopped Hard-
 Cooked Egg, page 160, chopped peanuts
 or almonds, crumbled crisp bacon,
 shredded coconut, minced cucumber,
 chopped tomato, diced banana and
 chopped apple

Thaw Basic Beef & Sauce. Melt butter in a small saucepan over low heat. Stir curry powder into butter. Cook gently 2 to 3 minutes. Carefully stir beef and sauce into butter mixture. Simmer gently 4 to 5 minutes. Remove from heat. Stir in sour cream, yogurt or lemon juice. Add salt. Warm slowly to serving temperature. Serve over rice with chutney and an assortment of condiments. Makes 2 servings.

Beef Stroganoff

Make one steak serve two! You can also prepare this from leftover steak.

1 (1/2-lb.) boneless sirloin, loin or
 tenderloin steak
1 tablespoon oil
1 to 2 tablespoons butter
1/4 cup minced onion or
 2 tablespoons minced shallots
1/2 cup sliced fresh mushrooms
1 tablespoon flour
1/2 cup beef stock

1/2 teaspoon Worcestershire sauce
1/4 teaspoon salt
Freshly ground black pepper to taste
Dash ground red pepper
1/2 cup dairy sour cream, room temperature
Buttered Noodles, page 101, or Steamed Rice,
 page 105
1 tablespoon minced parsley

Cut steak into 1/2" x 2" strips, 1/4-inch thick. Heat 1 tablespoon oil in a medium skillet over medium-high heat. Dry all surface moisture from steak strips with paper towels. Quickly fry in hot oil on both sides until lightly browned. Place on a plate. Reduce heat to medium-low and add 1 tablespoon butter to skillet. Sauté onion or shallots and mushrooms until translucent and tender. Place on plate with steak, leaving as much butter in skillet as possible. Add butter, if necessary, to make about 1 tablespoon. Blend in flour. Cook until frothy. Blend in beef stock, Worcestershire sauce, salt, pepper to taste and red pepper. Simmer and stir until thickened and smooth. Add beef, onions or shallots and mushrooms to sauce and heat through. Remove from heat and blend in sour cream all at once. Warm to serving temperature. Pour over noodles or rice. Garnish with minced parsley. Makes 2 servings.

Variation

Meatball Stroganoff, page 73.

Hamburger-Noodle Skillet

Create your own variations!

1 tablespoon oil
1/4 cup minced onion
1 garlic clove, crushed or minced
1/4 lb. lean ground beef
2/3 cup tomato juice
1/2 cup water, more if necessary

1/4 teaspoon oregano, basil or thyme
1/4 teaspoon salt
Pepper to taste
1 cup (1-1/2- to 2-oz.) uncooked
   wide egg noodles

Heat oil in an 8-inch skillet over medium heat. Briefly sauté onion and garlic. Add ground beef, breaking into chunks. Sauté until no longer pink. Stir in tomato juice, water, herb, salt and pepper. Bring quickly to a boil and stir in noodles. Bring to a boil again. Cover and slowly simmer 20 to 25 minutes. If mixture is dry, stir in a little water. If mixture is too moist, remove cover, bring to a boil and stir until desired consistency is reached. Makes 1 serving.

Variations

Hamburger-Noodle Meal: Sauté 1/4 cup minced celery with onion and garlic. Add 1/2 cup frozen peas, green beans or corn to finished dish. Stir, cover and cook 5 more minutes.
Hungarian Hamburger-Noodle Skillet: Omit herb. Sauté 2 to 3 tablespoons minced or slivered green pepper with onion and garlic. Stir 1/2 teaspoon paprika into mixture before adding ground beef. Stir 1/4 cup sour cream into finished dish.
Hamburger-Noodle Stroganoff: Omit herb. Sauté a few sliced mushrooms with onion. Stir 1/4 cup sour cream into finished dish.

Sukiyaki-Style Hamburger

If you don't have all these vegetables, use what you have!

1 tablespoon oil
1/4 lb. lean ground beef
2 slices medium onion, 1/4-inch thick
1 garlic clove, pressed or minced
1 celery stalk, sliced
2 or 3 green onions, cut in 1-inch pieces
3 or 4 medium mushrooms, sliced
1/8 medium green pepper, slivered
1/2 cup slivered cabbage

1 tablespoon soy sauce
1-1/2 teaspoons sugar
1/2 cup or less water
1/2 teaspoon beef stock granules
1/4 cup uncooked long-grain rice
1/4 to 1/2 cup frozen peas
Salt to taste
Soy sauce to taste

Heat oil in an 8-inch skillet over medium heat. Add ground beef, breaking into chunks. Sauté until no longer pink. Add onion, garlic, celery, green onions, mushrooms, green pepper and cabbage. Sauté briefly. Stir in 1 tablespoon soy sauce and sugar. Cook 30 seconds. Stir in water, beef stock granules and rice, reducing water if using a large volume of vegetables. Quickly bring to a boil. Cover and simmer 25 minutes. Stir in frozen peas. Cover and cook 5 more minutes. Add salt and soy sauce to taste. Makes 1 serving.

Curried Hamburger Meal

Curry was never easier, and seldom tasted better.

1 tablespoon oil
1/4 cup minced onion
1 garlic clove, pressed or minced
1/4 lb. lean ground beef
1/2 to 1 teaspoon curry powder
1/2 cup tomato juice
1/4 cup water, more if necessary
1/4 teaspoon salt
1/4 cup uncooked long-grain rice
1/2 cup frozen peas

2 tablespoons dairy sour cream or
    plain yogurt, if desired
Chutney
Assorted condiments, such as crumbled crisp
    bacon, chopped Hard-Cooked Egg, page
    160, chopped peanuts, toasted almonds,
    shredded coconut and raisins
Chopped vegetables and fruits such as
    green pepper, cucumber, green onion,
    tomato, banana and apple

Heat oil in an 8-inch skillet over medium heat. Briefly sauté onion and garlic. Add ground beef, breaking into chunks. Sauté until no longer pink. Stir in curry powder; cook 30 seconds. Add tomato juice, water, salt and rice. Mix and bring to a boil. Cover and simmer 25 minutes. Stir in peas and a little water if rice is dry. Cover and cook 5 more minutes. Before serving, stir in sour cream or yogurt, if desired. Serve chutney at the table. Sprinkle assorted condiments, chopped vegetables and fruits over curry. Makes 1 serving.

Hamburger-Spinach Scramble

This great skillet dinner is adapted from a specialty served in one of my favorite restaurants.

1 tablespoon oil
1 garlic clove, pressed or minced
1/4 cup minced onion or
    2 tablespoons minced shallots
1/2 cup sliced or chopped fresh mushrooms
1/4 lb. lean ground beef
1 teaspoon flour

1/4 cup drained, cooked and chopped spinach,
    or 1/3 cup leftover creamed spinach
1/4 teaspoon Worcestershire sauce
1/8 to 1/4 teaspoon salt
1/4 teaspoon basil, chervil or marjoram
1 egg

Heat oil in an 8-inch skillet over medium heat. Sauté garlic, onion or shallots and mushrooms until tender. Add ground beef, breaking into small chunks. Sauté until cooked through. Add flour and stir until absorbed. Stir in spinach, Worcestershire sauce, salt and herb. Cook and stir until mixture is bubbling and thickened. Push hamburger-spinach mixture aside and break egg into center of skillet. With a fork, quickly stir egg to scramble. Cook until almost set. Stir egg into hamburger-spinach mixture. Cook just until egg is set. Serve immediately. Makes 1 serving.

Variation

Hamburger Stretcher: Prepare in a large skillet. Use 4 eggs and double remaining ingredients, except ground beef. Beat eggs before pouring into hot skillet. Makes 2 servings.

Chili Skillet

Make a green salad with sour cream dressing to go with this colorful dish.

1 tablespoon oil
1/2 cup minced onion
1/4 cup chopped green pepper
1 garlic clove, pressed or minced
1/3 to 1/2 lb. lean ground beef
2 teaspoons chili powder or
   1 to 2 tablespoons chili seasoning mix
1/2 cup tomato juice
1 (8-oz.) can kidney beans

1/2 teaspoon oregano
1/2 teaspoon salt
1/4 cup uncooked long-grain rice
1/2 cup frozen whole kernel corn
1/4 cup chopped or sliced black olives,
   if desired
1/2 cup shredded Cheddar, longhorn or
   Monterey Jack cheese, lightly packed

Heat oil in a 10-inch skillet over medium heat. Briefly sauté onion, green pepper and garlic. Push to side of skillet. Add ground beef, breaking into chunks. Sauté until no longer pink. Stir in chili powder or chili seasoning mix and cook 30 seconds. Add tomato juice, undrained kidney beans, oregano, salt and rice. Stir and bring to a boil. Cover and simmer 25 minutes. Stir in corn and olives, if desired. Cover and cook 5 more minutes. Sprinkle cheese over top and cover just long enough to melt cheese. Makes 2 servings.

Liver à la Suisse

Sour cream does wonderful things for calf liver.

2 slices calf liver (about 1/2 lb.)
2 slices bacon, cut in half
1 small or medium onion, sliced
1/2 teaspoon tarragon

Salt and pepper to taste
1 to 2 tablespoons water
1/4 cup dairy sour cream

Cut any membranes or veins from liver. Rinse and drain on paper towels. Sauté bacon in a medium skillet until crisp. Remove from skillet. Add sliced onion to drippings in skillet. Add tarragon, salt and pepper. Sauté until onion is limp. Push to side of pan and add liver. Sauté on both sides until lightly browned. Sprinkle with salt and pepper. Cover and cook gently 5 to 10 minutes, depending on thickness of liver. To test doneness, cut into thickest portion; inside should no longer be red. Place liver on plates and quickly prepare sauce. Add 1 to 2 tablespoons water to skillet. Bring to a boil. Stir to loosen and dissolve pan brownings. Boil until syrupy. Remove from heat and blend in sour cream. Heat to serving temperature without boiling. Pour over liver. Garnish with bacon pieces. Makes 2 servings.

Variations

Liver in Mustard Sauce: Blend 1 teaspoon Dijon mustard or 1/2 teaspoon dry mustard into pan juices before adding sour cream.

Liver Hungarian-Style: Omit bacon and tarragon. Heat 2 tablespoons oil or Clarified Butter, page 159, in skillet. Sliver 1/4 green pepper. Sauté with onion. Stir 1 teaspoon paprika in 1 tablespoon ketchup into pan juices before adding sour cream.

Basic Ground Beef Mix

This mix lets you enjoy meat loaf, stuffed peppers or spaghetti & meatballs in minutes.

2 eggs
1/4 cup ketchup
1/4 cup water
1/2 cup minced onion
1 tablespoon Worcestershire sauce

1 teaspoon salt
1 cup Soft Breadcrumbs, page 164
   lightly packed
1 lb. lean ground beef

Beat eggs in a large bowl. Blend in ketchup, water, minced onion, Worcestershire sauce and salt. Mix in soft breadcrumbs. With a fork, mix ground beef with other ingredients. Divide into 4 or 5 single-serving portions for Individual Meat Loaves, Stuffed Peppers or Miniature Meatballs, see below. Cook within a day or freeze up to 3 months until ready to use. Makes about 4 cups.

BASIC GROUND BEEF MIX makes: Individual Meat Loaves, see below; Stuffed Peppers, page 73; Miniature Meatballs, page 73; Spaghetti & Meatballs, page 73; Appetizer Meatballs, page 73; and Meatball Stroganoff, page 73.

Individual Meat Loaves

Barbecue sauce makes it better.

About 1 cup Basic Ground Beef Mix, see above
Simple Barbecue Sauce, see below

Simple Barbecue Sauce:
2 tablespoons ketchup
1 teaspoon brown sugar

1/2 teaspoon prepared mustard

Preheat oven or toaster-oven to 350°F (175°C). Prepare Simple Barbecue Sauce. Shape Basic Ground Beef Mix into a small loaf or press into a tart pan. Spread barbecue sauce on top. Place on a small, shallow baking sheet or toaster-oven tray. Bake about 30 minutes. To freeze loaf before baking, wrap in foil without sauce. Freeze. Thaw, top with barbecue sauce and bake. If still frozen, bake 15 minutes at 400°F (205°C) then 20 minutes at 350°F (175°C). Makes 1 serving.

Simple Barbecue Sauce:
Blend ingredients in a small bowl.

Stuffed Peppers

Simplify this family favorite with your Basic Ground Beef Mix.

1 large green pepper	1/4 cup tomato-based sauce such as
Water	spaghetti sauce, marinara sauce,
About 1 cup Basic Ground Beef Mix,	tomato sauce or diluted ketchup,
page 72	chili sauce or tomato paste

Preheat oven or toaster-oven to 350°F (175°C). Trim a small slice from bottom of green pepper if needed so green pepper sits level. Cut top from pepper and remove all seeds and white membranes. In a small saucepan, cook green pepper 5 minutes in simmering water to cover. Drain and fill green pepper with Basic Ground Beef Mix. Trim top of pepper, if necessary, so mixture mounds over top. Place stuffed pepper in a 10-ounce custard cup or soufflé pot or in a foil tart pan. Pour sauce over. Bake 40 minutes. To freeze before baking, cool green pepper and fill. Place in foil pan, add sauce and wrap in foil. Freeze. Thaw, unwrap and bake. Makes 1 serving.

Miniature Meatballs

With these in your freezer, you can't go wrong.

About 2 cups Basic Ground Beef Mix, page 72

Preheat oven to 400°F (205°C). Shape Basic Ground Beef Mix into about eighteen 1-inch meatballs. Arrange on a shallow baking sheet and bake 15 minutes. Or heat 1-inch-deep oil to 350°F (175°C) in a deep-fryer or saucepan. Fry several meatballs at a time 3 to 4 minutes. Cool on foil-lined baking sheet and freeze. When frozen solid, put in a plastic bag, squeeze out air, twist-tie and freeze. Makes about 18 appetizer meatballs or 2 main dish servings.

Variations

Spaghetti & Meatballs: Cook 3 to 4 ounces spaghetti, see page 102. Drain. Heat 8 to 10 meatballs in 1 cup spaghetti sauce. Pour over spaghetti. Serve with grated Parmesan cheese. If desired, freeze meatballs and spaghetti sauce together in an airtight wide-mouth jar or freezer bag. Makes 1 serving.
Appetizer Meatballs: Warm 8 to 10 meatballs in a toaster-oven or small sauce warmer. Dip meatballs in sour cream seasoned to taste with salt and horseradish or mustard. Or serve with hot Barbecue Sauce, page 79, Cumberland Glaze, page 82, or Teriyaki Sauce, page 83.
Meatball Stroganoff: Prepare Beef Stroganoff, page 67, omitting steak and 1 tablespoon oil. Add 12 to 16 meatballs with onion and mushrooms to thickened beef stock.

Veal Piccata & Zucchini Sauté

Delicate and tangy at the same time, this dish is perfect for two!

1/4 cup flour	1/2 to 2/3 lb. veal scallops,
1 egg	1/4-inch thick (4 to 6 pieces)
1 large zucchini	1 lemon
3 tablespoons Clarified Butter, page 159,	1/4 cup chicken stock or water
or butter, more if necessary	1 tablespoon minced parsley
Salt to taste	2 teaspoons capers, if desired
Freshly ground black pepper to taste	

Spread flour in a pie plate or shallow dish. Beat egg in another shallow dish. Cut zucchini diagonally into lengthwise slices 1/4-inch thick. Heat about 2 tablespoons butter in a large skillet over medium heat. Lightly coat zucchini slices with flour, then dip in egg. Sauté zucchini in butter until lightly browned on both sides. Sprinkle with salt and pepper. Place on a heatproof plate in warm oven, about 150°F (65°C). If necessary, add butter to skillet to make about 2 tablespoons. Coat veal scallops with flour and dip in egg to coat. Sauté 2 to 3 minutes until golden brown. Turn and sprinkle with salt and pepper. Cook other side about 2 minutes until golden brown. Do not overcook. Cut 2 slices from center of lemon for garnish. Squeeze about 2 tablespoons juice from remaining lemon. Pour lemon juice over cooked veal in skillet and immediately place veal on plate in warm oven. Add 1 tablespoon butter and stock or water to lemon juice in skillet. Boil, and stir to loosen and dissolve any pan brownings. Set skillet aside. Arrange veal and zucchini in alternating rows on 2 warm heatproof dinner plates. Keep warm in oven until ready to serve. Before serving, boil pan juices until syrupy. Stir in parsley and capers, if desired. Pour over veal and zucchini. Garnish with lemon slices. Makes 2 servings.

Variation

Veal Piccata for One: Substitute 1 egg yolk for whole egg. Reduce other ingredients by half. Cook zucchini and veal at same time.

Wurst & Sauerkraut

Have your own Oktoberfest any month of the year!

1 tablespoon bacon drippings or oil	1/8 teaspoon salt
1/4 cup minced onion	1/4 teaspoon caraway seeds, if desired
1 (8-oz.) can sauerkraut, well-drained	Freshly ground black pepper
2 teaspoons brown sugar	4 wieners or 2 knackwurst (about 1/2 lb.)
1/3 cup dry white wine, beer or water	

Heat bacon drippings or oil in a medium saucepan over medium-low heat. Add onion. Sauté until tender. Stir in remaining ingredients except wieners or knackwurst. Cover and simmer 30 minutes. Add wieners or knackwurst. Cover and cook 15 more minutes. Makes 2 servings.

Baked Pork Chops & Dressing

The ideal dish for a chilly autumn evening.

1 to 2 recipes Basic Bread Dressing, page 108,
   or Sweet-Tart Bread Dressing, page 108
2 pork chops, 1-inch thick (about 3/4 lb.)

1/4 teaspoon rosemary
Salt and pepper to taste
Butter or bacon drippings

Spread dressing in a small shallow baking dish. Preheat oven to 325°F (165°C). Trim excess fat from chops. With a mortar and pestle, crush rosemary to a powder. Rub into both sides of each chop. Sprinkle with salt and pepper. Coat skillet with butter or bacon drippings. Heat over medium heat. Add chops to hot skillet. Brown on both sides. Arrange chops over dressing in baking dish. Bake 45 to 60 minutes, less for thinner chops. To test doneness, insert a knife into center of meat next to bone. Meat and juices should no longer be pink. Makes 2 servings.

Spaghetti Carbonara Madalena *Photo on page 118.*

Italian sausage distinguishes this version of Spaghetti Carbonara.

4 thick or 6 thin slices bacon (about 1/4 lb.)
2 fresh Italian sausages, regular or hot
   (1/2 to 2/3 lb.)
2 garlic cloves, pressed or minced
2 quarts water
1 tablespoon salt
1 tablespoon oil
1/2 lb. uncooked spaghetti

1 egg
1/2 cup grated Romano or Parmesan cheese
1/4 to 1/2 cup whipping cream or
   half-and-half
Freshly ground black pepper to taste
Freshly ground nutmeg to taste
1 tablespoon finely minced parsley

Slice bacon strips into 1/2-inch pieces. Sauté in a large skillet until crisp. Set aside on a plate. Squeeze Italian sausage from casing into hot bacon fat and break into small chunks. Sauté about 10 minutes over medium-low heat until cooked through. Add garlic and sauté briefly. Return bacon to skillet. While preparing bacon and sausage, combine water, salt and oil in a large saucepan. Bring to a full boil. Gradually add spaghetti, maintaining a boil, easing it into the water as it softens. Cook uncovered about 12 minutes until tender. Cooked spaghetti should cut cleanly with a spoon. Drain spaghetti in a strainer or colander. Return to saucepan over low heat or put in a warm chafing dish or electric skillet to finish at table. Toss hot bacon and sausage, including drippings, into spaghetti. Push spaghetti to sides of pan and break egg into center. Quickly scramble egg and stir it into spaghetti. Toss in grated cheese. Pour in 1/4 cup whipping cream or half-and-half. Mix. As cream is absorbed, add up to 1/4 cup more. Add black pepper and nutmeg. Garnish with minced parsley. Makes 2 servings.

Variation

Spaghetti Carbonara for One: Reduce by half all ingredients except egg.

Stir-Fry Meal

Use a wok or large skillet to fix this dish.

1 tablespoon soy sauce
2 tablespoons dry sherry
1/8 teaspoon salt
1/8 to 1/4 teaspoon ground ginger
6 to 8 oz. lean, boneless meat such as
   chicken, beef or shrimp
About 3 cups assorted cut vegetables

2 to 3 tablespoons oil
1 garlic clove, pressed or minced
1/4 cup chicken stock or beef stock
   or water
1 teaspoon cornstarch
2 to 4 tablespoons nuts, if desired
Steamed Rice, page 105

Combine soy sauce, sherry, salt and ginger in a small bowl. Cut meat into 1/2" x 1" pieces, about 1/4-inch thick. Stir into soy sauce mixture, cover and set aside. Prepare vegetables, cutting slow-cooking vegetables into smaller pieces and fast-cooking varieties into larger pieces. Heat a wok or large skillet over medium-high heat, 350°F (175°C). All at once, pour 2 tablespoons oil into pan and add garlic and vegetables. Reserve any vegetables that only need warming. With wooden spoons or stir-fry utensils, toss briskly 2 to 3 minutes until tender-crisp. Reduce heat and cover pan 1 to 3 minutes to steam slow-cooking vegetables. Place vegetables on a plate. Blend stock or water and cornstarch in a small bowl. Drain soy sauce marinade from meat into cornstarch mixture and blend. If necessary, add oil to wok to make about 1 tablespoon. When oil is hot, add meat. Stir-fry about 2 minutes until cooked through. Return vegetables to wok and add cornstarch mixture. Stir-fry briskly until sauce thickens and clears. Add nuts, if desired, and vegetables that only need warming. Stir-fry until heated. Serve with steamed rice. Makes 2 servings.

When To Add Stir-Fry Vegetables

For uniform cooking, add stir-fry vegetables in stages. Start with slow-cooking vegetables like carrots, green beans and broccoli. Then add pea pods, green pepper, asparagus, celery and onion rings.

Fast-cooking vegetables like cabbage, mushrooms, green onions, bean sprouts and zucchini can be added toward the end of cooking time. Tomato, water chestnuts and bamboo shoots only need to be warmed.

Broiled Ham & Cherry Sauce

A simple ham slice becomes a festive dinner party for two.

Cherry Sauce, see below
1/2 center-cut slice fully cooked ham
   (1/2 to 3/4 lb.)

Cherry Sauce:

1 (8-oz.) can pitted dark sweet cherries	Dash salt
1 tablespoon sugar	1 teaspoon cornstarch
1/8 to 1/4 teaspoon ground ginger	1 tablespoon kirsch (cherry brandy), if desired

Prepare Cherry Sauce and keep warm. Broil or pan fry ham slice just long enough to heat through. Cut in half, place on serving plates and pour sauce over. Makes 2 servings.

Cherry Sauce:
Drain and reserve syrup from cherries. Pour 1/3 cup syrup into a small saucepan. Add sugar, ginger and salt. Bring to a boil. Blend cornstarch into kirsch or 1 tablespoon cherry syrup. Gradually add cornstarch mixture to simmering cherry syrup mixture. Cook and stir until thickened and clear. Before serving, stir drained cherries into sauce. Heat to serving temperature.

Kinda Special Ham & Rice

This casserole is special enough for company but easy enough for week night dinners.

2 tablespoons butter	Pinch saffron, if desired
1/2 cup minced onion	1/4 cup dry white wine
1 cup sliced fresh mushrooms	2 tablespoons minced parsley
1/3 cup uncooked long-grain rice	1 cup frozen peas (about 5 oz.)
1/3 lb. ham, cut into 1/4- to 1/2-inch cubes	Salt and pepper to taste
(about 1 cup)	1/4 cup shredded Parmesan cheese,
3/4 cup chicken stock	lightly packed

Preheat oven to 350°F (175°C). Melt butter in a 10-inch skillet over medium heat. Add onion and mushrooms. Sauté until limp and translucent. Add rice. Sauté briefly. Stir in ham, chicken stock, saffron, if desired, white wine and parsley. Stir to blend. Bring to a full boil and pour into a 1-quart casserole. Cover and bake 30 minutes. While casserole is baking, thaw peas. Remove casserole from oven, stir in peas and salt and pepper. Sprinkle Parmesan cheese evenly over top. Bake uncovered 15 more minutes. Makes 2 servings.

Variation

For larger servings, increase rice to 1/2 cup and chicken stock to 1 cup.

Cornish Game Hen & Wild Rice

It's a scaled-down turkey for two! Ask the butcher to cut it in half for you.

1 (1-1/2-lb.) Cornish game hen
Wild Rice Stuffing, see below
Salt and pepper to taste
2 tablespoons butter

1/4 cup red currant jelly
2 tablespoons brandy or Cognac
Salt to taste

Wild Rice Stuffing:
1 tablespoon butter
2 tablespoons minced celery
2 tablespoons minced shallots or
   1/4 cup minced onion
2 tablespoons minced green pepper
1 tablespoon minced parsley
2/3 cup chicken stock or
   stock from simmered giblets

1/3 cup wild rice
1/2 teaspoon mixed herbs such as basil,
   chervil, marjoram or poultry seasoning
2 tablespoons Duxelles, page 161
   if desired
Salt to taste

Thaw game hen and remove giblets. Cut hen in half. Prepare Wild Rice Stuffing. Preheat oven to 375°F (190°C). Rinse and dry hen halves. Sprinkle salt and pepper on inner surfaces. Fill with Wild Rice Stuffing. Place a square of foil over each half; invert onto a small shallow baking sheet. To prepare ahead, completely cool stuffing before using and refrigerate stuffed hen halves up to 24 hours. Melt butter in a small saucepan and brush over hen halves. Bake 20 minutes. Add red currant jelly and brandy or Cognac to remaining butter in saucepan. Heat and stir until jelly is melted and mixture is smooth. Brush jelly glaze over hen halves. Bake 20 to 30 more minutes, basting with glaze every 10 minutes. Move foil and hen halves together onto serving plates; slip foil out. Bring remaining glaze to a boil and season with salt. Pour over hen halves. Makes 2 servings.

Wild Rice Stuffing:
Melt butter in a small saucepan over medium heat. Briefly sauté celery, shallots or onion and green pepper. Stir in parsley. Add chicken stock or stock made from giblets. Bring to a boil. Rinse wild rice in a small bowl and pour off rinse water. Add rice to boiling stock. Cover and slowly simmer 45 minutes until liquid is absorbed. Stir in duxelles, if desired, and salt.

Make giblet stock by simmering the neck and giblets of 1 chicken or Cornish game hen with 1 cup water and 1/4 teaspoon salt about 1 hour. Strain and boil liquid down to 2/3 cup.

Perfect Baked Chicken

Plain or fancy, baked chicken is a basic for singles and couples.

1 whole chicken leg, 2 drumsticks or thighs,
   or 4 wings
Oil or melted butter

Salt and pepper to taste
1/4 teaspoon herbs such as oregano, basil,
   thyme and tarragon

Preheat oven or toaster-oven to 375°F (190°C). Rinse chicken and dry on paper towels. Brush with oil or melted butter. Sprinkle with salt, pepper and herbs. Arrange chicken skin-side down in a small shallow baking dish. Bake 15 minutes. Turn and baste with pan drippings. Bake 10 to 45 more minutes, depending on size of chicken pieces, basting every 10 to 15 minutes. Bake whole legs a total of 35 to 60 minutes, thighs and drumsticks 25 to 50 minutes, and wings 25 to 40 minutes. To test doneness, insert a fork into thickest part of chicken; juices should be clear and amber. Makes 1 serving.

Oven Barbecued Chicken

Use the sauce on ham or ribs, too.

4 chicken drumsticks or thighs, or 8 wings
Barbecue Sauce, see below

Salt and pepper to taste

Barbecue Sauce:
1/4 cup ketchup
1 tablespoon vinegar
1 tablespoon brown sugar
1 teaspoon Worcestershire sauce

Dash Tabasco sauce or
   1/2 teaspoon prepared mustard
1 garlic clove, pressed or finely minced

Preheat oven to 375°F (190°C). Rinse chicken and dry on paper towels. Prepare Barbecue Sauce and brush over chicken pieces. Sprinkle with salt and pepper and refrigerate until time to cook. Arrange chicken skin-side down in a small shallow baking pan. Bake 15 minutes. Turn and baste with Barbecue Sauce. Bake 15 to 35 more minutes, depending on size of chicken pieces, basting every 10 to 15 minutes. To test doneness, insert a fork into thickest part of chicken; juices should be clear and amber. Makes 2 servings.

Barbecue Sauce:
Blend all ingredients in a small bowl.

Supremes of Chicken Véronique

Try this when seedless green grapes are in season.

2 tablespoons Clarified Butter, page 159,
  or butter
2 half chicken breasts, skinned and boned
2 tablespoons dry white wine,
  dry sherry or dry vermouth
1/4 to 1/2 teaspoon herbs such as tarragon,
  basil, chervil and thyme

1/4 teaspoon salt
1/4 to 1/2 cup whipping cream
1/2 cup fresh seedless green grapes,
  washed and stemmed

Heat butter in an 8-inch skillet over medium heat. Rinse chicken breasts and dry on paper towels. Quickly sauté until golden on both sides. Add wine, herbs and salt. Cover and simmer slowly about 5 minutes. To test doneness, press finger into thickest part of chicken breast; meat should spring back. Do not overcook. Place chicken breasts on a plate and cover loosely with skillet lid to keep warm. Quickly boil pan juices until syrupy. Add whipping cream. Boil until slightly thickened. Stir grapes into cream. Cook briefly to heat grapes through. Stir in any juices that have drained from the chicken breasts. Arrange chicken breasts on plates and spoon sauce over. Makes 2 servings.

Variations

Chicken Breasts in Wine Sauce: Omit grapes and whipping cream. Place cooked chicken breasts on plates, add 1 tablespoon butter to pan juices and cook until syrupy. Pour over chicken. Garnish with minced parsley.
Chicken Breasts in Mushroom Sauce: Omit grapes. Sauté 1/2 cup sliced fresh mushrooms in butter before cooking chicken breasts; set aside. Add to finished sauce before pouring over chicken.

Chicken Breasts in Curried Fruit

Pretty, palatable and practical! Can you beat that?

2 tablespoons Clarified Butter, page 159,
  or butter
2 half chicken breasts, skinned and boned
1/2 teaspoon curry powder
2 tablespoons dry white wine,
  dry sherry or dry vermouth

1/4 teaspoon salt
2 tablespoons raisins, if desired
1 (8-oz.) can fruit cocktail, well-drained
1 tablespoon brown sugar
2 tablespoons Toasted Almonds, page 165,
  slivered or sliced

Heat butter in an 8-inch skillet over medium heat. Add chicken breasts. Sauté until lightly golden on both sides. While sautéing chicken, stir curry powder into butter. Add wine, salt and raisins, if desired. Cover and simmer slowly over low heat about 5 minutes. To test doneness, press finger into thickest part of chicken breast; meat should spring back. Do not overcook. Place chicken breasts on a plate and cover loosely with skillet lid to keep warm. Quickly add fruit cocktail and brown sugar to pan juices and bring to a boil. Cook until syrupy. Place chicken breasts on plates. Pour sauce over. Garnish with toasted almonds. Makes 2 servings.

Supremes of Chicken Véronique, Anise Carrots, page 126, and Mushroom Rice Pilaf, page 105.

Cumberland Glazed Chicken

Red currant jelly, orange and mustard make this interpretation of an old English recipe.

2 whole chicken legs, or 4 drumsticks or
   thighs
Oil or melted butter

Salt and pepper to taste
Cumberland Glaze, see below
Salt to taste

Cumberland Glaze:
1/4 cup red currant jelly
1/2 teaspoon Dijon mustard
1 teaspoon grated orange peel

1/8 teaspoon ground ginger
1/8 teaspoon allspice, if desired

Preheat oven to 375°F (190°C). Rinse chicken and dry on paper towels. Brush with oil or melted butter. Sprinkle with salt and pepper. Arrange skin-side down in a small shallow baking dish. Bake 15 minutes, turn and bake 15 more minutes. Prepare Cumberland Glaze. Baste chicken with glaze. Bake up to 30 minutes, depending on size of chicken pieces, basting with glaze every 5 to 10 minutes. To test doneness, insert a fork into thickest part of chicken; juices should be clear and amber. If chicken browns well before cooked, cover loosely with foil. If pan juices begin to burn, reduce oven temperature and add a small amount of water to dish. Place cooked chicken on a plate. Skim excess fat from pan juices, blend into remaining glaze. If pan juices are thin, boil until syrupy. Season with salt. Pour over chicken. Makes 2 servings.

Cumberland Glaze:
Heat and stir red currant jelly in a small saucepan over medium-low heat until completely melted. Blend in remaining ingredients.

Variation

All-Jammed-Up Chicken: Omit Cumberland Glaze. Prepare glaze with 4 tablespoons strained apricot-pineapple, peach or apricot jam, 1 teaspoon Worcestershire sauce and 1/4 teaspoon ground ginger. Garnish with Toasted Coconut, page 165, if desired.

Instructions for skinning and boning chicken breast halves are found on page 163.

Yakitori

Broiled teriyaki chicken on skewers is delicious!

Teriyaki Sauce, see below
2 half chicken breasts, skinned and boned

4 green onions, cut in 1-inch lengths

Teriyaki Sauce:

2 tablespoons soy sauce
2 tablespoons dry sherry or Japanese sake
2 tablespoons brown sugar

1/4 teaspoon ground ginger
1 garlic clove, pressed

Prepare Teriyaki Sauce. Cut chicken in 1-inch pieces. Marinate in Teriyaki Sauce 3 to 4 hours if time permits. About 20 minutes before serving, alternate pieces of chicken and green onion on 4 short skewers. Baste with Teriyaki Sauce. Broil slowly, or barbecue over coals 10 to 15 minutes, turning and basting 3 or 4 times. Move away from heat or reduce heat if sauce starts to burn. Heat any remaining marinade. Serve over chicken. Makes 2 servings.

Teriyaki Sauce:
Blend all ingredients in a small bowl.

Honey-Glazed Chicken

The beautiful color of this chicken suggests the delightful flavor.

1 whole chicken leg, or 2 drumsticks or thighs
1 tablespoon butter, melted
Salt and pepper to taste
2 tablespoons honey

1/8 teaspoon ground ginger
1/8 teaspoon onion salt or garlic salt
1/2 teaspoon freshly ground lemon peel
Salt to taste

Preheat oven to 375°F (190°C). Rinse chicken and dry on paper towels. Brush with part of the melted butter. Sprinkle with salt and pepper. Arrange skin-side down in a small shallow baking dish. Bake 15 minutes. Blend honey, ginger and onion salt or garlic salt into remaining melted butter. Turn chicken. Spread generously with honey mixture, reserving at least 1 tablespoon. Bake 15 to 45 more minutes, depending on size of chicken pieces, basting with pan drippings every 10 minutes. Combine reserved honey mixture with lemon peel. Baste chicken with honey and lemon peel mixture twice during last 10 minutes. To test doneness, insert a fork into thickest part of chicken; juices should be clear and amber. If chicken browns well before cooked, cover loosely with foil. If pan juices begin to burn, reduce oven temperature. Place chicken on a plate. Skim excess fat from pan juices. Blend in any remaining honey mixture. If pan juices are thin, pour into a saucepan and boil until syrupy. Season with salt. Pour over chicken. Makes 1 serving.

Chicken à l'Orange

A cousin to Duck a l'Orange. Use the extra orange juice for Orange Rice Pilaf, page 105.

1 orange
About 2 tablespoons Clarified Butter,
 page 159, or butter
2 whole chicken legs or 4 chicken thighs
Salt to taste
1 tablespoon minced shallots

2 tablespoons dry white wine or dry sherry
1 tablespoon brown sugar or
 1 tablespoon honey
1/4 teaspoon tarragon
1 tablespoon orange-flavored liqueur
1 teaspoon cornstarch

Cut 2 slices from center of orange for garnish. Squeeze juice and grate peel from remaining orange; set aside. Melt butter in a medium skillet over medium heat. Rinse chicken and dry on paper towels. Sprinkle with salt. Place skin-side down in skillet. Sauté until golden brown. Turn chicken and add shallots at side of skillet. Sauté until translucent. In a small bowl, combine 2 tablespoons orange juice, wine or sherry, brown sugar or honey, and tarragon. Add to skillet. Stir to loosen and dissolve any pan brownings. Cover and simmer slowly about 30 minutes until chicken is tender. Place chicken on plates. Blend orange-flavored liqueur, reserved orange peel and cornstarch until smooth. Stir in pan juices. Bring to a full boil. Cook and stir until thickened and clear. Pour over chicken. Add orange slice twists for garnish. Makes 2 servings.

Chicken Soup

Enjoy this in good health!

2 cups Chicken Stock, page 162
2 tablespoons uncooked rice or 1/3 to
 1/2 cup leftover steamed rice
1 carrot, peeled and sliced
1 stalk celery, thinly sliced
1/4 onion, chopped

Raw, frozen or leftover cooked vegetables
 such as whole kernel corn, peas, diced
 zucchini, cut green beans, lima beans and
 peeled diced tomato
1/2 cup cooked chicken pieces
Pepper and seasoned salt to taste

Heat chicken stock to boiling in a medium saucepan. Add rice, carrot, celery, onion and other raw vegetables. Cover and simmer until tender. Add frozen or leftover cooked vegetables and chicken pieces. Cover and simmer 5 minutes. Add pepper and seasoned salt. Makes 2 main dish servings.

Cheese Fondue For Two

It's worth a special trip to a cheese shop to get well-aged cheese.

1/2 loaf French bread, or 2 French baguettes,
  or 6 to 8 French rolls
1/2 lb. aged Swiss cheese or combination of
  Swiss and Gruyere cheese
1 tablespoon flour
1 garlic clove

1 cup dry white wine such as Neuchâtel,
  Chablis or Reisling
Salt to taste
Freshly ground black pepper to taste
Freshly grated nutmeg to taste
2 tablespoons kirsch (cherry brandy)

Crisp bread or rolls by heating uncovered in 350°F (175°C) oven 5 to 10 minutes. Cool. Cut into 1-inch cubes, leaving a side of crust on each cube. Set aside in a napkin-lined basket. Coarsely shred cheese. Mix with flour. Prepare in a fondue pot at the table. Or prepare in a 1- to 2-quart stainless steel, enamel, earthenware or nonstick saucepan and serve from a warmer at the table. Cut garlic clove in half and rub entire inner surface of pot with cut sides. Heat wine in pot over low heat until bubbles begin to surface. Slowly add 1 handful of cheese at a time to hot wine, stirring constantly with a wooden fork or wire whip until melted. Each addition should be completely melted before the next is added. Season lightly with salt, pepper and nutmeg. Blend in kirsch. Cook gently, stirring constantly about 30 seconds. To serve, spear bread cubes with forks. Dip into fondue, stir around bottom of pot and swirl to remove without dripping. Cool slightly on plate before eating from fork. As fondue thickens, slowly blend in a little more warm wine. Serve with kirsch, dry white wine, coffee or tea. Makes 2 servings or 4 appetizer servings.

How To Make Cheese Fondue For Two

For perfect fondue, it's important to add the cheese gradually, stirring constantly. It is traditional to stir the fondue in a figure-8 motion.

With a fondue fork or dinner fork, spear bread cubes through the soft side into the crust. Dip into the fondue, stirring around bottom of the pot before removing.

Zucchini Frittata

This Italian-style omelet is a popular San Francisco luncheon dish.

1 tablespoon oil or Clarified Butter,
  page 159
1 small zucchini or 1/2 medium zucchini
  (about 1/4 lb.)
1/4 cup minced onion
2 tablespoons minced green pepper

1 garlic clove, pressed or minced
1/4 teaspoon salt
3 eggs
1/8 to 1/4 teaspoon oregano
1 teaspoon oil or Clarified Butter, page 159
1 to 2 tablespoons grated Parmesan cheese

Heat 1 tablespoon oil in an 8-inch skillet over medium heat. Add zucchini, onion, green pepper, garlic and salt. Sauté slowly, stirring frequently, until all are cooked through but not browned. Remove from heat. Preheat broiler. Beat eggs in a medium bowl. Blend in oregano and slightly cooled sautéed vegetables. Clean skillet. Add 1 teaspoon oil and tilt skillet to coat with oil. Heat until oil is almost smoking. Pour egg mixture into skillet, reduce heat to low and cook about 8 minutes until almost set but still fluid on top. Sprinkle with Parmesan cheese. Broil to set egg on top and brown lightly. Eggs should still be moist inside. Makes 1 serving.

Golden Crepes

Make up extras and freeze them for later.

1 egg
1/2 cup half-and-half, or
  2 tablespoons whipping cream plus
  milk to make 1/2 cup

1/8 teaspoon salt
1/3 cup unsifted flour,
  fork-stirred before measuring
Oil or Clarified Butter, page 159

Beat egg in a medium bowl. Blend in half-and-half or whipping cream plus milk. Add salt and flour. Stir to moisten and beat about 2 minutes until smooth. Or put all ingredients except oil in a blender, cover and blend 5 seconds. Scrape sides and blend 30 more seconds until smooth. Pour batter into a glass measuring cup. Cook immediately or cover and refrigerate 2 hours for improved body. Put a small amount of oil into an 8-inch, slope-sided skillet or crepe pan. Heat over medium to medium-high heat. Pour off any oil that will run off. Hold skillet in 1 hand and cup of batter in other. Pour about 3 tablespoons batter into center of skillet, swirling and tilting skillet to cover bottom evenly. Return to heat. Cook until top of crepe is dry and edges are browned and slightly curled. With a fork, pull edge of crepe away from skillet, pick up with fingers and turn. Or tilt and shake skillet to slide edge of crepe just beyond rim and flip crepe. Cook other side 3 or 4 seconds. Invert pan over a clean towel. Cook crepes from remaining batter, wiping pan as necessary to remove crumbs. Add more oil if crepes begin to stick. To freeze, wrap serving portions in plastic wrap, and wrap again in aluminum foil. Makes 5 or 6 crepes.

Main Dish Crepes

Four crepes and a rich sauce turn leftover meat or seafood into an elegant encore.

Cream Sauce, see below
1/2 to 3/4 cup chopped or
    ground cooked meat, poultry or seafood
    plus up to 1/4 cup cooked vegetables,
    see Fillings below

4 Golden Crepes, page 86
1/4 cup whipping cream
Shredded aged Swiss cheese or
    grated Parmesan cheese

Cream Sauce:
2 tablespoons butter
2 tablespoons flour
1/2 cup chicken stock or
    1/4 cup chicken stock plus 1/4 cup milk
2 tablespoons whipping cream

1 tablespoon dry sherry or dry white wine
2 tablespoons shredded aged Swiss cheese or
    1 to 2 tablespoons grated Parmesan cheese
Salt and pepper to taste

Prepare Cream Sauce; set aside. Combine filling ingredients with enough Cream Sauce to hold together, 2 to 4 tablespoons. Spoon about 1/4 of filling mixture along 1 side of each crepe. Roll into cylinders. Place in a shallow baking pan or 2 oval au gratin dishes. Blend whipping cream into remaining Cream Sauce. Pour over crepes to cover all but ends. Sprinkle lightly with shredded cheese. If desired, refrigerate overnight. Preheat oven to 350°F (175°C). Bake 15 to 20 minutes until heated through. If crepes were refrigerated, bake about 30 minutes. Broil until sauce and cheeses are lightly browned. Makes 2 servings.

Cream Sauce:
Melt butter in a small saucepan over medium heat until frothy. Stir in flour. Cook until frothy again. Stir in chicken stock or stock plus milk. Add whipping cream. Cook and stir until thickened and smooth. Stir in sherry or white wine and cheese. Cook gently, stirring constantly, until cheese is melted and sauce is smooth. Add salt and pepper.

Fillings
Ham: Combine ground or minced ham with sautéed mushrooms, shallots and green pepper.
Chicken or Turkey à la King: Combine minced chicken or turkey with Duxelles, page 161, or sautéed mushrooms, celery and onion, plus cooked peas and minced pimiento.
Chicken Livers: Combine chopped, cooked chicken livers with chopped Hard-Cooked Egg, page 160, or sautéed green onion.
Shellfish: Combine flaked or minced crab, lobster or shrimp with Duxelles, page 161, or sautéed mushrooms and shallots. Sprinkle sliced almonds over sauce before broiling.
Sole Véronique: Combine flaked poached fin fish with Duxelles, page 161, or sautéed mushrooms and shallots. Warm crepes in oven without sauce. Fold 1/2 cup seedless green grapes into thinned sauce, pour over crepes and broil until grapes are warm and sauce is lightly browned.
Salmon or Tuna: Combine flaked salmon or tuna with sautéed green onion and celery plus a few capers. Serve with lemon wedges.

Fish & Seafood

There's a growing wave of interest in fish cookery. People have discovered fish is high in protein and low in fat. Fish is easy to cook in minutes and most varieties come in single-serving portions. It is a food definitely worthy of your consideration.

Unfortunately, the interest in fish often gets snuffed out right at the market. I too have stood in front of a well-stocked fish counter and felt my enthusiasm dissolve as I stared at the mind-boggling number of varieties. Don't be intimidated! There is really an order in all this perplexity. With a few guidelines you can confidently embark on a great cooking adventure!

FATS AND FISH

When buying fish it isn't necessary to ask if it's tender. Fish is naturally tender. Ask whether the fish is lean or fat. The leanness may determine whether you need to add fat when cooking.

Compared to other sources of meat protein, it seems unfair to call any fish *fat*. Even the least lean of the fish listed below have less than half the fat of a beef loin steak of the same weight. Many have less than 1-percent fat. More often than not, the fish you buy will be on the lean side.

Lean varieties include:		
Cod	Halibut	Sea Bass
Flounder	Ocean Perch	Turbot
Haddock	Red Snapper	Whiting
Less lean types include:		
Butterfish	Salmon	Rainbow Trout
Mackerel	Shad	Pompano

Both lean and less lean fish can be fried with good results. Lean fish are at their best when poached or steamed. Less lean types are great broiled, baked or barbecued. You might start with a less lean, fresh fish, because the fat keeps it moist while you learn how often to baste, how much heat to use, how long to cook and how to test for doneness.

BASIC COOKING TECHNIQUES

Poaching—One of the fastest ways to cook fish, it is suitable for all varieties. Because of its bland appearance, poached fish needs interesting garnishes and colorful side dishes. Rich sauces are delicious with poached fish.

Frying—My preference for fairly thin, lean fillets. The batter, as in Fillet of Sole Amandine, holds the delicate fillets together and gives moisture and richness to the fish. Steaks and heavier fillets can be fried easily without batter.

Baking—Probably the easiest way to cook fish, it gives the best guarantee of good results. Lean varieties of fish benefit from occasional basting with butter which adds moisture and richness.

Broiling—Great for steaks with good fat content. Lean steaks need generous basting with fat. Steaks and thick fillets broil better than thin fillets. Do not turn thin fillets during broiling.

WHEN FISH IS FROZEN

I prefer fresh fish over frozen, but if the fresh fish looks a little dry and dull and has a bit too much aroma, I'd rather have good commercially frozen fish. Fish quick-frozen right after the catch should have a minimum of moisture loss when thawed. Buy it frozen solid so you have the choice of keeping it frozen or cooking it immediately. Never refreeze fish. Freeze fresh fish only when necessary. Home freezers cause larger, more destructive ice crystals to form. Use any frozen fish within a month to avoid surface drying and fishy flavor. Fish should be thawed in the refrigerator.

DO NOT OVERCOOK FISH

Overcooking is about the worst thing you can do to fish. It dries out the moisture and toughens the protein. The best test for checking doneness is the easiest: Stick a fork deep into the thickest part of a fillet or into the center of a steak and twist it gently. If the flesh breaks apart easily, the inner flesh has turned opaque and the juices are cloudy rather than clear, the fish is done.

SHELLFISH

A meal including shrimp, crab, lobster or scallops is obviously an event. If time is short you can buy these already cooked by experts, ready for use in hors d'oeuvres, seafood cocktails, salads and hot dishes.

Poached Fish

Ideal for cod, flounder, haddock, halibut, pompano, salmon, sea bass, sole or red snapper.

1 recipe Quick Court Bouillon, page 91, or
    Court Bouillon Supreme, page 92
1 (5- to 8-oz.) fish steak or about
    1/3 lb. fish fillets

Lemon wedge or Sour Cream Caper Sauce,
    page 115

Prepare Quick Court Bouillon or Court Bouillon Supreme. Place fish in boiling bouillon to barely cover. Bring to a boil again. Cover and reduce heat to maintain a very slow simmer. Cook fish about 3 minutes for thin fillets or 10 minutes for 1-inch steaks or fillets. Double cooking time if fish is frozen. To test doneness, insert a fork into thickest part of fish and gently twist; inner flesh should separate easily and look opaque. With a pancake turner, move fish to a plate. If desired, peel skin from steaks before serving. Garnish with lemon wedge or Sour Cream Caper Sauce. Makes 1 serving.

How To Poach Fish

These sole fillets in Court Bouillon Supreme are done. The flesh separates easily and is opaque throughout.

Remove the skin from poached salmon steaks by winding the skin around a fork. Curl and toothpick the "tails" to keep the shape during cooking.

Fillet of Sole Amandine

One of the best ways to serve delicate fillets.

1 egg yolk
2 to 3 tablespoons flour
1/3 lb. sole fillets or other fish fillets
Salt and pepper to taste
2 or more tablespoons Clarified Butter,
    page 159, or butter

1 to 2 tablespoons slivered blanched almonds
    or sliced almonds
2 teaspoons lemon juice
Lemon wedge

Beat egg yolk in a pie plate or shallow dish. Spread flour in another shallow dish. Rinse fish fillets and dry on paper towels. Dip 1 fillet at a time into egg yolk to coat. Sprinkle with salt and pepper. Dip in flour to coat. Shake off excess flour and place fillet on wax paper. Heat 1 to 2 tablespoons butter in a medium skillet. Add nuts. Sauté and stir until golden. Place on a side dish. Nuts will continue to brown slightly after removing from heat. Add more butter, if necessary to coat pan. Set heat on medium-high for thin fillets, or medium heat for thicker fillets. Sauté floured fillets 1 to 3 minutes until golden brown. Turn and sauté other side until done. To test doneness, insert fork into thickest part of fish and gently twist; inner flesh should separate easily and look opaque. Place fillets on a plate. Working quickly, remove any burned particles from skillet. Add more butter, if necessary, to make about 1 tablespoon. Add lemon juice; boil until syrupy. Toss nuts in lemon butter. Pour over fillets. Garnish with lemon wedge. Makes 1 serving.

Variations

Substitute chopped macadamia nuts or cashews for almonds.

Fillet of Sole Amandine for Two: Use whole egg instead of egg yolk and double remaining ingredients.

Amandine Sauce

Great with fish—or green beans, asparagus, broccoli, cauliflower, celery or Brussels sprouts.

2 tablespoons Clarified Butter, page 159,
    or butter
2 tablespoons slivered blanched almonds or
    sliced almonds

2 teaspoons fresh lemon juice
Salt and pepper to taste

Heat butter in a small skillet over medium-low heat. Add almonds. Sauté and stir until golden. Almonds will continue to brown slightly after removing from heat. Remove almonds from butter and sprinkle over prepared fish or vegetables. Stir lemon juice into butter. Raise heat and boil until syrupy. Pour over fish or vegetables. Season with salt and pepper. Serve immediately. Makes about 3 tablespoons, enough for 2 servings.

Variation

Stir pan juices from baked fish into butter with lemon juice.

Tartar Sauce

Enjoy it with fried, baked or broiled fish.

1/4 cup mayonnaise
1/2 teaspoon Dijon mustard or
   regular prepared mustard
1 tablespoon minced capers
1/4 teaspoon anchovy paste, if desired
1/8 teaspoon chervil

1 tablespoon sweet pickle relish or
   minced sweet or dill pickles
2 teaspoons minced parsley
1 teaspoon minced chives or green onion
1 Hard-Cooked Egg, page 160, chopped,
   if desired

Combine all ingredients. Refrigerate briefly to blend flavors. If made a day in advance, do not add parsley, chives or green onion until just before serving. Makes about 1/3 cup, enough for 2 servings.

Meuniere Sauce

The name is fancy, but the sauce is simple—and very good on fried and baked fish.

2 tablespoons Clarified Butter, page 159,
   or butter
2 teaspoons fresh lemon juice

Pan juices from baked fish, if desired
1 tablespoon minced parsley

Combine butter, lemon juice and any pan juices from baked fish, if desired, in a small saucepan. Boil until syrupy. Pour over fish and garnish with parsley. Or stir parsley into hot sauce before pouring over fish. Makes about 3 tablespoons, enough for 2 servings.

Quick Court Bouillon

Highly recommended for flavorful red snapper, sea bass or striped bass.

2 cups water
3/4 teaspoon salt
1/4 cup dry white wine or 1 tablespoon
   lemon juice or white wine vinegar

1/2 teaspoon leaf herbs such as parsley,
   thyme, tarragon and dill, if desired

Combine all ingredients in a medium stainless steel, enamel or nonstick skillet. Bring to a boil. If herbs are added, simmer 5 minutes before adding fish. Makes enough broth to poach 3/4-pound fish or 2 servings.

Fillet of Sole Mornay

With Mornay Sauce, poached sole is unexpectedly elegant.

2 tablespoons butter
2 tablespoons flour
1/2 cup chicken stock or strained
   Court Bouillon Supreme, see below
1/2 cup milk, half-and-half or
   whipping cream
Few drops Worcestershire sauce
Dash ground red pepper

1/4 cup grated Parmesan cheese or
   1/4 to 1/2 cup shredded aged Swiss
   or Gruyere cheese
Salt and pepper to taste
2 servings poached sole fillets or
   red snapper, page 89
Grated Parmesan cheese or shredded Swiss or
   Gruyere cheese

Melt butter in a small saucepan over medium heat until frothy. Stir in flour. Cook until frothy. Do not brown. Blend in chicken stock or strained Court Bouillon Supreme. Cook and stir until thickened and smooth. Blend in milk, half-and-half or whipping cream. Add Worcestershire sauce, ground red pepper and 1/4 to 1/2 cup cheese. Cook gently, stirring constantly, until cheese is melted and sauce is smooth and hot. Add salt and pepper to taste. Arrange warm poached fillets on heatproof plates or in au gratin dishes. Pour sauce over fish to cover. Lightly sprinkle Parmesan, Swiss or Gruyere cheese over top. Broil until lightly browned and bubbling. Makes 2 servings.

Variations

Sole Mornay with Baby Shrimp: Sprinkle about 1 ounce warmed, cooked cocktail shrimp over each serving of poached sole before pouring sauce over.
Fillet of Sole Véronique: Stir 1/2 cup fresh seedless grapes into sauce. Heat long enough to warm grapes. Reduce or omit cheese, if desired.

Court Bouillon Supreme

This broth makes salmon, halibut, cod or other mild fish fit for royalty.

2 cups water
3/4 teaspoon salt
1/4 cup dry white wine
1/4 medium carrot, thinly sliced,
   (less than 1/4 cup)
1/2 stalk celery including leaves,
   thinly sliced (about 1/3 cup)

1/4 medium onion, chopped
2 whole cloves
4 whole peppercorns
1/2 bay leaf
2 sprigs parsley
1/4 teaspoon thyme
1/4 teaspoon tarragon

Combine all ingredients in a medium stainless steel, enamel or nonstick skillet. Bring to a boil. Cover, reduce heat and simmer 10 minutes before adding fish. After poaching fish, strain broth to use in a sauce for fish or freeze in an airtight container for later use. Makes enough broth to poach 3/4-pound fish or 2 servings.

Tender Baked Fish

Fish bakes fast and seldom browns; breadcrumbs give a finished look.

1 or more tablespoons butter
1 to 2 teaspoons lemon juice
1/2 teaspoon grated onion, if desired
1/3 to 1/2 lb. fish fillets or fish steak

Salt and pepper to taste
Paprika
Buttered Breadcrumbs, page 161,
  if desired

Preheat oven to 350°F (175°C). Melt 1 tablespoon butter in a medium shallow baking dish in pre-heating oven. Mix lemon juice and grated onion, if desired, into melted butter. Dip fish into butter mixture to coat. Sprinkle with salt and pepper. Arrange in baking dish. Bake 5 to 20 minutes, depending on thickness, basting lean fish with pan juices every 5 minutes. If fish absorbs butter, add more as desired. To test doneness, insert a fork into thickest part of fish and gently twist; inner flesh should separate easily and look opaque. Sprinkle with paprika and buttered breadcrumbs, if desired, during the last 3 minutes of baking. Place on a plate and pour any pan juices over fish. If juices are thin, boil until syrupy. Makes 1 serving.

Salmon With Egg & Caper Sauce

A most attractive and appetizing combination!

1 tablespoon butter
1 tablespoon flour
1/3 cup milk, chicken stock or strained
  Court Bouillon Supreme, page 92
1/3 cup dairy sour cream
1/4 teaspoon Dijon mustard

Salt and pepper to taste
1 to 2 teaspoons capers
1 Hard-Cooked Egg, page 160,
  coarsely chopped
2 poached salmon steaks, page 89,
  or broiled or baked salmon

Melt butter in a small stainless steel, enamel or nonstick saucepan over medium heat until frothy. Stir in flour. Heat until frothy again. Do not brown. Blend in milk, chicken stock or strained Court Bouillon Supreme. Cook and stir until thickened and smooth. Remove from heat and add sour cream all at once, blending immediately. Blend in mustard. Add salt and pepper. Fold in capers and hard-cooked egg. Keep sauce warm. Cook salmon steaks and arrange on individual plates. Pour egg and caper sauce over. Makes 2 servings.

Variation

Quick Egg & Caper Sauce: Substitute 1/3 cup canned white sauce for butter, flour and milk, chicken stock or Court Bouillon Supreme. Heat white sauce. Blend in other sauce ingredients.

Cold Poached Salmon & Sauce Verte

Make this in the morning for an elegant late luncheon on the terrace.

2 poached salmon steaks, page 89
Sauce Verte, see below

Whole lettuce leaves, butter lettuce
   preferred

Sauce Verte:

2 tablespoons drained, cooked chopped
   spinach
1 tablespoon minced parsley
2 green onions with fresh green tops

1/4 teaspoon tarragon
1/8 teaspoon chervil
1/3 cup mayonnaise
Salt to taste

Poach salmon steaks. While warm, peel off skin and scrape surface with broad side of a knife to remove white film. Cover and chill. Prepare Sauce Verte; chill. At serving time, arrange salmon steaks on lettuce-lined serving plates. Top with Sauce Verte.

Sauce Verte:

Finely chop spinach, parsley and green onions. Mix with tarragon, chervil, mayonnaise and salt. Refrigerate to blend flavors.

Variation

Substitute mayonnaise, Sauce Gribiche, page 47, or Tartar Sauce, page 91, for Sauce Verte.

Basted Broiled Fish

Broiling can be tricky, so baste the fish often to keep it moist.

About 2 tablespoons butter
1 (1/3-lb.) fish fillet or steak, about
   1 inch thick
Salt and pepper to taste
About 1 tablespoon oil

Lemon juice, if desired
1 lemon slice, if desired
Hollandaise Sauce, page 120, or
   Sauce Bearnaise, page 64

Melt butter in a small saucepan. Preheat broiler and broiler pan. Rinse and dry fish. Brush both sides with melted butter. Sprinkle with salt and pepper. Generously coat center of hot broiler pan with oil. Place fish on pan and sprinkle with lemon juice, if desired. Broil 10 to 15 minutes, basting several times and turning once. Do not turn thinner fillets. To test doneness, insert a fork into thickest part of fish and gently twist; inner flesh should separate easily and look opaque. With a pancake turner, move fish to a plate. Garnish with lemon slice, if desired. Serve with Hollandaise Sauce or Sauce Bearnaise. Makes 1 serving.

Scallops Newburg

Good things come in small portions! Divide among 4 scallop shells for appetizers.

Creamy Sauce, see below
2 tablespoons butter
1/4 lb. mushrooms, sliced
2 tablespoons minced shallots
1/2 lb. fresh scallops
1/2 cup dry sherry or dry white wine

Up to 1/4 cup whipping cream or
   half-and-half
Grated Parmesan Cheese or Buttered
   Breadcrumbs, page 164
Salt and pepper to taste

Creamy Sauce:
1 tablespoon butter
1 tablespoon flour
1/2 cup milk or half-and-half
1/8 teaspoon salt

Dash ground red pepper
1/4 teaspoon thyme
1/4 teaspoon Worcestershire sauce

Prepare Creamy Sauce. Set aside. Melt butter in a small skillet over medium-low heat. Add mushrooms. Sauté briefly. Add minced shallots. Sauté until mushrooms and shallots are translucent. Rinse scallops and dry on paper towels. Cut larger scallops into bite-size pieces. Add to mushrooms and shallots. Sauté about 2 minutes, stirring constantly, until scallops begin to firm. Add sherry or white wine. Cover, reduce heat and simmer 2 to 3 minutes. With a slotted spoon, move scallops and mushrooms to 2 small au gratin dishes. Raise heat under wine and boil until about 1/4 cup wine remains. Blend into Creamy Sauce. Add up to 1/4 cup whipping cream or half-and-half to thin sauce to desired consistency. Add salt and pepper. Pour sauce over scallops and mushrooms. To delay serving, stir scallops and mushrooms into sauce in saucepan and refrigerate. At serving time, heat gently to serving temperature, stirring constantly, and spoon into baking dishes. Lightly sprinkle cheese or buttered breadcrumbs over sauce. Broil until browned and bubbly. Makes 2 servings.

Creamy Sauce:
Melt butter in a small stainless steel, enamel or nonstick saucepan. Heat until frothy; stir in flour. Heat until frothy again. Do not brown. Add milk or half-and-half. Cook and stir over medium-low heat until thickened and smooth. Stir in salt, ground red pepper, thyme and Worcestershire sauce.

Cucumber Sauce

Light, rich and refreshing with fish or fish sticks.

2 tablespoons mayonnaise
2 tablespoons dairy sour cream
1 teaspoon lemon juice
1/8 teaspoon salt

Dash pepper
1/4 cup shredded or finely minced,
   peeled and seeded cucumber

Combine all ingredients. Refrigerate until serving time. Makes about 1/3 cup, enough for 2 servings.

Scampi

There's absolutely no reason for restaurants to have a corner on this classic.

8 to 12 raw jumbo shrimp in the shell
   (2/3 to 3/4 lb.)
1/4 cup butter (1/2 stick)
2 garlic cloves, pressed or minced
About 2 tablespoons fresh lemon juice

Salt to taste
Freshly ground black pepper to taste
1 to 2 tablespoons minced parsley
Buttered Breadcrumbs, page 164,
   if desired

Wash shrimp and remove "legs" and shells, leaving tails attached. If desired, devein shrimp by making a shallow cut down center back of each shrimp. Open cut and rinse away exposed vein. Melt butter in a 10-inch skillet over medium heat. Stir in garlic. Sauté briefly, but do not brown. Add shrimp. Sauté 1 to 2 minutes on each side until shrimp turn pink and flesh is opaque and firm. Pour lemon juice over shrimp. Sprinkle with salt and pepper. Place shrimp on plate. Working quickly, raise heat and boil pan juices until syrupy. Stir in minced parsley. Pour over shrimp. Garnish with buttered breadcrumbs, if desired. Serve immediately. Makes 2 servings.

How To Make Scampi

To remove the vein from shelled shrimp, make a shallow cut along the back curve of the shrimp, open the cut and rinse out the vein.

Sauté the shrimp on both sides until they turn pink and the flesh becomes opaque and firm.

Side Dishes

Potatoes, pasta, rice and bread are those wonderful foods that go with everything and help everything else go together. Their mild flavors create transitions between salty foods, sour foods, spicy foods and sweet foods. Besides this, they are a source of important nutrients.

These bland diplomats of the dinnerplate can play another role in a menu, too. Because they don't have strong flavors, they are perfect to season up when you want to keep the rest of the meal simple. When you are building a meal around the natural flavor of some superb meat or vegetable, introduce extra flavors by adding sauces and seasonings to these starch foods.

POTATOES

Each variety of potato has its virtues and limitations. My choice for a good basic stock potato is the Idaho Russet, also called the Russet Burbank potato. It is ideal for baking, excellent for mashing and frying, and satisfactory for boiling. When you have no particular menu in mind, buy an Idaho Russet. If you plan to boil potatoes to serve plain, creamed or in a salad, select a potato such as a White Rose, Cobbler, Katahdin, Red La Soda or Red Pontiac.

Buy potatoes in a size you will consume in a single meal. Leftover potatoes can be refrigerated a day or so, but they do not freeze well in home freezers. Many packaged frozen and dried potato products can be prepared in small quantities. Tips on storage are found on pages 10 and 11.

PASTA

Among the estimated 150 varieties of pasta, the most versatile is the wide egg noodle.

It's almost impossible to get a consistent measure of noodles when measuring a single serving in a measuring cup. Curly noodles fit into a cup differently than straight ones. One serving of uncooked noodles can weigh as little as 1-1/2 ounces or as much as 2-2/3 ounces. I strongly advise using a 1-pound (450 gram) scale for measuring.

Spaghetti is also difficult to measure. Package directions always assume you'll cook the whole amount. If you don't have a scale, select a serving size of 1-1/2 to 4 ounces per person and divide the package accordingly. Tie off or rubber band the portions and store them for future use.

Leftover noodles and spaghetti can be frozen and reheated with good results. Freeze them in foil tart pans with 1 tablespoon water and cover with a double thickness of aluminum foil. Reheat in the covered foil pan at 350°F (175°C) about 40 minutes, or thaw and heat about 30 minutes.

RICE

I think rice is compatible with more main dishes than any other side dish, except possibly bread. Converted long-grain white rice is the best basic stock rice. Its advantage over potatoes or pasta is that the cooking time is not critical. When the rest of the meal requires a lot of last minute preparations or the exact serving time is unknown, rice can be cooked completely in advance. It can be held over low heat or cooled and reheated later. If it gets a little dry, steaming it with a tablespoon or 2 of water will bring it back.

Leftover long-grain rice, either plain or pilaf, freezes and reheats beautifully. Freeze leftover rice in any wide-mouth freezer container. To reheat, put the rice in a small covered saucepan, add 1 to 2 tablespoons water, cover and warm over low heat. Stir once or twice as rice thaws. Leftover rice will keep in the refrigerator up to one week.

BREADS & DRESSINGS

No side dish could be easier than bread. To add new tastes to bakery bread, spread with flavored butters and toast or broil. There are times when the fresh, hot, homemade breads found in this chapter can make a meal extra special.

Dressings and stuffings are a practical way to use bread all year, not just on holidays. They use up the odds and ends of your bread collection and do a good job of cleaning up vegetable scraps. Use the recipes here to create dressings to suit your particular main dish and your special tastes.

Potatoes Anita   **Photo on page 63.**

Serve this little sister of Potatoes Anna with your finest steak or lamb chop.

1 large Idaho Russet potato or other all-purpose potato (about 3/4 lb.)	**Salt and pepper to taste**
	Minced parsley
2 to 3 tablespoons Clarified Butter, page 159	

Peel potato and slice very thin. Heat butter in a heavy 8-inch skillet. Dry potato slices on paper towels. Arrange overlapping slices in a ring on bottom of skillet. Fill in center with overlapping slices. Sprinkle with salt and pepper. Arrange a second layer with remaining slices. Invert a small heatproof plate over potatoes and place a heavy object, such as a can of water, on the plate to weight it down. Sauté potatoes over medium heat until underside is golden brown and slices are molded together. Remove weight and plate. Carefully turn potatoes all at once. Cook until browned and cooked through. Cut in half and place on plates. Pour butter remaining in pan over potatoes. Garnish with minced parsley. Makes 2 servings.

Basic Baked Potatoes

Leftover baked potatoes make delicious fried potatoes for breakfast.

1 medium-large Idaho Russet potato or other baking potato (about 2/3 lb.)	**Salt and pepper to taste**
	Topping, if desired, see below
Oil, butter or bacon drippings	**Garnish, if desired, see below**

Preheat oven or toaster-oven to 425°F (220°C). Scrub and dry potato. Rub potato skin with oil, butter or bacon fat to keep skin soft. Pierce with a fork or knife to let steam escape during baking. Place potato on a small shallow baking sheet or toaster-oven tray. Bake about 45 minutes until a fork can easily be inserted into center of potato or potato is tender when squeezed. To serve, roll hot potato on counter top, pressing gently with heel of hand. Slit skin from end to end and push ends toward center to open slit. Fluff potato with a fork. Sprinkle with salt and pepper. Add topping and garnish, if desired. Makes 1 serving.

Toppings

Butter, sour cream, plain yogurt, Sour Cream & Cheese Sauce, page 115, or sieved cottage cheese. For main dish baked potatoes, top with creamed chipped beef, creamed tuna or chicken, Quick Beef Stroganoff, page 66, or creamed diced ham.

Garnishes

Crumbled crisp bacon, chopped chives or green onions, crumbled blue cheese, shredded Cheddar cheese, slivered Toasted Almonds, page 165, Toasted Sesame Seeds, page 165, Buttered Bread-crumbs, page 164, or minced parsley.

Stuffed Baked Potatoes

The best of both—baked potato flavor and creamy mashed potato texture.

1 Basic Baked Potato, page 99
2 tablespoons butter
1/4 cup dairy sour cream
Up to 2 tablespoons milk, half-and-half or
 whipping cream

1 green onion, minced
1 tablespoon crumbled crisp bacon
Salt and pepper to taste
2 to 3 tablespoons shredded
 Cheddar cheese

Bake potato, but do not roll on counter top. Leave oven at 425°F (220°C). Cut hot potato in half lengthwise. Scoop pulp into a medium bowl, leaving enough pulp inside the skin to hold potato's shape. With a wire whip or electric mixer, beat hot potato until almost smooth. Add butter and sour cream. Beat until blended. Add milk, half-and-half or whipping cream to moisten potato mixture. Stir in green onion and crumbled bacon. Season with salt and pepper. Spoon mixture into potato skins, forming smooth mounds. If desired, refrigerate up to 24 hours. To serve immediately, place stuffed potato halves in a small shallow baking pan, sprinkle with cheese and bake 10 minutes. To reheat if refrigerated, preheat oven to 325°F (165°C); warm in oven 20 to 25 minutes, sprinkle with cheese and bake 5 more minutes. Makes 2 servings.

How To Make Stuffed Baked Potatoes

Carefully scoop pulp from baked potato halves, leaving 1/8- to 1/4-inch pulp next to the skin to retain shape of potato.

Fill potato skins with seasoned potato mixture, forming smooth mounds. Sprinkle with cheese and bake 10 minutes until heated through and cheese is melted.

Boiled Potatoes   *Photo on page 93.*

Try them with your own creamy variations.

1 to 2 cups water
1/2 teaspoon salt
1/2 to 3/4 lb. potatoes such as
   White Rose or Idaho Russet

Salt and pepper to taste

Pour 1/2-inch-deep water into a small saucepan. Add 1/2 teaspoon salt. Bring to a full boil. Scrub and rinse potatoes. Leave whole or cut in quarters. Add to boiling water. Cover and reduce heat to maintain a slow boil. Cook until tender, 15 to 25 minutes for quarters, 25 to 45 minutes for whole potatoes. Drain; reserve liquid for soup stocks or sauces. Return potatoes in saucepan to low heat to evaporate remaining moisture. Remove from heat. Peel potatoes. Sprinkle with salt and pepper. Serve plain or with sauce or garnish. Makes 2 servings.

Variations

Parsley Potatoes: Heat 2 to 3 tablespoons butter until frothy, but not browned. Roll hot peeled potatoes in butter and sprinkle with 1 tablespoon minced parsley.
Creamed Potatoes: Prepare Sour Cream Sauce, page 115, or use 1/2 cup of any cream sauce. If desired, stir in shredded aged Cheddar cheese or a small amount of mustard. Cut hot, peeled potatoes into cubes. Fold into sauce.

Buttered Noodles

A delightful staple you can use many ways.

1 quart water
1-1/2 teaspoons salt
1 tablespoon oil
2 cups uncooked wide egg noodles
   (3 to 4 oz.)

2 tablespoons Clarified Butter, page 159,
   or butter
Salt and pepper to taste
Poppy seeds or minced parsley,
   if desired

Combine water, 1-1/2 teaspoons salt and oil in a medium saucepan. Bring to a full boil. Gradually add noodles, maintaining a boil. Reduce to a slow boil. Cook uncovered 8 to 10 minutes, stirring once, until tender. Drain in a strainer or colander. Add butter to saucepan. Heat until frothy. For noodles in browned butter, heat clarified butter until amber. Remove from heat. Add drained noodles. Gently stir or toss to coat noodles with butter. Add salt and pepper. Garnish with poppy seeds or minced parsley, if desired. Makes 2 servings.

Fettucine Alfredo

good

Main dish or side dish, it will be the main attraction!

double recipe

1 quart water
1-1/2 teaspoons salt
1 tablespoon oil
2 cups uncooked wide egg noodles
   (3 to 4 oz.)
2 tablespoons butter (1/4 stick)

1/2 cup whipping cream
1/4 1/2 cup freshly grated or shredded
   Parmesan cheese *+ 1/4 c cheddar cheese*
Dash freshly ground black pepper
Dash freshly grated nutmeg, if desired

Combine water, salt and oil in a medium saucepan. Bring to a full boil. Gradually add noodles, maintaining a boil. Reduce heat to a slow boil. Cook uncovered 8 to 10 minutes, stirring once, until tender. Drain in a strainer or colander. Return noodles to saucepan, or put in a warm chafing dish or electric skillet to finish at table. Fold in butter until melted. Pour in whipping cream. Sprinkle with Parmesan cheese. Fold and stir until cream is partially absorbed and cheese is melted. Just before serving, add pepper and nutmeg, if desired. Makes 2 servings.

Simple Spaghetti

Add a little of this and a little of that, and spaghetti goes versatile!

2 quarts water
1 tablespoon salt
1 tablespoon oil

3 to 4 oz. uncooked spaghetti,
   spaghettini or vermicelli

Combine water, salt and oil in a large saucepan. Bring to a full boil. Gradually add spaghetti, maintaining a boil. Ease spaghetti into the water as it softens. Cook uncovered until tender, about 12 minutes for spaghetti, 10 minutes for spaghettini or 7 minutes for vermicelli. Cooked spaghetti should cut cleanly with a spoon. Drain in a strainer or colander. Makes 2 side dish servings or 1 main dish serving.

Variations

Buttery Parmesan Spaghetti: Add 1 to 2 tablespoons butter and freshly ground black pepper to taste. Toss until butter is melted. Toss about 1/4 cup grated Parmesan cheese with spaghetti.
Garlic Pasta: Briefly sauté 2 cloves pressed or minced garlic in 1 to 2 tablespoons butter. Add to spaghetti with 1 tablespoon minced parsley and freshly ground black pepper. Toss. Serve with grated Parmesan cheese.
Spaghetti in Mushroom Cream: Sauté 1/2 cup sliced mushrooms in 2 tablespoons butter until translucent and tender. Stir in 1/4 cup whipping cream. Heat to boiling. Add salt and freshly ground black pepper to taste. Toss with spaghetti. Serve with grated Parmesan cheese.

Noodles Polonaise

Breadcrumbs turn ordinary noodles into something special!

1 quart water	2 tablespoons Clarified Butter, page 159,
1-1/2 teaspoons salt	or butter
1 tablespoon oil	1/4 cup Soft Breadcrumbs, page 164
1-1/2 cups uncooked wide egg noodles,	1 tablespoon minced parsley, if desired
(about 3 oz.)	Salt and pepper to taste

Combine water, salt and oil in a medium saucepan. Bring to a full boil. Add noodles, stir once and boil gently 8 to 10 minutes until tender. Drain in a strainer or colander. Immediately add 1 table-spoon butter and soft breadcrumbs to saucepan. Sauté until breadcrumbs are crisp and golden brown. Remove pan from heat. Add remaining tablespoon of butter. Stir to melt. Toss in noodles. Add minced parsley, if desired, and salt and pepper. Toss again. Makes 2 servings.

Variation

Quick Noodles Polonaise: Omit soft breadcrumbs. Reduce butter to about 1-1/2 tablespoons. Stir 2 tablespoons Buttered Breadcrumbs, page 164, into hot butter before tossing with noodles.

Noodles Romanoff

A satisfying main dish, too.

1 quart water	1/2 cup cottage cheese
1-1/2 teaspoons salt	1/8 teaspoon onion salt
1 tablespoon oil	1 (2-oz.) can sliced mushrooms, drained,
1-1/2 cups uncooked wide egg noodles	or 3 tablespoons Duxelles, page 161
(about 3 oz.)	1/4 cup Buttered Breadcrumbs, page 164
1/2 cup dairy sour cream	

Preheat oven to 350°F (175°C). Combine water, salt and oil in a medium saucepan. Bring to a full boil. Gradually add noodles, maintaining a boil. Reduce to a slow boil. Cook uncovered 8 to 10 minutes, stirring once, until tender. While noodles are cooking, combine remaining ingredients, except buttered breadcrumbs, in a medium bowl. Drain cooked noodles in a strainer or colander. Fold into sour cream mixture. Spoon into two 10-ounce soufflé pots, au gratin dishes, casseroles or one 3-cup casserole. Sprinkle buttered breadcrumbs over top. Bake uncovered 20 to 25 minutes until bubbly. Makes 2 servings.

Variation

Tuna & Noodles Romanoff: Drain and flake 1 (3-1/2-ounce) can tuna. Fold into sour cream mixture before folding in noodles.

Steamed Rice

Serve steamed rice with curries and Oriental stir-fry dishes.

1 cup water
1/4 teaspoon salt

1/2 cup uncooked long-grain rice or
  brown rice

Combine water, salt and rice in a small saucepan. Cover tightly and bring to a boil. Reduce heat to a very slow simmer. Cook white rice about 15 minutes, or brown rice 40 minutes, until all water is absorbed. Do not lift lid during cooking. If rice is dry or too firm, add 1 to 2 tablespoons water; cover and cook until absorbed. Makes 2 servings.

Variations

Parsley-Lemon Rice: Stir 1 tablespoon butter, 1 tablespoon finely minced parsley and 1/4 teaspoon freshly grated lemon peel into cooked rice. Cover 2 minutes to blend flavors.
Mushroom Rice: Stir 2 tablespoons Duxelles, page 161, 1 tablespoon butter and 1/4 teaspoon thyme, marjoram or chervil into cooked rice. Cover 2 minutes to blend flavors.
Orange Mint Rice: Stir 1 tablespoon butter, 1/2 teaspoon freshly grated orange peel and 1/4 teaspoon dry mint leaves or 1 teaspoon finely minced fresh mint leaves into cooked rice. Cover 2 minutes to blend flavors.

Rice Pilaf *Photo on page 80.*

Check the variations for some exotic suggestions.

1 to 2 tablespoons Clarified Butter,
  page 159, or butter
1/2 cup uncooked long-grain rice

2 tablespoons minced shallots or
  1/4 cup minced onion
1 cup chicken stock

Heat butter in a small saucepan over medium heat. Add rice and shallots or onion. Sauté until rice is golden. Add chicken stock. Bring to a boil. Reduce heat to a slow simmer. Cover and cook 15 to 20 minutes. To delay serving, reduce heat to lowest setting and add 1 to 2 tablespoons water occasionally to replace lost moisture. Makes 2 to 3 servings.

Variations

Saffron Rice Pilaf: Mix up to 1/16 teaspoon ground saffron with stock before adding to rice.
Orange Rice Pilaf: Substitute 1/4 cup orange juice for part of the stock. Stir 1/4 to 1/2 teaspoon grated orange peel into finished pilaf. Cover 2 minutes to blend flavors.
Middle Eastern Rice Pilaf: Add dash cinnamon to stock. Fold 2 to 3 tablespoons slivered Toasted Almonds, page 165, and 2 to 3 tablespoons softened raisins into finished pilaf. Serve with shish kebab or lamb chops.
Mushroom Rice Pilaf: Stir 1/4 cup sautéed sliced mushrooms or 2 to 3 tablespoons Duxelles, page 161, into finished pilaf.

Fried Rice

Here's an opportunity to use leftover rice and bits of leftover meats.

1 to 2 tablespoons oil or bacon drippings
1 cup plain Steamed Rice, page 105
2 teaspoons soy sauce
1 to 2 green onions, sliced

1 egg
2 to 3 tablespoons minced cooked meat
    such as ham, pork, chicken, bacon,
    brown-and-serve sausage or shrimp

Heat oil or bacon drippings in an 8-inch skillet. Add steamed rice. Stir-fry until rice is hot and mixed with oil or drippings. Add soy sauce; mix well. If rice is dry, add 1 to 2 tablespoons water; cover and cook gently until water is absorbed. Stir in green onion. Push rice to side of skillet. Beat egg separately or break into skillet and quickly scramble with a fork. As egg sets, stir gently to let uncooked egg flow underneath. Stir cooked egg into rice, breaking egg into small pieces. Stir in minced cooked meats. Heat through. Makes 2 servings.

How To Make Fried Rice

The scrambled egg should be completely cooked before breaking into pieces and mixing with rice. Add the minced cooked meat last.

A handsome dish, even without these green onion plumes, Fried Rice is perfect with All-Jammed-Up Chicken, page 82, or broiled fish.

Wild Rice

Chewy and flavorful. Enjoy this on special occasions.

1 tablespoon butter
1 to 2 tablespoons minced shallots

1 cup chicken stock
1/2 cup wild rice

Melt butter in a small saucepan over low heat. Add shallots. Sauté briefly but do not brown. Add chicken stock. Bring to a boil. In a small bowl, rinse wild rice in water. Pour off water. Stir wild rice into boiling stock. Cover and reduce heat to a very slow simmer. Cook 40 to 50 minutes until rice is tender and liquid is absorbed. If rice is dry, add 1 to 2 tablespoons water, cover and steam until absorbed. Makes 2 to 3 servings.

Variation

Wild & White Rice: Reduce wild rice to 1/4 cup. After 20 minutes cooking, add 1/4 cup long-grain white rice. Cook 30 more minutes.

Savory Bread Dressing

Perfect with delicately flavored meats like chicken breasts, fish, game hens and veal.

2 tablespoons butter or bacon drippings
1/4 cup minced celery, including leaves
1 to 2 tablespoons minced shallots
2 tablespoons minced green pepper
1/2 cup sliced or chopped fresh mushrooms
    or 2 tablespoons Duxelles, page 161
2 tablespoons minced parsley
About 2 tablespoons finely diced or crumbled
    cooked ham, bacon or sausage, if desired

2 tablespoons chopped nuts such as pecans,
    cashews, walnuts or Toasted Almonds,
    page 165, or 1 tablespoon Toasted Sesame
    Seeds, page 165
1/4 teaspoon sage or thyme
1/4 teaspoon basil, marjoram or oregano
1 cup Soft Breadcrumbs, page 164
Salt and pepper to taste

Preheat oven to 325°F (165°C). Melt butter or bacon drippings in a medium skillet over medium-low heat. Add celery, shallots, green pepper and fresh mushrooms. Sauté until all are tender. Or sauté celery, shallots and green pepper, then stir in duxelles. Add parsley, cooked meat, if desired, nuts or sesame seeds and herbs. Lightly stir in soft breadcrumbs. Add salt and pepper. Spoon into a 2-cup casserole. Cover and bake 30 minutes. For a crisp top, uncover during last 10 minutes. Makes 2 servings.

Variations

Chicken Dressing: Add 1/8 to 1/4 teaspoon additional herbs such as thyme, rosemary or tarragon. If desired, add a dash of ginger, nutmeg or cinnamon.

Fish Dressing: Omit sage. Add 1/4 teaspoon tarragon or dill weed. If desired, add small amounts of crushed rosemary, thyme and crushed anise or fennel seed. For spicy flavor, add a dash of allspice or a mixture of cinnamon, nutmeg and cloves.

Veal Dressing: Add 1/8 teaspoon crushed rosemary. Substitute thyme or tarragon for other herbs.

Basic Bread Dressing

Consider this recipe as a guide and make your own versions.

1 to 2 tablespoons butter or bacon drippings
1/4 cup minced celery, including leaves
2 tablespoons minced onion
2 tablespoons minced parsley

1/4 to 1/2 teaspoon mixed herbs such as
    sage, thyme, marjoram and oregano
1 cup Soft Breadcrumbs, page 164
Salt and pepper to taste

Preheat oven or toaster-oven to 325°F (165°C). Melt butter or drippings in an 8-inch skillet over medium-low heat. Add celery and onion. Sauté until tender. Stir in parsley and mixed herbs. Lightly stir in soft breadcrumbs. Add salt and pepper. Spoon into a 10-ounce casserole. Cover and bake about 30 minutes. For a crisp top, uncover during last 10 minutes. Makes 1 to 2 servings.

Variation

Moist Bread Dressing: Add 1 to 2 tablespoons stock, water, milk or cream before baking.

Sweet-Tart Bread Dressing

A special dressing for pork, duckling and other rich meat.

1 tablespoon butter
1/2 cup minced, peeled apple
1/4 cup minced celery, including leaves
2 tablespoons minced onion
2 tablespoons minced parsley
1/4 teaspoon sage or thyme
1/4 teaspoon rosemary
Dash cinnamon

Dash nutmeg
Dash ginger
1/2 teaspoon grated orange peel, if desired
2 tablespoons chopped, softened, dried
    prunes, apricots or raisins, if desired
1 cup Soft Breadcrumbs, page 164
Salt and pepper to taste

Preheat oven to 325°F (165°C). Melt butter in a medium skillet over medium-low heat. Add apple, celery and onion. Sauté until all are tender. Stir in parsley, herbs, spices, orange peel and fruit, if desired. Lightly stir in soft breadcrumbs. Add salt and pepper. Spoon into a 10-ounce casserole. Cover and bake 30 minutes. For a crisp top, uncover during last 10 minutes. Makes 1 to 2 servings.

Variations

Pork Dressing: Add crushed caraway seed and thyme to taste with a dash of anise or cumin.
Duck Dressing: Add 1/4 teaspoon basil, marjoram or oregano.

Extra Special Biscuits

The wonderful flavor and texture come from the cream.

2/3 cup buttermilk biscuit mix
1/4 cup whipping cream

Preheat oven to 450°F (230°C). In a small bowl, mix buttermilk biscuit mix and whipping cream to form a soft dough. Beat vigorously 15 strokes. On a lightly floured surface, shape dough into a ball. Knead 5 times. Pat out 1/2-inch thick. Cut biscuits with a 2-inch cookie cutter. Arrange on ungreased baking sheet. Reshape dough scraps and cut again. Bake 8 to 10 minutes until golden brown. Makes 4 to 6 biscuits.

Variations

Sesame Biscuits: Brush tops with milk or cream and sprinkle with sesame seeds before baking.
Drop Biscuits: Do not knead. Beat dough and drop by spoonfuls onto ungreased baking sheet. Makes 4 biscuits.

Popovers

You can make this batter ahead and refrigerate it up to 24 hours before baking.

1 egg
1 egg white, if desired
1/2 cup milk or half-and-half

1/2 cup flour
1/4 teaspoon salt

Place four 5- or 6-ounce ungreased custard cups in standard oven and preheat to 425°F (220°C). Beat egg in a medium bowl. Add egg white for increased volume, if desired. Blend in milk or half-and-half. Stir in flour and salt until moistened. Beat until smooth. When custard cups are hot, pour about 1/4 cup batter into each custard cup. Bake 20 minutes. Reduce temperature to 350°F (175°C) and bake 10 to 15 more minutes until popovers are puffed, crisp and well-browned. To delay serving, turn off heat and let popovers stand in oven about 10 minutes. If desired, wrap and freeze popovers. Thaw and bake uncovered at 350°F (175°C) about 5 minutes. Makes 4 popovers.

Variation

Blender Method: Put all ingredients in blender and blend until smooth.

Onion-Cheese Loaf   ***Photo on page 45.***

Especially good with a main dish salad or a simple steak-and-salad dinner.

2 tablespoons butter
1/3 cup minced onion
1 egg yolk or 1 egg white
1/3 cup milk

1 cup buttermilk biscuit mix
1/2 cup shredded sharp Cheddar cheese,
    lightly packed

Preheat oven to 400°F (205°). Line a 7" x 3" or a 9" x 5" loaf pan lengthwise with wax paper, see page 134. Set aside. Melt butter in a small skillet over medium heat. Sauté onion until translucent and tender but not browned. Beat egg yolk or egg white in a medium bowl. Blend in milk. Add buttermilk biscuit mix. Stir to moisten and beat about 50 strokes. Stir in half the onion and half the cheese. Pour batter into loaf pan. Drizzle remaining onion over batter. Sprinkle remaining cheese evenly over top. Bake 20 to 25 minutes until edges separate from pan. Makes 3 to 4 servings.

Garlic-Cheese Butter

The classic!

2 tablespoons butter
1 garlic clove, pressed or minced

4 slices bread
1 tablespoon grated Parmesan cheese

Melt butter in a small saucepan over low heat. Add garlic. Sauté briefly but do not brown. Dip surface of bread into melted butter. Or cool butter and spread on bread. Sprinkle Parmesan cheese over buttered surfaces. Toast in toaster-oven or broil until bubbly and lightly browned. Makes 4 servings.

Variations

Curried Garlic Butter: Omit Parmesan cheese. Add 1/4 teaspoon curry powder to butter with garlic.
Garlic & Blue Cheese Butter: Blend 1 tablespoon mashed blue cheese into cooled garlic butter.

Spread flavored butters, including Chili Butter, page 125, on halves of individual hard rolls, English muffins, or hamburger buns. Or cut hot dog rolls lengthwise into breadsticks and spread butter on cut surfaces. To serve flavored butters as quick hot canapé spreads, use the technique described in the recipe for Blue Cheese Crisps, page 35.

Herbed Butter

Mix butter with different herbs and enjoy it on bread, potatoes and even popcorn!

2 tablespoons butter
1 teaspoon minced shallots
1/2 teaspoon mixed herbs such as marjoram,
    tarragon, chervil, basil and oregano

1 to 2 teaspoons finely minced parsley
4 slices bread

Melt butter in a small saucepan over low heat. Stir in shallots. Sauté briefly but do not brown. Remove from heat. Stir in herbs and parsley. Spread on bread. Toast in toaster-oven or broil until bubbly and lightly browned. Makes 4 servings.

Dilled Mustard Butter

Serve it with a fish dinner.

2 tablespoons butter, room temperature
1/2 teaspoon prepared mustard

1/4 teaspoon dill
4 slices bread

Blend butter, mustard and dill in a small bowl. Spread on bread. Toast in toaster-oven or broil until bubbly and lightly browned. Makes 4 servings.

Sesame-Cheddar Butter

Especially good on whole-wheat breads and rolls.

2 tablespoons butter, room temperature
2 tablespoons shredded sharp Cheddar cheese
1 teaspoon Toasted Sesame Seeds, page 165

Few drops Worcestershire sauce
Dash ground red pepper
4 slices bread

Blend butter, cheese, sesame seeds, Worcestershire sauce and red pepper in a small bowl. Spread on bread. Toast in toaster-oven or broil until bubbly and lightly browned. Makes 4 servings.

Vegetables

Unless you eat in the finest restaurants, it's almost impossible to get a good selection of well-prepared vegetables. Few vegetables can be cooked in quantity without breaking up, getting crushed or losing their aesthetic appeal.

At home it's possible to give vegetables special care. By preparing vegetables in small quantities just before they are served, you can preserve the appetizing color, texture and nutrients. With sauces and garnishes, you can add the touches that will make vegetables even more interesting.

WHICH VEGETABLES TO SERVE

The choice of vegetables for any particular menu depends on your personal preference, nutritional goals and most of all your choice of main dish.

Vegetables can have a big impact in providing balance and contrast to your meals. Look for a vegetable with a flavor and color that will enhance your main dish and other courses. Consider the best shape and size to complement the other foods. If the other foods are going to be large, select a vegetable that can be cut into small pieces.

If more than one vegetable is being served, avoid serving two from the same family or two starchy vegetables. Don't serve two with the same color or shape, unless you want a special effect. White vegetables work best as the second vegetable.

COOKING GREEN VEGETABLES

Almost all foods are mildly acid, but the acid in green vegetables can cause them to discolor. To avoid discoloring and produce beautiful green vegetables in minutes, use this cooking technique:
- Put enough water in a medium saucepan to generously cover the vegetables to be cooked. Allow 1 to 1-1/2 quarts for 2 servings. Add 1-1/2 teaspoons salt for each quart of water.
- Bring water to a full rolling boil.
- Add the vegetables gradually so the water maintains a boil. The green color of the vegetables should develop immediately. If the vegetables tend to float, roll them in the water until the green color develops overall.
- Reduce the heat to maintain a slow boil and cook the vegetables uncovered until tender. Drain and serve.

Sauces made of tomato, lemon juice, vinegar, sour cream, yogurt or any other acid will discolor green vegetables in minutes, so add these sauces just before serving.

COOKING WHITE VEGETABLES

White vegetables, such as cauliflower and onions, benefit from being cooked in a moderate amount of water with a little vinegar or lemon juice added. Cook these vegetables covered. Cauliflower will remain snowy white and firm. Onions will keep their white color but they will not soften as readily.

COOKING ORANGE VEGETABLES

Carrots and other orange vegetables will survive all the abuses green and white vegetables cannot. They don't fall apart when slightly overcooked and they keep their lovely orange color no matter how long they wait to be served. Even their supply of vitamin A, for which orange vegetables are famous, stays intact throughout the cooking process. Carrots, winter squash, sweet potatoes and yams are wonderful to serve when you don't have time to worry about vegetables.

SAUCES FOR VEGETABLES

A beautifully cooked vegetable can be enjoyed without any sauce at all, or with just a little lemon juice and a few herbs. But sauces enhance vegetables and add variety to the total meal. Besides the sauces in this chapter, Amandine Sauce, page 90, adds a special flavor to certain vegetables.

One small problem is keeping the sauce *on* the vegetable rather than in the bottom of the pan or all over the dinner plate. These tips should help:
- Dry the cooked vegetables. Draining vegetables does not leave them dry. Return the pan of drained vegetables to the heat a few seconds to boil off remaining moisture. The surface moisture on the vegetables will evaporate as steam.
- Butter sauces should be free of watery liquid. Otherwise the butter or other fat will not cling to the vegetables. The watery portion will wet the surface of the vegetables and the sauce will slide right off. Use either Clarified Butter, page 159, which already has the watery portion removed, or heat regular butter just until the watery portion boils off. If lemon juice, wine, stock or any other watery

liquid is added, boil the butter mixture again until syrupy.

- Prepare most butter sauces in the same pan as the vegetables. Push the drained vegetables to the side or make the sauce in the pan while the vegetables are draining in a colander. Let the sauce cool slightly before combining so the vegetables will not fry and stick to the pan. Never prepare an acid sauce in the same pan with a green vegetable.

- Toss the vegetables in the butter sauce or pour the sauce over them. If the butter sauce becomes watery after mixing with the vegetables, serve the vegetables with a slotted spoon or tongs, boil the sauce down again and pour it over the vegetables.

- Pour creamy sauces over cooked vegetables or mix the sauce into the vegetables when serving.

FROZEN VEGETABLES

Frozen vegetables are waste-free, take up little storage space, require practically no preparation and keep for a long time. Peas, mixed vegetables, whole kernel corn and lima beans should rattle in the package, making them easier to separate for single servings. Packages that do not rattle have probably thawed and refrozen, so don't buy them. Specialty mixed vegetables with sauces included can add tremendous interest to meals for 2.

CANNED VEGETABLES

An 8-ounce can of almost any vegetable is a convenient size for 1 or 2. A few cans on the shelf provide instant variety and are always ready for unexpected meals. Larger cans may be used, but you should have a plan to use the excess.

FRESH VEGETABLES

Fresh vegetables are a good buy because they are usually sold by weight. A handful of beans costs the same per bean as a bushel. You should select the freshest and best looking vegetables you can find. Some tips:

Asparagus—Choose spears with tightly closed heads, straight, firm dark green stalks, and very little white woody end. Fatter and smoother stalks are more tender.

Broccoli—Select firm stalks with compact dark green or purplish-green flowerets.

Brussel Sprouts—They should be small, compact and bright green with fresh-looking leaves.

Cauliflower—Heads should be compact, white and unblemished.

Green Beans—They should be firm and slender.

CHOOSE VEGETABLES BY COLOR
Green

Artichokes	Green Beans	Greens:
Asparagus	Green Peppers	Beet Tops
Broccoli	Lima Beans	Chicory
Brussels	Pea Pods	Collard
Sprouts	Peas	Dandelion
Cabbage	Spinach	Kale
Celery	Summer	Mustard
Chayote	Squash	Swiss Chard
Squash	Zucchini	Turnip Tops

White

Anise (Fennel)	Jerusalem	Onions
Belgian Endive	Artichokes	Parsnips
Cauliflower	Kohlrabi	Turnips
Celery Root (Celeriac)	Leeks	

Orange

Carrots	Winter Squash	Yams
Sweet Potatoes		

Yellow

Corn	Rutabaga	Yellow Squash

Red & Purple

Beets	Red Onions	Tomatoes
Red Cabbage	Red Peppers	

CHOOSE VEGETABLES BY TYPE
Cabbage Family

Broccoli	Cabbage	Collard
Brussels	Cauliflower	Kohlrabi
Sprouts		

Onion Family

Green Onions	Leeks	Onions

Starchy Vegetables

Corn	Lima Beans	Sweet Potatoes
Dry Beans	Peas	Lentils

MISCELLANEOUS VEGETABLES

Bean Sprouts	Eggplant	Mushrooms

Green Beans & Bacon-Onion Dressing

Try the dressing on Brussels sprouts, cauliflower, cabbage, spinach or fried potatoes.

Bacon-Onion Dressing, see below
1/2 to 3/4 lb. fresh green beans
1 quart water

1-1/2 teaspoons salt
Salt and pepper to taste

Bacon-Onion Dressing:
1 to 2 slices bacon
2 to 3 tablespoons minced onion

Prepare Bacon-Onion Dressing. Set aside. Wash beans and break off ends. Leave whole or cut into 2-inch lengths. Combine water and salt in a medium saucepan. Bring to a full boil. Drop beans into boiling water. Reduce to a slow boil. Cook uncovered about 7 minutes until beans are tender. To test doneness, cut a bean with a fork against side of pan; bean should cut easily. Drain immediately. Toss with Bacon-Onion Dressing. Add salt and pepper. Makes 2 servings.

Bacon-Onion Dressing:
Cut bacon into 1/4-inch pieces. Sauté in a small skillet over medium-low heat until limp. Add onion. Sauté until bacon and onion are cooked through and tender.

Sour Cream Sauce

More flavorful than a plain cream sauce.

1 tablespoon butter
1-1/2 teaspoons flour
1/4 cup milk

1/8 teaspoon seasoned salt
1/4 cup dairy sour cream

Melt butter in a small saucepan over medium heat until frothy. Stir in flour. Heat until frothy again. Blend milk and seasoned salt into mixture. Simmer and stir over low heat until thickened and smooth. Remove from heat. Add sour cream all at once; blend in immediately. Warm to serving temperature. Pour over or mix with asparagus, broccoli, cauliflower, Brussels sprouts, peas or potatoes. Makes about 1/2 cup, enough for 2 servings.

Variations

Sour Cream Caper Sauce: Stir 2 teaspoons capers into sauce. Good with poached fish.
Sour Cream & Cheese Sauce: Add 1/4 cup lightly packed, shredded, aged Cheddar cheese to sauce before adding sour cream. Heat gently, stirring constantly, until cheese is melted. Serve over cauliflower or baked potato.
Sour Cream Mustard Sauce: Blend 1 teaspoon Dijon mustard into sauce. Serve on cauliflower, broccoli, Brussels sprouts or cabbage.

Buttered Peas

Serve versatile peas plain, sauced, spiced or herbed!

2 cups water
1/2 teaspoon salt
1-1/3 cups frozen peas (about 6 oz.)
1 to 2 tablespoons Clarified Butter,
   page 159, or butter

1/4 teaspoon basil, if desired
Salt and pepper to taste

Combine water and salt in a medium saucepan. Bring to a full boil. Add frozen peas. Return to a boil then reduce to a simmer. Cover and cook 1 minute. Drain. Push peas to side of pan. Place butter and basil, if desired, in pan. Heat briefly to boil off any moisture. Stir peas into butter. Add salt and pepper. Cover and keep warm over very low heat up to 5 minutes. To delay serving, remove from heat and set lid ajar to cool; reheat to serve. Makes 2 servings.

Variations

Peas à la Crème: Substitute 1/4 cup whipping cream for butter. Boil until syrupy.
Peas and Mushrooms: Stir 1 to 2 tablespoons Duxelles, page 161, into buttered peas. Add 1 tablespoon minced pimiento, if desired.
Curried Peas: Stir 1/4 teaspoon curry powder into butter. Cook 1 minute before mixing with peas.
Minted Peas: Sauté 1 tablespoon minced shallots in butter until translucent and tender. Stir in peas and 1 teaspoon finely minced fresh mint or 1/2 teaspoon dry mint. Cover and remove from heat. Let stand 1 to 2 minutes to blend flavors.
Miscellaneous Additions: Substitute savory, marjoram, oregano, dill weed or rosemary for basil. Add chopped cashews, pecans, walnuts or Toasted Almonds, page 165.

Peas à l'Orange *Photo on page 93.*

Even a popular vegetable needs a new look now and then.

2 cups water
1/2 teaspoon salt
1-1/3 cups frozen peas (about 6 oz.)
1 tablespoon butter

1/2 teaspoon chicken stock granules
1/4 to 1/2 teaspoon freshly grated orange peel
1/4 teaspoon tarragon
Pinch sugar

Combine water and salt in a medium saucepan. Bring to a full boil. Add peas. Return to a boil. Reduce heat to a simmer. Cover and cook 1 minute. Drain peas in a colander or strainer. Combine remaining ingredients in saucepan. Warm over low heat. Stir in drained peas. Cover and keep warm over very low heat 2 minutes to blend flavors. Makes 2 servings.

Gordy's Cabbage

Here's something you can do with that last wedge of cabbage.

1 tablespoon butter
1 cup finely shredded cabbage,
   lightly packed

1 tablespoon water
1/4 teaspoon soy sauce
Salt and pepper to taste

Melt butter in an 8-inch skillet over medium heat. Immediately add cabbage. Cook and stir until cabbage is limp and coated with butter. Add water. Cover and reduce heat to a simmer. Cook about 3 minutes until cabbage is tender. Stir in soy sauce and salt and pepper. Boil off any excess liquid. Makes 1 serving.

Asparagus Polonaise

Try Butter Polonaise over broccoli, photo on page 63, Brussels sprouts, spinach and cauliflower.

Butter Polonaise, see below
3/4 lb. asparagus
About 1-1/2 quarts water

About 2 teaspoons salt
Salt and pepper to taste

Butter Polonaise:
2 tablespoons Clarified Butter, page 159,
   or butter
1/2 to 1 tablespoon minced shallots,
   if desired

2 to 3 tablespoons Soft Breadcrumbs,
   page 164
1/2 teaspoon lemon juice
2 teaspoons minced parsley

Prepare Butter Polonaise. Set aside. Snap off base end of each asparagus stalk at its natural breaking point. Discard base or reserve for cream soup. Wash and drain asparagus spears. Put 1-inch-deep water in a large skillet. Add 1-1/2 teaspoons salt for each quart of water. Bring to a full boil. Add asparagus, rolling spears in water to develop color on all sides. Return to a boil. Reduce to a slow boil. Cook uncovered about 5 minutes until asparagus is tender. To test doneness, insert a fork into thickest part of largest spear; fork should slip in easily. Drain immediately. Return asparagus to low heat to boil off any remaining moisture. Arrange on plates. Spoon Butter Polonaise over. Sprinkle with salt and pepper. Makes 2 servings.

Butter Polonaise:
Heat butter in a small saucepan over medium-low heat. If desired, stir shallots into butter. Immediately add soft breadcrumbs. Sauté and stir until golden brown and crisp. Mix in lemon juice and parsley.

Variation

Quick Butter Polonaise: Heat 1 to 2 tablespoons butter. Stir in 1 to 2 tablespoons Buttered Breadcrumbs, page 164.

Zucchini Italiano

Quick, easy and perfect with spaghetti and meatballs or lasagne.

1 medium zucchini (about 1/3 lb.)
1 tablespoon olive oil or oil
1 small garlic clove, minced or pressed
1/8 to1/4 teaspoon salt

1/4 teaspoon oregano
1 tablespoon water, if desired
2 tablespoons shredded Parmesan cheese

Trim ends from zucchini and slice 1/8-inch thick. Heat oil in an 8-inch skillet. Stir in garlic. Add zucchini, salt and oregano. Stir-fry over medium heat until zucchini slices are tender and slightly translucent. To speed cooking, add 1 tablespoon water; cover and steam briefly. Sprinkle with Parmesan cheese. Cover briefly to melt cheese. Makes 1 serving.

Buttered Zucchini

Slice zucchini thick or thin, or straight, diagonally or lengthwise, or dice or shred it.

1 quart water
1-1/2 teaspoons salt
2 medium zucchini (about 2/3 lb.)

1 to 2 tablespoons Clarified Butter,
   page 159, or butter
Salt and pepper to taste

Combine water and salt in a medium saucepan. Bring to a full boil. Trim ends from zucchini and cut as desired. Drop into boiling water. Reduce to a slow boil. Cook uncovered 3 to 5 minutes until a fork can easily be inserted into thickest piece. Zucchini should still be opaque. Drain immediately. Push zucchini to side of pan and add butter. Heat briefly to boil off any moisture. Toss zucchini with butter. Add salt and pepper. Makes 2 servings.

Variations

Zucchini with Vermouth & Walnuts: Drain cooked zucchini in a colander or strainer. Sauté 2 to 3 tablespoons coarsely chopped walnuts in butter until golden. Remove walnuts. Add 2 tablespoons dry vermouth to butter; boil until syrupy. Cool slightly. Toss zucchini with vermouth-butter mixture. Add salt and pepper. Heat to serving temperature. Garnish with walnuts.
Lemon-Dill Zucchini: In a small saucepan, combine butter, 2 teaspoons lemon juice and 1/4 teaspoon dill. Boil until syrupy. Just before serving, toss with hot, well-drained zucchini.
Zucchini au Gratin: Spoon hot buttered zucchini into an au gratin dish or small shallow baking dish. Sprinkle Buttered Breadcrumbs, page 164, grated sharp Cheddar cheese or grated Parmesan cheese evenly over top. Heat in oven, toaster-oven or broiler to warm crumbs or melt cheese.

Cauliflower & Curried Cheddar Topping

An acid, like lemon juice or vinegar, keeps cauliflower snowy white and firm.

Curried Cheddar Topping, see below
1/2 lb. cauliflower flowerets or
   1 small head cauliflower

1 to 2 cups water
2 teaspoons lemon juice or white wine vinegar
1/2 teaspoon salt

Curried Cheddar Topping:
2 tablespoons mayonnaise
1/2 teaspoon Dijon mustard
1/4 teaspoon curry powder

1/4 cup shredded Cheddar cheese,
   lightly packed

Prepare Curried Cheddar Topping. Set aside. Core cauliflower and pull off all leaves. Break off flowerets or leave small head whole. Wash and drain. Combine water, lemon juice or vinegar and salt in a medium saucepan. Bring to a full boil. Add cauliflower. Cover and return to a boil. Reduce to a slow boil. Cook until cauliflower is tender, about 8 minutes for flowerets or 10 minutes for small head. To test doneness, insert a fork into stem of a large floweret or into center of head; cauliflower should give only slight resistance. Preheat oven to 400°F (205°C). Drain cauliflower. Arrange in a heatproof casserole or au gratin dish. Spread Curried Cheddar Topping over cauliflower. Bake 5 minutes until topping is warm and cheese melts. Makes 2 servings.

Curried Cheddar Topping:
Combine all ingredients in small bowl. Stir until blended.

Hollandaise Sauce

A little trouble, but it's terrific!

1 egg yolk
2 teaspoons fresh lemon juice
2 teaspoons water

Dash salt
1/4 cup cold butter

In a small stainless steel, enamel or nonstick saucepan, blend egg yolk, lemon juice, water and salt. Half-fill a larger saucepan or bowl with cold water and place near range. Cut cold butter into 8 to 10 chunks and place near range. Add 2 chunks butter to egg yolk mixture. Whip constantly over very low heat. Do not overcook egg yolk. Raise pan from heat at any time to slow cooking. If sauce begins to granulate or curdle, immediately immerse bottom of pan in cold water, whipping briskly. When first chunks of butter are blended into mixture, add remaining butter 1 chunk at a time, whipping constantly until each is blended. When sauce is thickened and smooth, add more salt or lemon juice to taste, if desired. Serve immediately. To delay serving, immerse bottom of pan in cold water to stop cooking, then rewarm gently, whipping constantly. Serve with artichokes, broccoli or asparagus. Makes about 1/3 cup, enough for 2 servings.

Broccoli & Caper Butter

Here's a delicious way to serve broccoli—or asparagus, Brussels sprouts, cauliflower and cabbage.

Caper Butter, see below
2 medium stalks broccoli (about 3/4 lb.)
1-1/2 quarts water

2 teaspoons salt
Salt and pepper to taste

Caper Butter:
2 tablespoons Clarified Butter,
   page 159, or butter

2 teaspoons capers
1/4 teaspoon thyme or oregano

Prepare Caper Butter; keep warm in saucepan. Slash heavy broccoli stems. To peel stems, slip knife blade under skin at base of stalk, lift and pull back toward flowers. Save any small flowerets pulled off for stir-fry dishes, salads or dippers. Combine water and salt in a medium saucepan. Bring to a full boil. Holding broccoli by stalk end, plunge flowers into boiling water about 5 seconds. Release stalks and let flowers float to surface. Reduce heat to a slow boil. Cook uncovered about 5 minutes until stalks are tender. To test doneness, insert a fork into thickest part of stalk; broccoli should give only slight resistance. Drain immediately. Return broccoli to low heat to boil off any remaining moisture. Carefully lift broccoli to plates. Pour Caper Butter over and sprinkle with salt and pepper. Makes 2 servings.

Caper Butter:
Combine butter, capers and thyme or oregano in a small saucepan. Cook over medium heat until all moisture from capers and butter evaporates.

Carefree Creamed Spinach

No one will guess it was so easy!

1 (10 oz.) pkg. frozen chopped spinach
Boiling salted water
1/4 cup (2 oz.) cream cheese, whipping cream
   or dairy sour cream

Onion salt, garlic salt or seasoned salt
   to taste
Duxelles, page 161, if desired

Cook spinach in boiling salted water according to package directions. Drain well in a strainer or colander. Return spinach to saucepan. Blend in cream cheese, whipping cream or sour cream. Heat to serving temperature. Stir in onion salt, garlic salt or seasoned salt and duxelles, if desired. Makes 2 or 3 servings.

> *One cup well-drained, chopped cooked spinach can be substituted for a cooked and drained 10-ounce package of frozen chopped spinach.*

Steamed Fresh Spinach

Sometimes the simplest way is the best.

1 large bunch fresh spinach (about 1 lb.)	Salt and pepper to taste
Water	Buttered Breadcrumbs, page 164
1 teaspoon salt	2 lemon wedges
1 to 2 tablespoons butter or bacon drippings	

Break off stems and damaged or yellowed parts of spinach leaves. Fill sink with water; add 1 teaspoon salt. Dunk spinach repeatedly in water to wash well. Shake off excess water. Pack leaves into a medium saucepan. Do not add water. Cover and cook over medium-low heat until leaves wilt to bottom of pan. Stir once and cook 1 to 2 more minutes. Drain off juices. Chop spinach, if desired. Add butter or bacon drippings. Cook until melted and excess moisture is boiled off. Add salt and pepper to taste. Garnish with buttered breadcrumbs. Serve with lemon wedges. Makes about 2 servings.

Artichokes & Lemon Dip

Artichokes are also delicious with Hollandaise Sauce, melted butter or plain mayonnaise.

Lemon Dip, see below	2 garlic cloves, peeled and halved
Water	2 tablespoons oil
Salt	1 bay leaf, if desired
2 slices lemon, 1/2-inch thick	2 large artichokes

Lemon Dip:

3 tablespoons dairy sour cream	Few gratings fresh lemon peel
3 tablespoons mayonnaise	1/8 teaspoon salt
1 tablespoon lemon juice	

Prepare Lemon Dip; refrigerate. In a large pot or Dutch oven, put enough water to float artichokes. Add 1-1/2 teaspoons salt per quart of water. Squeeze juice from lemon slices into water; drop slices into water. Add garlic, oil and bay leaf, if desired. Bring water to a full boil. Cut 1 inch from top of each artichoke and cut off all but 1 inch of stem. With kitchen shears, cut tips from leaves. Pull off any unattractive leaves at base. Wash and drain artichokes. Holding by stem ends, plunge artichokes into boiling water 5 seconds. Release and let stem sink to bottom. Cover and reduce heat to a simmer. Cook about 40 minutes, until a fork can be inserted into base. Drain upside-down. Trim stems even with base. Stand upright. Serve with Lemon Dip in a side dish. Or remove choke and place small cup of Lemon Dip in center of artichoke. To remove choke, carefully spread artichoke leaves away from center. Pull out inner immature leaves, exposing choke. With a spoon, scrape the choke from the heart. Makes 2 servings.

Lemon Dip:
Blend all ingredients in a small bowl.

Creamed Spinach in Tomato Cups

Delicious and colorful with your next steak dinner.

1 (10-oz.) pkg. frozen chopped spinach
Boiling salted water
1 tablespoon butter
2 tablespoons minced shallots
1/2 cup chopped or sliced fresh mushrooms
1 tablespoon flour
1/2 cup whipping cream
1/4 teaspoon basil

1/2 teaspoon Worcestershire sauce
Dash nutmeg, if desired
Salt and pepper to taste
2 medium-small tomatoes or 1 large tomato
Salt to taste
2 tablespoons Buttered Breadcrumbs,
    page 164
1 tablespoon shredded Parmesan cheese

Cook frozen chopped spinach in boiling salted water according to package directions. Drain well in a strainer or colander; set aside. Melt butter in a medium saucepan over medium heat. Add shallots and fresh mushrooms. Sauté until tender. Blend in flour. Cook a few seconds. Stir in drained spinach, whipping cream, basil and Worcestershire sauce. Cook and stir until thickened. Add nutmeg, if desired, and salt and pepper. Remove from heat. Preheat oven to 350°F (175°C). Cut tops from small tomatoes or cut large tomato in half. Cut a small slice from bottoms if necessary so tomatoes sit straight. Scoop seeds and pulp from tomatoes. Sprinkle insides with salt. Spoon warm spinach into tomato cups. Refrigerate extra spinach for later use. Combine buttered breadcrumbs and cheese. Press into creamed spinach. Place tomato cups in a small shallow baking pan. Bake in preheated oven about 8 minutes until tomato is warm and cheese is melted. Makes 2 servings.

How To Make Artichokes & Lemon Dip

Select round, compact, heavy artichokes with tightly closed leaves. Trim top, stem and leaf tips. Brown blemishes on the leaves do not harm artichoke flavor.

Remove the choke from artichoke to make room for dressing, salad or stuffing. Spread leaves from center, pull out inner leaves and use a spoon to scrape out fibrous choke.

Country-Style Creamed Spinach

I like it best with corn on the cob, sliced tomatoes and baked chicken.

1 (10-oz.) pkg. frozen chopped spinach
Boiling salted water
2 slices bacon, diced
1/4 cup minced onion
1 garlic clove, crushed or minced
1 tablespoon flour
1/4 cup milk, half-and-half or
   whipping cream

1/4 teaspoon Worcestershire sauce
Pinch sugar
Salt to taste
1 Hard-Cooked Egg, page 160, chopped,
   if desired

Cook frozen chopped spinach in boiling salted water according to package directions. Drain well in a strainer or colander; set aside. Sauté diced bacon in a medium saucepan until limp. Add onion and garlic. Sauté until onion is tender. Blend in flour. Cook a few seconds. Mix in drained spinach and milk, half-and-half or whipping cream. Add Worcestershire sauce and sugar. Cook and stir until thickened. Add salt to taste. Garnish with chopped egg, if desired. Makes 2 or 3 servings.

Brussels Sprouts & Lemon-Sesame Butter

Try the sauce on green beans, zucchini, summer squash, cabbage or spinach.

Lemon-Sesame Butter, see below
1/2 lb. Brussels sprouts
1 quart water

1-1/2 teaspoons salt
Salt and pepper to taste

Lemon-Sesame Butter:

1 to 2 tablespoons Clarified Butter,
   page 159, or butter

2 teaspoons sesame seeds
1 to 2 teaspoons lemon juice

Prepare Lemon-Sesame Butter; set aside. Trim stalks of Brussels sprouts close to base of heads without loosening fresh leaves. Wash and drain. Combine water and 1-1/2 teaspoons salt in a medium saucepan. Bring to a full boil. Add Brussels sprouts; return to a boil. Reduce to a slow boil. Cook uncovered until Brussels sprouts are tender. To test doneness, insert a fork into center of a large sprout; it should give only slight resistance. Drain. Return to low heat to boil off any remaining water. Add Lemon-Sesame Butter; toss. Add salt and pepper. Serve immediately. Makes 2 servings.

Lemon-Sesame Butter:
Combine butter and sesame seeds in a small saucepan. Cook gently over medium-low heat, stirring frequently, until sesame seeds turn golden brown. Add lemon juice. Boil quickly until syrupy.

Chili Corn on the Cob *Photo on page 114.*

Cooking the inner husks with the corn heightens the flavor.

Chili Butter, see below
2 ears fresh corn on the cob

Water
Salt and pepper to taste

Chili Butter:
2 tablespoons butter, room temperature
1/2 teaspoon chili powder

1/8 teaspoon onion salt or garlic salt

Prepare Chili Butter; set aside. Pull off and discard outer layer of corn husks. Pull off inner husks and place in a medium or large saucepan. Add enough water to float corn. Bring to a full boil over high heat. Clean silk from ears of corn by brushing with a vegetable brush under running water. Break ears in half, if desired. Place in boiling water. Reduce to a slow boil. Cover and cook 3 to 5 minutes. Drain corn. Serve with Chili Butter and salt and pepper to taste. Makes 2 servings.

Chili Butter:
Blend ingredients and allow time for flavors to blend. Refrigerate if made more than 2 hours in advance. Serve at room temperature. Also good with whole kernel corn.

Party Yams

Colorful orange shells stuffed with spicy mashed yams or sweet potatoes.

2 medium oranges
1 (8- to 9-oz.) can yams or sweet potatoes
1/4 teaspoon cinnamon
1 to 2 tablespoons butter

1/2 to 1 tablespoon brown sugar
Salt to taste
1 to 2 tablespoons broken toasted pecans
Miniature marshmallows

Preheat oven to 350°F (175°C). Cut tops from oranges about 1/2 inch above center. From tops, squeeze 2 tablespoons juice and grate 1/4 teaspoon peel. Set aside. Cut pulp from bottom portion of oranges and pull out inner membranes without damaging peel. Reserve pulp to use for breakfast or in a fruit salad. Cut a small slice from bottoms of orange shells if necessary so oranges sit straight. Drain yams or sweet potatoes. Place in a small saucepan. Mash lightly. Add cinnamon, orange juice and peel. Warm over medium heat until bubbling and heated through. Add butter, brown sugar and salt. Stir in pecans. Pack mixture into orange shells, mounding over top. At this point, refrigerate up to 24 hours, if desired. To serve immediately, bake 10 minutes, then press miniature marshmallows onto surface and heat until browned. If refrigerated, bake 20 minutes before adding marshmallows. Makes 2 servings.

Baked Sweet Potatoes

So good and so good for you.

1 yam or sweet potato	**Butter to taste**
Butter or oil	**Salt and pepper to taste**

Preheat oven or toaster-oven to 350°F (175°C). Scrub yam or sweet potato well; dry. Rub skin with butter or oil. Place in a small shallow baking pan. Bake 45 to 60 minutes until a fork slips easily into center. Cut a slit down center and press open. Or cut in half lengthwise. Add butter, salt and pepper. Makes 1 or 2 servings.

Buttered Carrots *Photo on page 80.*

Carrots are marvelously versatile. Try all the variations!

2 large or 4 small fresh carrots	**1/2 teaspoon sugar**
(about 1/2 lb.)	**1/4 teaspoon salt**
1/4 cup water	**1 to 2 tablespoons butter**

Peel carrots with a vegetable peeler. Prepare carrots whole, shred or dice them, cut in half or in sticks, or slice straight or diagonally. Combine water, sugar and salt in a small saucepan. Bring to a boil. Add carrots. Cover and reduce to a simmer. Cook 3 to 4 minutes for shredded carrots, or up to 20 minutes for whole carrots. To test doneness, insert a fork into thickest piece of carrot; cooked carrots should give only slight resistance. Add butter. Raise heat. Cook uncovered until almost all liquid has evaporated. Makes 2 servings.

Variations

Anise Carrots: Add 1 to 2 tablespoons anise-flavored liqueur to finished carrots. Boil rapidly until syrupy.

Carrots à la Crème: Omit butter. Add 2 tablespoons whipping cream to finished carrots. Boil rapidly until cream thickens slightly.

Carrots à l'Orange: Add 1 to 2 teaspoons sugar or honey and 1/2 teaspoon freshly grated orange peel or tangerine peel to carrots with butter. Or stir 1 to 2 tablespoons orange marmalade or orange-flavored liqueur into finished carrots. Boil rapidly until syrupy.

Gingered Carrots: Add 1 tablespoon honey and 1/8 teaspoon ground ginger with butter. Boil rapidly until syrupy. Garnish with Toasted Sesame Seeds, page 165, if desired.

Carrots Vichy: Increase sugar to 1 teaspoon. Sprinkle finely minced parsley over finished carrots.

Carrots du Jour: Add herbs such as basil, marjoram, mint, dill, sage or thyme. Or add spices such as cloves, curry, ginger, mace or nutmeg. Or add flavors such as coconut, red currant jelly or mint jelly.

Broiled Tomatoes

If you're going to be pressed for time, make these a day ahead.

1 large tomato or 2 small tomatoes
Seasoned salt to taste

Crumb Topping, see below

Crumb Topping:
1/8 teaspoon seasoned salt
1/4 teaspoon basil or oregano
1 to 2 teaspoons minced parsley

1 tablespoon grated Parmesan cheese
1/4 cup Buttered Breadcrumbs, page 164

Preheat oven or toaster-oven to 350°F (175°C). Trim stem end from large tomato and cut tomato in half crosswise. Or cut tops off small tomatoes. Cut a small slice from bottoms, if necessary, so tomatoes sit straight. Trim a small amount of pulp from each tomato cup and reserve in a small bowl. Cut criss-crossing slits through pulp of tomatoes and sprinkle with seasoned salt. Prepare Crumb Topping. Press into tomato cups, mounding over top. At this point, refrigerate up to 24 hours, if desired. To serve, place tomato cups in a small shallow baking dish. Bake 8 to 10 minutes until warmed through. Broil until top is browned, if desired. Makes 2 servings.

Crumb Topping:
Blend seasoned salt and basil or oregano into reserved tomato pulp. Stir in parsley and Parmesan cheese. Toss buttered breadcrumbs into Parmesan cheese mixture.

How To Make Broiled Tomatoes

Trim a little pulp from each tomato cup to make room for the topping. Combine the trimmed pulp with the crumb topping to add moisture.

Make criss-cross cuts into the surface of the tomatoes and sprinkle with seasoned salt. Spoon the crumb topping onto the tomatoes and pack down to form a smooth mound.

Beets in Sour Cream

Great as a chilled salad too!

1 (8-oz.) can beets, any cut
1/4 cup dairy sour cream, room temperature
1/4 teaspoon prepared horseradish

1/8 teaspoon seasoned salt
1/4 teaspoon dill weed

Put beets and juice into a small saucepan. Bring to a boil over high heat. Reduce heat. Simmer until beets are heated through. Combine sour cream and remaining ingredients in a medium bowl. Drain juice from beets. Gradually add hot beets to sour cream mixture. Return beets and sour cream to saucepan. Warm briefly and gently, stirring constantly. Serve immediately. Makes 2 servings.

Orange Beets *Photo on page 114.*

Very pretty on the plate and palatable to the taste buds.

1 tablespoon butter
1 tablespoon minced onion or shallots
1 tablespoon orange marmalade

1 (8-oz.) can beets, any cut, well-drained
Salt and pepper to taste

Heat butter in a small saucepan over medium heat. Sauté minced onion or shallots in butter until tender and translucent. Stir in orange marmalade and beets. Cover and warm over low heat until heated through. Add salt and pepper. Makes 2 servings.

Lemony Harvard Beets

Here's a lemon twist to an old classic.

2 tablespoons brown sugar
2 tablespoons lemon juice
1 tablespoon butter
Dash ginger

Few gratings lemon peel
1 (8-oz.) can beets, any cut
1/2 teaspoon cornstarch
Salt to taste

Combine brown sugar, lemon juice, butter, ginger and lemon peel in a small saucepan. Drain beets, reserving 1 tablespoon juice. Add beets to saucepan. Bring to a boil. Cover and simmer until heated through. Blend cornstarch and reserved beet juice until smooth. Mix into hot beets. Simmer and stir until thickened and clear. Add salt. To delay serving, remove from heat and reheat later. Makes 2 servings.

Cakes & Pastries

Good baking is a genuine accomplishment. The skill and art involved make it both fun and satisfying. But if you love to bake, baking for 1 or 2 can be a real frustration. Whenever you bake you are faced with 12 tempting servings of some irresistible treat that you feel you must use up before you can bake again. You can freeze individual servings, but eventually your freezer may become filled with misshapen packages of unknown contents or vintage. When I found myself eating high calorie goodies when they were past their prime just because I wanted to get rid of them, I knew something had to be done.

My solution was to develop recipes for cakes and pastries that would make 2 to 4 servings. Now, when the last serving is eaten, instead of a sense of relief, I feel virtuously happy knowing that I haven't over-indulged. When I feel like baking again there's nothing to hold me back. If you enjoy baking and you like a little variety in your dessert menu, or if you simply have no will power, these recipes are for you!

ABOUT BAKING PANS

The most useful baking pan for small cake recipes is a 7" x 3" nonstick aluminum junior loaf pan. Cakes baked in this pan from the recipes in this chapter will be small sheet cakes, 1/4 the size of a 13" x 9" cake and only about 1-1/2-inches tall. Because of the higher sides of these pans, top browning may be reduced.

A small baking sheet is also useful. Buy the smallest you can find for baking cream puffs, meringues, shortcakes, biscuits or a few cookies.

Other handy pans include a 6-cup muffin pan and a 9" x 5" loaf pan. An 8-inch square baking pan and a 9-inch round layer pan will handle double recipes of the quarter-size cakes with slight changes in baking times. Small aluminum foil loaf pans and shallow rectangular roll pans are useful for baking cakes or for other small projects.

Shiny aluminum foil pans reflect heat, which slows baking, so place them on a small baking sheet in the oven to attract heat.

Glass, iron and dark metal baking pans absorb more heat and produce heavier crusts. To compensate, reduce oven temperatures by 25°F (15°C).

If you have ample freezer space, mix up some of your favorite recipes and divide the batter among smaller pans for baking and freezing. Or, depending on the number of eggs, cut some recipes in half or thirds and bake them in smaller pans:

A Recipe Calling For	Can Be Baked In
1 (13" x 9") pan or 2 (9 inch) round pans	4 (7" x 3") loaf pans or 3 (9" x 5") loaf pans or 2 (8-inch) square pans or 24 cupcake cups.
1 (9-inch) square pan or 1 (11" x 7") pan	3 (7" x 3") loaf pans.
1 (9-inch) round pan or 1 (8-inch) square pan	2 (7" x 3") loaf pans.

LINING THE LOAF PAN

Removing sheet cakes from loaf pans can be more difficult than removing cakes from shallow pans. This technique for lining loaf pans will help:
- Tear off a 6- to 10-inch piece of wax paper. Fold the cut edges of the paper to the center making a long strip of double- or triple-thick wax paper the width of the loaf pan.
- Fit the folded paper, loose edges down, into the pan from end to end, letting the ends of the paper project up the ends of the pan, see page 134. Keep the paper pressed against the ends of the pan while adding batter.
- To remove the partially cooled cake from the pan, loosen the sides of the cake with a knife, then gently lift one end of the wax paper to ease the cake from the bottom of the pan. Pick up both ends of the paper to remove the cake. Peel the paper from the ends and bottom of the cake.

MEASURING INGREDIENTS ACCURATELY

In cake baking, more than any other type of cooking, accurate measuring is vital. When ingredient proportions are incorrect, the results will show it. If the amount of sugar, liquid, fat or baking powder is too great, the cake will collapse.

If the flour proportion is too high, the cake will be bready and the center will be humped and cracked. Too much baking soda will cause the cake to turn gray, dry and off-flavored. With too little baking soda it won't rise or brown properly. A slight variation can make a major difference in small batches. So use proper measuring equipment and level with a straight-edge spatula.

TO SIFT OR NOT TO SIFT

If you sift a level cup of flour scooped from a freshly opened package or a canister, you could end up with as much as 1-1/3 cups of sifted flour. If a recipe calls for 1 cup of sifted flour, this difference could cause the recipe to fail. The purpose of sifting flour is to give a consistent measure. Sift flour directly into the measuring cup and level it. If you do not have a sifter or a larger strainer, lighten the flour in the canister by stirring it briskly with a fork. Then spoon it into a measuring cup and level it. Baking mixes should be spooned into the measuring cup and leveled without sifting.

MORE BAKING TIPS

• Use superfine sugar instead of granulated sugar, if possible. It dissolves faster and gives better texture, especially in meringues.

• Bring all ingredients to room temperature. Batters will mix faster, and sugar, salt and leavening will dissolve better.

• Keep an oven thermometer in the oven as a constant check of temperature.

• Bake most foods in the center of the oven. The oven shelf should usually be in the middle position.

• If more than one pan is in the oven at the same time, allow at least a 1-inch space between the pans, and between the oven walls and the pans.

STORING CAKES

If a cake will be served within a day or two, keep it at room temperature in a tightly closed container. Most cakes should be frozen for longer storage. Only cakes with cream or custard fillings or frostings should be refrigerated. Cool temperatures cause changes in the flour that may make cake or bread seem dry, stale and raw-tasting. Freezing will protect cakes longer without side effects. Plain cakes and breads can be safely thawed and refrozen repeatedly without a loss in quality.

Enclose cakes or breads for freezing in plastic bags or aluminum foil, and exclude as much air as possible. Wrap frosted cakes first in plastic wrap, then in foil.

Clockwise from bottom left: Nut Pound Cake, page 132, Viennese Chocolate Torte, page 132, Carrot Cupcakes, page 134, Meringue Kisses, page 141, Cream Puffs, page 142, Lemon-Glazed Cake and Rum-Glazed Cake, page 133, and Individual Meringue Tortes, page 141, with Strawberries Chantilly, page 155.

Half-Pound Cake

Actually it's only 6 ounces—but it's a pound cake anyway!

1/4 cup butter, room temperature	1/4 teaspoon vanilla extract
1/4 cup superfine or granulated sugar	1/3 cup sifted flour
1 egg	Powdered sugar, if desired

Preheat oven to 325°F (165°C). Line a 6" x 3" aluminum foil loaf pan with wax paper, see page 134. With an electric mixer, beat butter in a small bowl until soft and light. Gradually add sugar, beating until light and fluffy. Beat egg in another small bowl. Gradually add to the butter-sugar mixture, beating until light and fluffy. Stir in vanilla. Stir in flour to moisten; beat until light and smooth. Spoon batter into prepared pan and distribute evenly. Bake about 55 minutes until edges separate from pan. Top should be golden and spring back when lightly touched in center. Cool in pan 15 minutes. Loosen sides and remove by lifting ends of wax paper. Cool on a wire rack. Sprinkle with powdered sugar, if desired. Makes 4 servings.

Variations

Nut Pound Cake: Stir 2 to 3 tablespoons finely minced walnuts or pecans into batter.
Lemon or Orange Pound Cake: Stir 1/2 teaspoon freshly grated lemon or orange peel into batter.

Viennese Chocolate Torte *Photo on page 131.*

Reminiscent of luscious Austrian pastries!

Viennese Chocolate Frosting, see below	1 to 2 tablespoons Toasted Almonds,
1 Half-Pound Cake, see above	page 165, sliced, if desired
1 to 2 tablespoons apricot jam	

Viennese Chocolate Frosting:

1/2 cup chocolate chips	1 egg yolk
1/4 cup butter, room temperature	1/4 teaspoon vanilla extract

Prepare Viennese Chocolate Frosting. Slice Half-Pound Cake into 4 horizontal layers. Press apricot jam through a fine tea strainer to puree. Spread a thin layer of apricot puree and a layer of Viennese Chocolate Frosting on lower 3 layers. Stack layers. Frost sides and top with remaining frosting. Sprinkle toasted almonds over top, if desired. Makes 4 servings.

Viennese Chocolate Frosting:
In a small heavy saucepan, warm chocolate chips gently over very low heat, stirring constantly until chocolate is melted. Cool to room temperature. Combine butter, egg yolk and vanilla in a small bowl. Whip until light and fluffy. Gradually add cooled chocolate, whipping until blended.

Lemon-Glazed Cake *Photo on page 131.*

This is a modified version of a popular cake.

1/2 cup sifted flour
1/4 teaspoon salt
1/8 teaspoon baking soda
1/4 cup butter, room temperature
1/2 cup superfine or granulated sugar

1/2 teaspoon vanilla extract
1 egg
1/4 cup dairy sour cream, room temperature
Lemon Glaze, see below

Lemon Glaze:
1 tablespoon butter
1/2 cup sugar

2 tablespoons fresh lemon juice
1/2 to 1 teaspoon freshly grated lemon peel

Preheat oven to 350°F (175°C). Line a 7" x 3" loaf pan with wax paper, see page 134. Sift together flour, salt and baking soda. Set aside. With an electric mixer, beat butter in a medium bowl until creamy. Add sugar. Beat until light and airy. Add vanilla and egg. Beat until fluffy. Stir in half the flour mixture to moisten. Beat until smooth. Add sour cream. Beat until smooth. Stir in remaining flour mixture to moisten. Beat about 30 seconds until smooth and thickened. Spread in prepared pan. Bake 30 to 35 minutes until edges separate from pan and top springs back when lightly touched in center. While cake is baking, prepare Lemon Glaze; keep warm. With a fork, pierce holes in top of hot cake at 1/2-inch intervals. Slowly drizzle warm Lemon Glaze over cake. If glaze runs off cake, brush with pastry brush until absorbed. Serve warm or cooled. Makes 3 or 4 servings.

Lemon Glaze:
Combine butter, sugar, lemon juice and grated lemon peel in a small saucepan. Simmer and stir until sugar is dissolved and mixture is syrupy. If hot glaze is too thick, stir in 1 tablespoon water.

Variation
Rum-Glazed Cake: Use 1/4 cup granulated sugar and 1/4 cup light brown sugar instead of 1/2 cup superfine sugar. Omit Lemon Glaze ingredients. Prepare Rum Glaze with 1 tablespoon butter, 2 tablespoons dark rum and 1/4 cup firmly packed light brown sugar. Top cake with Sweetened Whipped Cream, page 149.

Carrot Cake *Photo on page 131.*

The moistness depends on the smallness of the carrot shreds and your own careful measuring.

1/2 cup sifted flour
1/4 teaspoon salt
1/2 teaspoon cinnamon
1/4 teaspoon baking soda or
   3/4 teaspoon baking powder
1 egg
1/4 cup oil

1/2 cup granulated sugar or
   light brown sugar, firmly packed
1/2 teaspoon vanilla extract
2/3 cup (4-1/2 oz.) finely shredded or blender-
   ground peeled carrots, lightly packed
2 tablespoons finely chopped walnuts
Cream Cheese Frosting, page 136

Preheat oven to 350°F (175°C). Line a 7" x 3" loaf pan with wax paper, see below. Sift together flour, salt, cinnamon and baking soda or baking powder. Baking soda makes a darker cake while baking powder makes a lighter, more carrot-flavored one. Set aside. With a wire whip or electric mixer, beat egg in a medium bowl. Beat in oil, granulated or brown sugar and vanilla until smooth. Stir in flour mixture to moisten. Beat until smooth. Stir in carrots and walnuts. Pour into prepared pan. Bake 40 to 45 minutes until cake springs back when lightly touched in center. Cool in pan 15 minutes. Loosen sides and remove by lifting ends of wax paper. Cool on a wire rack. Prepare frosting. Frost cooled cake. Makes 3 or 4 servings.

Variation

Carrot Cupcakes: Line a muffin pan or custard cups with paper liners. Fill each cup 2/3 full. Bake about 25 minutes. Makes 8 cupcakes.

How To Make Carrot Cake

Line loaf pans as shown here to make the small cakes in this chapter. The lining technique is described on page 129.

For most accurate measure, weigh 4-1/2 ounces carrots and grind in blender. Or grate or finely shred carrots to measure 2/3 cup, lightly packed.

Quarter Cake

It's one quarter of a regular size cake, so you and your guest can eat the whole thing!

1 egg
2 tablespoons oil
1/4 cup water

1 cup yellow cake mix, any brand calling for
2 eggs and 1-1/3 cups liquid

Preheat oven to 350°F (175°C). Line a 7" x 3" loaf pan with wax paper, see page 134. Beat egg in a medium bowl. Beat in oil and water. Stir in cake mix to moisten. Whip 1 to 1-1/2 minutes until smooth. Pour into prepared loaf pan. Bake 25 minutes until edges separate from pan and cake springs back when lightly touched in center. Cool in pan 15 minutes. Remove by lifting ends of wax paper. Cool on a wire rack. Makes 3 or 4 servings.

Variations

Chocolate Chip Cake: Finely chop 2 tablespoons chocolate chips in blender. Stir into batter.
Cherry Cake: Finely chop 6 maraschino cherries to make 2 tablespoons. Stir into batter.
Nut Cake: Stir 2 tablespoons chopped Toasted Walnuts or Toasted Almonds, page 165, into batter.
Lemon Cake or Orange Cake: Stir 1/2 teaspoon grated lemon peel or orange peel into batter.

Lemon Curd

This traditional English condiment makes a delightful filling, topping or spread.

2 to 3 fresh lemons
1/2 cup butter (1 stick)

1-1/2 cups sugar
5 whole eggs or 10 egg yolks

Finely grate peel from lemons to make about 2 tablespoons; set aside. Squeeze juice from lemons to make 1/2 cup. Combine lemon juice, butter and sugar in top of a stainless steel, glass or enamel double boiler. Heat over simmering water, stirring occasionally, until sugar is dissolved. Beat eggs or egg yolks in a medium bowl. Gradually add hot sugar mixture to eggs, stirring constantly until blended. Return to double boiler and stir in lemon peel. Cook over simmering water, stirring constantly with a rubber spatula until opaque, smooth and thickened enough to hold a shallow swirl. Pour into several small, clean glass jars. Cool. Cover tightly and refrigerate up to 6 weeks. Use to fill tart shells, Meringue Tortes or Hard Meringues, page 141. Or use to top plain cake, layer in a parfait or spread on toast. Makes about 2-1/2 cups.

Variation

Lemon Cream: Whip 1/2 cup whipping cream until stiff but not brittle. Fold 1/3 cup Lemon Curd into whipped cream until blended. Use as filling for Cream Puffs, page 142.

Cream Cheese Frosting

The perfect frosting for carrot cake and fruit pulp cakes.

3 tablespoons (1-1/2 oz.) cream cheese,
  room temperature
1 tablespoon butter, room temperature

1/2 teaspoon vanilla extract
3/4 to 1 cup unsifted powdered sugar

Combine cream cheese, butter and vanilla in a small bowl. With an electric mixer, beat until light and fluffy. Gradually add 3/4 cup powdered sugar, beating until light and easy to spread. Add additional powdered sugar in small amounts for more body. Makes about 2/3 cup frosting, enough for one 7" x 3" cake.

Buttercream Frosting

To vary the flavor, add grated lemon or orange peel, or substitute other flavor extracts for vanilla.

2 tablespoons butter, room temperature
1-1/2 to 3 teaspoons milk, half-and-half or
  whipping cream

1/2 teaspoon vanilla extract
3/4 to 1 cup unsifted powdered sugar

Combine butter, 1-1/2 teaspoons of the milk, half-and-half or whipping cream, vanilla and about 1/2 cup of the powdered sugar in a small bowl. With an electric mixer, beat until smooth. Add 1/4 cup more powdered sugar. Beat until light and easy to spread. Beat in additional milk, half-and-half or whipping cream in small amounts to soften frosting. Or beat in additional powdered sugar in small amounts for more body. Makes about 1/2 cup frosting, enough for one 7" x 3" cake.

Milk Chocolate Frosting

Add either more whipping cream or powdered sugar to get the consistency you want.

2 to 3 tablespoons whipping cream
2 rounded tablespoons chocolate chips
2 tablespoons butter, room temperature

1/2 teaspoon vanilla extract
Dash salt
1/2 to 3/4 cup unsifted powdered sugar

Combine 2 tablespoons whipping cream and chocolate chips in a small saucepan over low heat. Heat gently, stirring constantly until chocolate is melted and blended with cream. Cool to room temperature. Combine chocolate mixture, butter, vanilla and salt in a medium bowl. With an electric mixer, beat until smooth. Gradually add 1/2 cup powdered sugar. Beat until smooth and easy to spread. Beat in additional whipping cream in small amounts to soften frosting. Or beat in small amounts of powdered sugar for more body. Makes about 2/3 cup frosting, enough for one 7" x 3" cake.

Strawberry Shortcakes

Gourmet and down-home cooking meet in this irresistible dessert.

1 pint fresh strawberries
1 tablespoon superfine or granulated sugar
2 tablespoons orange-flavored liqueur

1 recipe Shortcakes Supreme, page 138
Orange Whipped Cream, see below
Finely shredded orange peel

Orange Whipped Cream:
1/2 cup whipping cream
1 tablespoon superfine or granulated sugar
Pinch grated orange peel

Dash salt
1/4 teaspoon vanilla extract

Select 2 prettiest strawberries for garnish; wash and refrigerate. Wash, hull and slice remaining strawberries into a medium bowl. Mix in sugar and orange-flavored liqueur. Cover and refrigerate 2 hours. Bake Shortcakes Supreme; cool. At serving time, prepare Orange Whipped Cream. Place a shortcake on each of 2 dessert plates. Top each with 1/4 of the strawberries with juice and a spoonful of Orange Whipped Cream. Repeat with remaining shortcakes and strawberries. Spoon remaining Orange Whipped Cream over top. Garnish with a few shreds of orange peel and reserved whole strawberries. Makes 2 servings.

Orange Whipped Cream:
Combine all ingredients in a medium bowl and chill with beaters if time permits. At serving time, whip cream until stiff but not brittle.

Spicy Peach Shortcakes

Enjoy this shortcake year-round.

1 recipe Shortcakes Supreme, page 138
1 (8-oz.) can sliced peaches

Spicy Whipped Cream, see below

Spicy Whipped Cream:
1/2 cup whipping cream
1 tablespoon brown sugar
1/4 teaspoon cinnamon

1/8 teaspoon ground ginger
Dash salt
1/4 teaspoon vanilla extract

Prepare Shortcakes Supreme. Drain peaches. Prepare Spicy Whipped Cream. Place a shortcake on each of 2 dessert plates. Top each with about 1/3 of the drained peaches and a spoonful of Spicy Whipped Cream. Lightly press another shortcake on top of peaches and whipped cream and spoon remaining Spicy Whipped Cream over. Garnish with remaining peach slices. Makes 2 servings.

Spicy Whipped Cream:
Combine all ingredients in a medium bowl and chill with beaters if time permits. At serving time, whip cream until stiff but not brittle.

Shortcakes Supreme

Better than shortcakes made from scratch!

2/3 cup buttermilk biscuit mix
2 tablespoons superfine or granulated sugar

1/4 cup whipping cream

Preheat oven to 425°F (220°C). Lightly oil a small baking sheet. Blend baking mix and sugar in a medium bowl. Add whipping cream. Stir to moisten dry ingredients. Beat 15 strokes. Spoon dough into 4 mounds at least 3 inches apart on prepared baking sheet. With the back of a spoon, flatten dough into 3-inch circles. Bake 10 to 12 minutes until golden brown. Makes 2 servings.

Cinnamon-Apple Cake

A la mode or with whipped cream, you'll love it.

2 tablespoons butter
2 to 3 tablespoons coarsely chopped walnuts
1/4 cup light brown sugar, firmly packed
1 tablespoon whipping cream
1/2 teaspoon cinnamon
Dash salt

1 medium cooking apple such as Rome
  Beauty or Golden Delicious
  (about 1/2 lb.)
Baking Mix Cake Batter, see below
Sweetened Whipped Cream, page 149, or
  vanilla ice cream or whipping cream

Baking Mix Cake Batter:
1 egg
1 tablespoon oil
1/4 cup milk

1/2 teaspoon vanilla extract
1/4 cup superfine or granulated sugar
3/4 cup buttermilk biscuit mix

Preheat oven to 350°F (175°C). Melt butter in an 8-inch ovenproof skillet. Briefly sauté walnuts in butter over medium heat. Remove from heat. Blend in brown sugar, 1 tablespoon whipping cream, cinnamon and salt. Spread evenly over bottom of pan. Peel, quarter and core apple. Cut each quarter into 4 or 5 slices. Arrange slices in a spiral on top of nut mixture, with 2 to 4 slices in center. Press slices into nut mixture. Prepare Baking Mix Cake Batter. Pour over apples, spreading to cover. Bake about 25 minutes until edges separate from pan and cake springs back when lightly touched in center. Cool in pan 10 minutes. Loosen sides with a knife. Place an 8- or 9-inch plate upsidedown over pan and invert cake onto plate. Rearrange apples and glaze, if necessary. Serve warm with Sweetened Whipped Cream, ice cream or whipping cream. Makes 3 or 4 servings.

Baking Mix Cake Batter:
Beat egg in a medium bowl. Beat in oil. Blend in milk, vanilla and sugar. Stir in buttermilk biscuit mix to moisten. Beat vigourously 1 to 1-1/2 minutes until smooth.

Ginger-Peachy Cake

An 8-ounce can of fruit makes the meal.

2 tablespoons butter
1/4 cup light brown sugar, firmly packed
Dash salt
1 (8-oz.) can sliced peaches

Few dashes ground ginger
Quarter Cake batter, page 135
Sweetened Whipped Cream, page 149,
  or whipping cream, if desired

Preheat oven to 350°F (175°C). Melt butter in a 7" x 3" loaf pan. Blend in brown sugar and salt. Spread evenly over bottom of pan. Drain peach slices and arrange over brown sugar mixture. Lightly sprinkle with ginger. Prepare Quarter Cake batter. Pour over peaches and distribute evenly. Bake about 30 minutes until edges separate from pan and top springs back when lightly touched in center. Cool in pan 10 minutes. Loosen sides with a knife. Place a plate upside down over pan and invert cake onto plate. Rearrange peach slices and glaze, if necessary. Serve warm with Sweetened Whipped Cream or whipping cream, if desired. Makes 3 or 4 servings.

Variation

Apricot-Almond Upside-Down Cake: Substitute 1 (8-ounce) can apricot halves for peaches. Arrange drained apricot halves, rounded-side down on brown sugar mixture. Sprinkle 2 tablespoons slivered or sliced Toasted Almonds, page 165, between apricot halves.

How To Make Cinnamon-Apple Cake

If the apple is large, cut thinner slices to ensure complete cooking. Arrange apple slices in a spiral that will look attractive when the cake is inverted.

Invert the baked cake onto a salad plate and rearrange slices and glaze if necessary. Serve warm with topping.

Pineapple-Rum Upside-Down Cake

Always a family favorite.

Sour Cream Cake Batter, see below
2 tablespoons butter
1/4 cup light brown sugar, firmly packed
1 tablespoon dark rum
Dash salt

1 (8-oz.) can pineapple slices
4 maraschino cherries, cut in half
Ice cream, Sweetened Whipped Cream,
    page 149, or whipping cream

Sour Cream Cake Batter:
1/2 cup sifted flour
1/4 teaspoon salt
1/8 teaspoon baking soda
1/4 cup butter, room temperature

1/2 cup superfine or granulated sugar
1/2 teaspoon vanilla extract
1 egg
1/4 cup dairy sour cream, room temperature

Prepare Sour Cream Cake Batter. Preheat oven to 350°F (175°C). Melt butter in a 9" x 5" loaf pan. Blend brown sugar, rum and salt into butter. Spread evenly over bottom of pan. Drain pineapple slices. Arrange 3 slices side by side in pan. Cut fourth slice into quarters; arrange pieces between slices along sides of pan. Place a maraschino cherry half, rounded side down, in the center of each pineapple slice. Cut remaining cherry halves in half again and arrange around outside of pineapple slices. Pour Sour Cream Cake Batter over fruit and distribute evenly. Bake 30 to 35 minutes until edges separate from pan and top springs back when lightly touched in center. Cool in pan 10 minutes. Loosen sides with a knife. Place a serving plate upside down over pan and invert cake onto plate. Rearrange pineapple slices, cherries and glaze, if necessary. Serve warm with ice cream, Sweetened Whipped Cream or whipping cream. Makes 3 or 4 servings.

Sour Cream Cake Batter:
Sift together flour, salt and baking soda; set aside. With an electric mixer, beat butter in a medium bowl until creamy. Add sugar. Beat until light and airy. Add vanilla and egg. Beat until fluffy. Stir in half the flour mixture to moisten. Beat until smooth. Add sour cream. Beat until smooth. Stir in remaining flour mixture to moisten. Beat about 30 seconds until smooth.

Variation

Bananas Foster Upside-Down Cake: Omit pineapple and maraschino cherries. Blend 1/8 teaspoon cinnamon into brown sugar mixture. Peel 1 large banana and cut into 1/3-inch slices. Press slices into brown sugar mixture in bottom of baking pan. Press pecan halves or pieces into brown sugar mixture between banana slices. Pour batter over and bake.

Individual Meringue Tortes *Photo on page 131.*

An elegant dessert shell to frame fruit, ice cream or pudding.

1 egg white, fresh or frozen
Pinch salt
1/16 teaspoon cream of tartar or
   1/4 teaspoon lemon juice
1/3 cup superfine or granulated sugar or
   1/3 cup light brown sugar, firmly packed
1/4 teaspoon vanilla or other extract

2 to 3 tablespoons finely crushed soda
   crackers or fine dry breadcrumbs
1/4 cup finely minced walnuts, pecans,
   hazelnuts, macadamia nuts, toasted
   almonds or shredded coconut
Fillings & Toppings, see below

Preheat oven to 250°F (120°C). Cut a piece of unglazed, brown grocery bag paper to cover a small baking sheet. Draw two 4-inch circles on the paper. Put egg white in a medium bowl. Place bowl in a larger bowl of warm water to warm egg white to about 85°F (30°C). With an electric mixer, whip egg white to a froth. Sprinkle salt and cream of tartar or lemon juice over egg white. Beat at high speed to blend. Gradually add sugar, beating constantly, until meringue holds stiff peaks and sugar is dissolved. Add vanilla or other extract. Beat until stiff again. Fold in crumbs and nuts. Spoon equal amounts of batter into the circles on paper-lined baking sheet. With the back of a spoon, shape each mound to fit each circle, leaving a slightly raised rim. Bake 45 minutes for slightly soft interior or 1 hour for crisp interior. Do not brown. Slide brown paper with meringues onto a wire rack. When cooled, slip a spatula under meringues to lift from paper to plates. Add filling and topping. To delay serving, store in airtight containers. To freeze, separate with a layer of foil and overwrap with foil. Makes 2 tortes.

Fillings & Toppings

Peach Melba: Fill with canned or sweetened fresh sliced peaches. Drizzle Melba Sauce, page 158, over torte. Top with Sweetened Whipped Cream, page 149.

Heavenly Lemon: Fill with Lemon Curd, page 135. Top with Sweetened Whipped Cream, page 149.

Strawberry Sundae: Fill with ice cream. Top with sweetened sliced and crushed fresh strawberries or fill with Strawberries Chantilly, page 155.

Spring Berry: Fill with sweetened fresh strawberries, blueberries or raspberries. Top with Sweetened Whipped Cream, page 149.

Chocolate Mousse: Fill with chilled Magnificent Mousse au Chocolat, page 153. Top with Sweetened Whipped Cream, page 149.

Variations

Meringue Kisses: Drop meringue batter by teaspoonfuls onto paper-lined baking sheet. Bake 20 to 25 minutes for soft, chewy kisses, or 30 minutes for crisp kisses. Makes 16 to 18 kisses.

Hard Meringues: Reduce sugar to 1/4 cup. Do not use brown sugar. Omit crumbs and nuts. Add food color to tint, if desired. Shape into circles. Bake 1 hour. Turn oven off and leave meringues in oven 1 hour to dry. Serve like Individual Meringue Tortes.

Cream Puffs *Photo on page 131.*

This easy favorite is versatile as a dessert, entree or appetizer.

1/4 cup water	1 egg
2 tablespoons butter	Chocolate Whipped Cream, see below
1/8 teaspoon salt	Powdered sugar
1/4 cup flour	

Chocolate Whipped Cream:

2 mounded tablespoons chocolate chips	2/3 cup whipping cream
2 teaspoons sugar	1/2 teaspoon vanilla extract
Dash salt	1/2 teaspoon instant coffee powder, if desired

Preheat oven to 425°F (220°C). Put water, butter and salt in a small saucepan. Bring to a boil, breaking butter into pieces to speed melting. As soon as butter is melted and water is boiling, add flour all at once. Stir vigorously until mixture clings together and resembles cornmeal mush. Remove from heat immediately. Work quickly to avoid moisture loss. Beat eggs and gradually add to slightly cooled flour mixture, beating well. Spoon batter into 2 or 3 mounds at least 3 inches apart on an ungreased baking sheet. Bake 15 minutes. Reduce heat to 325°F (165°C). Bake 20 to 25 more minutes until crisp and golden brown. Turn off oven. Stick a sharp knife into side of each puff to release steam. Close oven about 20 minutes to let puffs dry. Cool on a wire rack. Prepare Chocolate Whipped Cream. Slice off tops of puffs. Press inside dough to bottom and sides. Fill puffs with Chocolate Whipped Cream. Replace tops. Sprinkle with powdered sugar. Freeze unfilled puffs, if desired. Thaw, fill and reheat at 325°F (165°C) about 5 minutes. Makes 2 or 3 puffs.

Chocolate Whipped Cream:
Combine chocolate chips, sugar, salt and 2 to 3 tablespoons of the whipping cream in a small saucepan. Warm and stir over very low heat until chocolate chips are melted and blended into cream. Remove from heat. Gradually blend in remaining cream, vanilla and instant coffee powder, if desired. Pour into a medium bowl. Refrigerate with beaters. When chilled, whip until stiff.

Variations

Dessert Puffs: Omit Chocolate Whipped Cream. Fill puffs with desired flavor of ice cream or pudding. Top with sweetened crushed strawberries, liqueur, Hot Fudge Sauce, page 155, or Melba Sauce, page 158. Or fill with Raspberry Fool, page 158, Lemon Cream, page 135, or Sweetened Whipped Cream, page 149.

Entree Cream Puffs: Omit Chocolate Whipped Cream and powdered sugar. Fill with desired Main Dish Crepes filling, page 87, or chicken, tuna, shrimp, crab or ham salad.

Appetizer Puffs: Preheat oven to 400°F (205°C). Drop batter by half teaspoonfuls onto baking sheet. Bake 15 minutes. Turn oven off and dry 15 minutes. Fill as desired. Makes 12 to 16 small puffs.

Dinner Desserts

In case you haven't guessed, I adore desserts! For me a meal has not ended unless I've had my little bit of sweet. These desserts are light enough to top off a substantial meal without overdoing it. They are built around nutritional foods like fruits, eggs and dairy products, plus a few extras such as chocolate, brandy or a maraschino cherry.

CHEESE & FRUIT

A dessert of cheese and fruit is superbly simple and nutritious! Americans often serve fruit and cheese with dry wine or coffee. The French serve cheese first with fresh, crusty French rolls, butter and dry wine, followed by fruit and the rest of the wine. In England the cheese is served with plain crackers, a sweet wine and fruit.

Whichever pattern you choose, for best flavor serve dessert cheeses at room temperature. Cover them with a glass dome or plastic wrap to contain their aroma until they are served. Almost any cheese will do. My favorites are the dessert cheeses like Camembert or Port du Salut, but the blue-vein cheeses, Cheddars or Monterey Jack are equally suitable. Try new cheeses as you discover them.

The fruit should be selected to complement the cheese. Grapes, pears and apples are classic choices. Pineapple and honeydew are remarkably compatible. Use seasonal fruits. In the winter add nuts in the shell and dry fruits. Try green grapes with Camembert, apples with Cheddar or Swiss, pineapple with Port du Salut or pears with blue cheese.

FRUIT DESSERTS

Few desserts are as elegant as those made from fresh fruit. A stemmed glass of raspberries or a wedge of melon with a simple garnish is equal to the most impressive entree you might serve. Have fun during summer when so many fresh fruits are available. In winter, turn fresh or canned fruits into hot, crispy desserts.

Peaches, pears, bananas, apples, nectarines and avocados will darken after they are cut. To prepare these fruits in advance, toss the cut fruit in lemon, orange or grapefruit juice, or stir it into a sauce made with sour cream or yogurt. Sweeten the sauce with honey or brown sugar, if you like.

ICE CREAM

Served plain, ice cream is an effortless dessert. With a little thought it becomes a special dessert like Cherries Jubilee, Baked Alaska or Peach Melba.

Take care of ice cream to preserve its flavor and creamy texture. Buy only what you can use in a month and never let it thaw or refreeze. After you have scooped what you need from the carton, press a sheet of plastic wrap against the surface of the ice cream to prevent the formation of icy frost.

FLAMING DESSERTS

There is no more exciting conclusion to an elegant dinner than a flaming dessert. This excitement is simple to produce with a little know-how.

Equipment—You will need a chafing dish, skillet, saucepan or server of metal or heatproof glass. Serving dishes can be elegant or basic, but they must be able to withstand the heat of the flames and the cold of the ice cream at the same time. Do not use your fine crystal. I suggest silver-plated stemmed dishes.

You'll need a ladle with a handle that angles away from the bowl. The handles on most sauce ladles aim straight up, which puts your hand in direct line with the flames. If you use a ladle, you'll need a candle. Or you can use a small, long-handled syrup, butter or sauce warmer, preferably with its own candle warmer. With this you'll need a long match.

Liquor—The best liquors for flaming are dark rum or brandy, including Cognac and flavored brandies like Grand Marnier or kirsch. However, any liquor with an alcohol content of 80-proof (40 percent) or more should give good results. If the alcohol content of the basic liquor is over 80 proof, a little liqueur can be added for flavor. Choose a liquor that complements the food being flamed.

Safety—Make certain there is nothing that could catch fire within reach of the flames. Consider curtains and draperies, overhead lighting fixtures and table decorations, surfaces and coverings. Keep the flame at a distance from yourself and your guest. Do not attempt to carry a flaming dish from the kitchen to the table. Either complete the flaming in the kitchen or do it at the table.

Procedure—

• Have all equipment and ingredients, except the ice cream, on a tray or tea cart to take to the table. Many flaming dishes, such as Bananas Foster, can be prepared entirely at the table. Others are prepared in the kitchen and taken hot to the table for final flaming and serving.

• Dim the lights. Flaming is effective only in a darkened room. If there are too many lights it is sometimes impossible to see the flames, which can be dangerous.

• Warm the liquor. Sometimes you can simply pour the liquor over the hot food and ignite it with a match after giving it a moment to warm. But for more certain results, warm all or part of the liquor separately in a small sauce warmer and light it with a long match. Or warm 1 to 2 tablespoons in a ladle over a candle and ignite by dipping the edge of the ladle into the flame. The remainder of the liquor is poured over the hot food and allowed to warm a moment before pouring on the flaming ladle of liquor.

The liquor will not ignite if the food is not hot enough, or if the liquor warms so long that the alcohol evaporates, or if it is diluted by the sauce.

• Ignite the liquor and pour it over the hot food. Shake the pan or stir the sauce to keep the flames alive. The larger the pan surface, the bigger the blaze will be, so add the liquor accordingly.

• As the flames die, serve and enjoy.

How To Make Flaming Desserts

This stainless steel butter warmer is ideal for warming liquor to be flamed. Ignite with a long match and pour over dessert or sauce to be flamed.

A ladle with a handle that angles away from the bowl can also be used to warm liquor for flaming. Ignite the warm liquor by tipping the bowl into the flame.

Dessert Crepes

Ordinary ingredients become special treats when wrapped in crepes.

1 egg	1/2 cup sifted flour
1 egg yolk	1 tablespoon melted butter
2/3 cup milk	Oil or Clarified Butter, page 159,
1 teaspoon sugar	more if needed
Dash salt	Fillings & Toppings, see below

Beat egg and egg yolk in a medium bowl. Blend in milk, sugar and salt; stir in flour to moisten. Add melted butter and beat about 2 minutes until smooth. Pour batter into a glass measuring cup. Cover and refrigerate 2 hours. Put a small amount of oil into an 8-inch slope-sided skillet or crepe pan. Heat over medium to medium-high heat until oil is almost smoking. Pour off any oil that will run off. Hold skillet in one hand and cup of batter in other. Pour about 3 tablespoons batter into center of skillet, swirling and tilting skillet to cover bottom evenly. Return to heat. Cook until top of crepe is dry and edges are browned and slightly curled. With a fork, pull edge of crepe away from skillet, pick up with fingers and turn. Or tilt and shake skillet to slide edge of crepe just beyond rim and flip crepe. Cook other side 3 or 4 seconds; invert skillet over a clean towel to release crepe. Cook crepes from remaining batter, wiping pan as necessary to remove crumbs. Add more oil if crepes begin to stick. Fill and top crepes. Allow 2 to 3 crepes per serving. To freeze plain crepes, wrap serving portions in plastic wrap and wrap again in aluminum foil. Makes about 8 crepes.

Fillings & Toppings

Crepes Chocolate: Fill crepes with Chocolate Whipped Cream, page 142, and sprinkle with powdered sugar. Or spoon chocolate ice cream in a line down the side of a crepe. Roll and freeze. Serve with Hot Fudge Sauce, page 155.

Strawberry Crepes: Wash, quarter and sweeten strawberries. Fold into Sweetened Whipped Cream, page 149. Spoon onto crepes and roll. Sprinkle with powdered sugar. Substitute sweetened raspberries, peaches, bananas or other fresh fruits for strawberries, if desired.

Lemon Crepes: Spread a thin layer of Lemon Curd, page 135, over crepes. Roll and sprinkle with powdered sugar.

Jam Crepes: Spread jams, jellies or preserves over crepes. Fold or roll. Sprinkle with powdered sugar.

Variation

Blender Method: Put egg, egg yolk, milk, sugar, salt and flour in a blender. Cover and blend 5 seconds. Scrape sides. Add melted butter. Blend 30 more seconds. Pour into measuring cup. Cover and refrigerate 2 hours. Cook as above.

For delicious breakfast pancakes, serve crepes with syrup and butter, or canned or sweetened fresh fruit and Sweetened Whipped Cream, page 149.

Cherries Jubilee

Not much trouble—but what an effect!

1 (8-oz.) can dark, sweet pitted cherries
1 tablespoon sugar
Dash cinnamon
Dash cloves or 4 whole cloves
1 (3-inch) strip lemon peel

1 teaspoon cornstarch
1 tablespoon water
2 large scoops vanilla ice cream
2 tablespoons kirsch (cherry brandy)

Drain juice from cherries into a small saucepan. Add sugar, cinnamon, cloves and strip of lemon peel. Simmer uncovered until juice measures about 1/4 cup. Remove whole cloves, if used, and lemon peel. In a small bowl, blend cornstarch and water until completely smooth. Drizzle into simmering cherry juice, stirring constantly until clear and thickened. Add drained cherries. Heat to serving temperature. Pour into a small chafing dish. Place ice cream in 2 heat-roof dessert dishes. At table, warm kirsch in a small long-handled pot or in a ladle over a candle. Ignite warmed kirsch with a long match. Pour over cherries. Shake or stir until flames subside. Ladle cherries and sauce over ice cream. Makes 2 servings.

Variation

Quick Cherries Jubilee: Omit sugar, cornstarch and water. Heat 1/4 cup red currant jelly in small saucepan or chafing dish. Add lemon peel, cinnamon and cloves. Simmer and stir until jelly is melted and smooth. Drain cherries. Add to melted jelly. Heat to serving temperature. Ignite as directed.

Strawberries Romanoff

Follow a rich meal with this beautiful dessert.

1 pint fresh strawberries
1 tablespoon honey
2 tablespoons orange-flavored liqueur

1/4 teaspoon freshly grated orange peel,
   if desired
Sweetened Whipped Cream, page 149

Hull strawberries. Wash and drain on paper towels. Cut berries in half for better flavor. Combine with honey, liqueur and half the grated orange peel, if desired. Cover and refrigerate 1 to 2 hours. To serve, spoon berries and juice into 2 stemmed dessert glasses. Top with Sweetened Whipped Cream. Garnish with remaining grated orange peel, if desired. Makes 2 servings.

Crepes Suzette

Finish it with showmanship at the table.

1 medium orange with bright orange skin
3 tablespoons sugar
2 tablespoons orange-flavored liqueur
1/4 cup butter

6 Dessert Crepes, page 145, or
  6 Golden Crepes, page 86
2 tablespoons orange-flavored liqueur
2 tablespoons brandy or cognac

Finely grate orange peel to make 1 teaspoon. Squeeze juice from orange to make 1/4 to 1/3 cup. Combine grated orange peel, orange juice, sugar and 2 tablespoons orange-flavored liqueur. At table if desired, put butter in a large electric skillet or in a chafing dish with fairly hot alcohol flame. Place within reach, the orange peel mixture, crepes, a tablespoon and fork to handle crepes, orange-flavored liqueur, brandy, a 1-ounce measure, a long match to ignite brandy and 2 serving plates and forks. Melt butter. Stir in orange peel mixture. Boil until smooth and slightly thickened. Reduce to a slow simmer. Dip crepes 1 at a time in syrup placing spotted side down first, then attractive side down. Fold in half and then in quarters to form wedge with attractively browned side showing. Push folded crepe to side of skillet or chafing dish. Repeat until all crepes have been dipped, folded and stacked to the side. Arrange folded crepes to cover bottom of skillet or chafing dish. Pour 2 tablespoons orange-flavored liqueur over, then brandy. Let brandy warm slightly. Ignite with a long match. Shake pan gently until flames subside. Simmer sauce, spooning over crepes, until thickened and syrupy again. Makes 2 servings.

Bananas Foster

Celebrate Mardi Gras anytime with this New Orleans specialty.

2 tablespoons butter
1 large or 2 small, firm bananas
1/4 cup light brown sugar, firmly packed
Dash nutmeg or cinnamon
1/4 teaspoon grated orange peel

2 tablespoons banana liqueur, if desired
1/4 cup dark rum or other rum
2 large scoops vanilla ice cream
Toasted Almonds, page 165, slivered or
  sliced, if desired

Melt butter over medium heat in an electric skillet. Peel bananas and halve lengthwise or slice diagonally 3/4-inch thick. As soon as butter froths, add bananas. Sauté quickly on each side until lightly browned. Add brown sugar, nutmeg or cinnamon, orange peel, banana liqueur, if desired, and 2 tablespoons of the rum. Stir until blended. Boil until syrupy. Place ice cream in 2 heatproof dessert dishes. Warm remaining 2 tablespoons rum in a small long-handled pot or in a ladle over a candle. Ignite with a long match. Pour over bananas. Shake until flames subside. Spoon bananas and sauce over ice cream. Garnish with toasted almonds, if desired. Makes 2 servings.

Variation

Pineapple Flambé: Substitute 1/4 medium pineapple for bananas. Omit orange peel and banana liqueur. Peel and core pineapple. Slice 1/2-inch thick. Sauté in butter and ignite as directed. Substitute brandy for rum, if desired.

Fresh Fruit à la Suisse

No topping goes better with berries and summer fruits than sour cream and brown sugar.

1/2 to 1 cup prepared fresh strawberries, kiwi, grapes, raspberries, apples, nectarines, peaches, figs, pears, bananas, pineapple or apricots

1/4 cup dairy sour cream
2 teaspoons light brown sugar

Place fruit in a dessert dish. Blend sour cream and brown sugar in a small bowl. Spoon over fruit or mix with fruit. Makes 1 serving.

Sweetened Whipped Cream

The all-time favorite dessert topping.

1/3 cup whipping cream
2 teaspoons superfine or granulated sugar

1/4 teaspoon vanilla extract
Dash salt

Combine ingredients in a small bowl, and chill with beaters if time permits. Beat with an electric mixer or wire whip until thickened and doubled in volume. Makes two 1/3-cup servings.

Variations

Chocolate Whipped Cream: Substitute 2 tablespoons instant hot chocolate powder for sugar.
Spiced Whipped Cream: Substitute brown sugar for granulated sugar. Add a dash each of ground cinnamon, cloves and ginger.
Favorite Flavor Whipped Cream: Substitute almond, peppermint, banana or other extract for vanilla. Add grated lemon or orange peel.

Whipped Crème Fraîche

Better than whipped cream on fruit desserts.

1/4 cup whipping cream
2 tablespoons dairy sour cream
1 tablespoon superfine or granulated sugar

1/4 teaspoon vanilla extract
Dash salt

Combine all ingredients in a small bowl, and chill with beaters if time permits. Beat with an electric mixer or wire whip until thickened and doubled in volume. Serve over fruit. Makes two 1/3-cup servings.

Apple Brown Betty

One apple and a little tired bread team up to deliver this delicious dessert.

1 tablespoon butter
1/3 cup Soft Breadcrumbs, page 164,
   lightly packed
2 tablespoons light brown sugar
Dash salt
1/4 teaspoon cinnamon
1 medium cooking apple (about 1/2 lb.)

1 to 3 teaspoons granulated sugar
1/2 teaspoon lemon juice
1/8 teaspoon grated lemon peel
Vanilla ice cream, whipping cream or
   Sweetened Whipped Cream, page 149,
   if desired

Preheat oven to 375°F (190°C). Melt butter in a small saucepan. Remove from heat. Add soft breadcrumbs. Stir to mix well. In a small bowl, combine brown sugar, salt and cinnamon. Blend until no lumps remain. Lightly mix in buttered breadcrumbs; set aside. Peel and core apple. Finely chop and put in a 2-cup soufflé pot or casserole. Add granulated sugar, lemon juice, lemon peel and 1/4 cup of the crumb mixture. Mix well; pat down in casserole. Sprinkle remaining crumbs evenly over top. Bake about 45 minutes until apples are tender and top is browned. Serve warm with vanilla ice cream, whipping cream or Sweetened Whipped Cream, if desired. Makes 1 or 2 servings.

Variation

Easy Brown Betty: Omit apple, granulated sugar, lemon juice and lemon peel. Lightly drain one 8-ounce can fruit cocktail or sliced peaches. Mix with 1/4 cup crumb mixture in one 10-ounce or two 6-ounce soufflé pots, custard cups or casseroles. Sprinkle with remaining crumbs. Bake 30 minutes.

Peach Pudding Cake

Another wonderful way to use just a little bit of yellow cake mix.

2 tablespoons butter
1 (8-oz.) can sliced peaches
2/3 cup yellow cake mix, any brand calling
   for 2 eggs and 1-1/3 cups liquid

2 tablespoons chopped nuts
Sweetened Whipped Cream, page 149,
   if desired

Preheat oven to 350°F (175°C). Melt butter in a small saucepan. Drain syrup from peaches. Arrange peaches in a 2-cup soufflé pot or casserole. Spread dry cake mix evenly over fruit. Sprinkle with nuts. Drizzle with melted butter. Bake 40 to 45 minutes. Serve warm or cooled with Sweetened Whipped Cream, if desired. Makes 2 servings.

Variations

Fruit Cocktail Pudding Cake: Substitute one 8-ounce can fruit cocktail for peaches.
Applesauce Pudding Cake: Substitute 2/3 cup applesauce for drained peach slices.

Lemon Pudding Fluff

Moist, tangy and bound to be repeated!

1/2 cup sugar
2 tablespoons flour
1/8 teaspoon salt
2 tablespoons lemon juice (about 1/2 lemon)
1/2 to 1 teaspoon freshly grated lemon peel
   (about 1/2 lemon)

1 egg
1/2 cup milk
Sweetened Whipped Cream, page 149, or
   ice cream, if desired

Put 3/4-inch-deep water in an 11" x 7" shallow baking pan. Place in oven. Preheat oven to 350°F (175°C). Blend sugar, flour and salt until free of lumps. Prepare lemon juice and peel; set aside. Separate egg, putting egg white into a small bowl and egg yolk in a medium bowl. With an electric mixer, whip egg white until it holds stiff peaks but is not dry; set aside. Beat egg yolk. Gradually blend in milk, sugar mixture, lemon juice and lemon peel. Fold in beaten egg white until blended but not quite smooth. Pour into two 10-ounce soufflé pots, custard cups or casseroles. Place in hot water bath in oven. Bake 45 to 50 minutes until puffed and lightly browned. Serve warm or cooled with Sweetened Whipped Cream, if desired. Makes 2 servings.

Pineapple-Oatmeal Crunch

Breakfast cereal can be a basic ingredient.

2 tablespoons butter
1 (1-oz.) packet instant oatmeal
1/4 cup light brown sugar, firmly packed
Dash salt

1/2 teaspoon cinnamon
1 (8-oz.) can crushed pineapple
Sweetened Whipped Cream, page 149,
   if desired

Preheat oven to 375°F (190°C). Melt butter in a small saucepan. Remove from heat. Blend in instant oatmeal. Add brown sugar. Blend until no lumps remain. Sprinkle with salt and cinnamon. Stir until blended. Drain 3 tablespoons juice from pineapple and discard. Put pineapple and remaining juice into 2-cup soufflé pot or casserole. Blend in 1/4 cup of the oatmeal mixture. Spread remaining oatmeal mixture over the top. Bake 30 minutes. Serve warm or at room temperature, with Sweetened Whipped Cream or ice cream, if desired. Makes 2 or 3 servings.

Variation

Apple-Oatmeal Crunch: Omit pineapple. Peel, core and thinly slice 2 cooking apples such as Pippin, McIntosh or Golden Delicious. Mix with 2 tablespoons sugar, 1 teaspoon lemon juice, 1/4 teaspoon grated lemon peel and 1/4 cup of the oatmeal mixture. Spoon into a 3- or 4-cup soufflé pot or casserole; pack down. Spread remaining oatmeal mixture over top. Bake 45 minutes until apples are tender. Makes 3 servings.

Magnificent Mousse au Chocolat

Get fancy!

1/4 cup whipping cream
1/4 cup chocolate chips
1 egg
1/2 teaspoon vanilla or other extract
Dash salt

1 tablespoon superfine or granulated sugar
Sweetened Whipped Cream, page 149,
   if desired
Toasted Almonds, page 165, if desired

Combine whipping cream and chocolate chips in a small saucepan. Warm over low heat, stirring constantly, until chocolate is melted and mixture is smooth and blended. Remove from heat. Separate egg, putting egg white into a small bowl and egg yolk into a medium bowl. Beat together egg yolk and vanilla or other extract. Gradually add warm chocolate mixture, stirring constantly until blended. Cover and refrigerate. When chocolate mixture is partially firm, whip egg white until frothy. Add salt. Continue whipping, gradually adding sugar, until egg white holds stiff peaks and sugar is dissolved. Whip chilled chocolate mixture until smooth and light. Fold beaten egg white into chocolate mixture until blended. Spoon into two 6-ounce soufflé pots or dessert dishes. Refrigerate 2 to 3 hours until firm. Garnish with Sweetened Whipped Cream and toasted almonds, if desired. Makes 2 servings.

Variation

For a lighter mousse, melt chocolate in 1 tablespoon dark rum and 1 tablespoon of the cream. Chill remaining cream. After adding whipped egg white to chocolate mixture, whip chilled cream. Fold into chocolate and egg white mixture.

Pots de Crème

The traditional pots de crème must be cooked with great care. This is an easier version!

1 egg
1/3 cup chocolate chips
1/2 teaspoon vanilla extract, or
   1 to 2 teaspoons dark rum

1/4 cup milk
1/4 cup whipping cream
1 tablespoon sugar
Dash salt

Combine egg, chocolate chips and vanilla or rum in a blender. Cover and blend 15 seconds. Combine milk, whipping cream, sugar and salt in a small saucepan over medium heat. Bring to a boil, stirring frequently. Pour over chocolate mixture in blender and blend 3 minutes. Scrape sides and blend 30 more seconds. Pour into two 6-ounce soufflé pots or dessert dishes. Refrigerate overnight until firm. Makes 2 servings.

Variation

Substitute 1/2 cup half-and-half for milk and whipping cream. Add 2 tablespoons butter to saucepan to boil with half-and-half. Omit salt.

Gramma's Baked Custard

Perfection requires a little extra care and some experience.

1 egg
2 tablespoons sugar or honey
1/2 teaspoon vanilla extract

1/8 teaspoon salt
3/4 cup milk or half-and-half
Nutmeg, if desired

Put 3/4-inch-deep hot water in a 9" x 5" loaf pan. Place in oven. Preheat oven to 325°F (165°C). Lightly beat egg in a medium bowl. Blend in sugar or honey, vanilla and salt. Blend in milk or half-and-half. Pour into two 6-ounce custard cups or soufflé pots. Sprinkle with nutmeg, if desired. Place cups in hot water bath in oven. Bake 40 to 45 minutes until a knife inserted just off center comes out clean. A watery residue indicates overbaking. Cool before serving. Makes 2 servings.

Variation

For richer flavor and color, substitute 2 egg yolks for 1 egg. Increase baking time about 10 minutes.

Sundae Specials

Ice cream is delicious, nutritious and economical.

Crunchy cookie crumbs, granola, crushed
   macaroons, chopped toasted nuts or
   Toasted Coconut, page 165, as desired

Ice cream or sherbet, any flavor
Toppings, see below
Garnishes, see below

Put a spoonful of cookie crumbs, granola, crushed macaroons, nuts or coconut in a small dessert dish as desired. Top with ice cream or sherbet. Or roll scoops of ice cream in crumbs or other ingredients. Spoon topping over ice cream or sherbet and add 1 or more garnishes. Makes 1 serving.

Toppings

Hot Fudge Sauce, page 155, Melba Sauce, page 158, or any sundae sauce

Jam or fruit preserves, plain or thinned with orange-flavored liqueur, almond-flavored liqueur, rum, kirsch (cherry brandy) or other brandy

Honey, maple syrup or molasses

Garnishes

Sweetened Whipped Cream, page 149

Chopped Toasted Almonds, page 165, Toasted Walnuts, page 165, cashews, peanuts or pecans

Toasted Coconut, page 165 or Toasted Sesame Seeds, page 165

Chocolate chips, shaved chocolate or instant hot chocolate powder

Maraschino cherries, chopped candied ginger or raisins

Crushed peanut brittle, peppermint or other hard candies

Hot Fudge Sauce

For quick hot chocolate, blend 2 tablespoons of this sauce with 3/4 cup hot milk.

1/4 cup whipping cream, half-and-half or
  evaporated milk
1/4 cup sugar

1/4 cup chocolate chips
Dash salt
1/2 teaspoon vanilla extract

Combine whipping cream, half-and-half or evaporated milk with sugar, chocolate chips and salt in a small saucepan. Bring to a gentle boil over medium heat, stirring constantly. Cook 1 to 2 minutes until sauce is thickened and smooth. Stir in vanilla. Cool slightly before serving. Refrigerate leftover sauce. To reheat, add a small amount of water; simmer gently, stirring constantly until smooth. Makes 1/2 cup sauce.

Variations

Milk Chocolate Sauce: For lighter body and flavor, double the amount of liquid.
Creative Flavor Sauces: Add cinnamon or cloves before cooking. After cooking, blend in instant coffee, flavored liqueurs, dark rum, brandy, grated orange or lemon peel or bitters.

Pears Hélène

If you have a small sauce warmer, serve the sauce at the table.

2 canned pear halves or 4 quarters with syrup
1 teaspoon vanilla extract
2 large scoops vanilla ice cream

Hot Fudge Sauce, see above
Toasted Almonds, page 165,
  if desired

Combine pears and pear syrup with vanilla. Cover and refrigerate 3 to 4 hours. At serving time, arrange pears with a scoop of vanilla ice cream in each of 2 stemmed dessert dishes. Pour Hot Fudge Sauce over. Garnish with toasted almonds, if desired. Makes 2 servings.

Strawberries Chantilly *Photo on page 131.*

The strawberry-raspberry blend is superb.

1 pint fresh strawberries
1/4 cup Melba Sauce, page 158

Few drops kirsch (cherry brandy), if desired
Sweetened Whipped Cream, page 149

Hull strawberries. Wash and drain on paper towels. Mix whole berries with Melba Sauce and kirsch, if desired. Spoon into clear glass dessert dishes. Top with a small amount of Sweetened Whipped Cream. Makes 2 servings.

Perfect Baked Alaskas depend on super-cold ingredients. Freeze the scoops of ice cream and cookies or cake slices before frosting with meringue.

How To Make Individual Baked Alaskas

Assemble Baked Alaskas on boards for insulation during baking. Whip meringue until stiff, but not brittle, and spread smoothly over ice cream, attaching completely to cookie. Deep swirls and peaks will burn.

Melba Sauce, page 158, is a perfect topping for Individual Baked Alaskas made with vanilla, peach, strawberry or macadamia nut ice cream.

Individual Baked Alaskas

Do the basic preparation the day before.

2 large scoops ice cream, any flavor
2 large, round, flat crisp cookies

Meringue, see below
Topping, as desired

Meringue:
2 egg whites, fresh or frozen
1/8 teaspoon salt
1/8 teaspoon cream of tartar or
   1/2 teaspoon lemon juice

1/4 cup superfine or granulated sugar
1/2 teaspoon vanilla extract

Wash a 3/4-inch-thick, 10" x 6" plain wooden board or 2 small unfinished decoupage plaques. Place in freezer at coldest setting. Scoop ice cream onto aluminum foil. Place with cookies in freezer to harden. Before serving, preheat oven to 475°F (245°C). Prepare Meringue. Place cookies on board or plaques. Center a scoop of ice cream on each. Working quickly, spread meringue evenly and smoothly over ice cream, covering ice cream and cookies completely. At this point, freeze up to 24 hours, if desired. To bake, place board or plaques on a small baking sheet. Place in center of oven. Bake 2 to 3 minutes until meringue is golden brown. Serve immediately. Top with Hot Fudge Sauce, page 155, Melba Sauce, page 158, Cherries Jubilee sauce, page 146, crushed sweetened strawberries or a liqueur. Makes 2 servings.

Meringue:
Put egg whites in a medium bowl. Place bowl in a larger bowl of warm water to warm egg whites to about 85°F (30°C). With an electric mixer, whip until frothy. Sprinkle salt and cream of tartar or lemon juice over whites and beat at high speed to blend. Continue beating, gradually adding sugar, until meringue holds stiff peaks and sugar is dissolved. Add vanilla. Beat until blended.

Variations
Specialty Baked Alaskas: Omit crisp cookies. Place ice cream on spongecake cups for shortcake, or on 3/4-inch-thick slices of pound cake cut into 3- to 4-inch rounds, or on large brownies, bar cookies or 3/4-inch slices of jellyroll cake.
Crunchy Baked Alaskas: Roll scoops of ice cream in granola cereal, chopped peanuts or macadamia nuts, Toasted Coconut, page 165, or finely chopped Toasted Almonds or Toasted Walnuts, page 165. Or roll scoops of ice cream in crushed peppermint candies, peanut brittle or other hard candy. Freezer temperature should be colder than 0°F (-20°C) if ice cream is rolled in crushed candy.

1 teaspoon lemon juice equals 1/4 teaspoon cream of tartar in making meringues.

Melba Sauce *Photo on page 156.*

This versatile raspberry sauce will keep for ages—if it has the chance!

1 (10-oz.) pkg. frozen raspberries
1/2 cup red currant jelly
1/4 cup sugar

1 tablespoon lemon juice
1/4 teaspoon finely grated lemon peel
Dash salt

Thaw raspberries. Place in a medium saucepan. Cover and gently simmer 15 minutes. Put through a fine strainer into a glass measuring cup, pressing gently to extract as much juice as possible. Discard seeds and pulp. Add water to juice, if necessary, to make 2/3 cup. Return juice to clean pan. Add remaining ingredients. Simmer and stir until jelly melts, sugar dissolves and mixture is smooth. Pour into an airtight jar. Cool. Cover and refrigerate until ready to use. For a thicker sauce, either add more jelly or do not dilute juice from raspberries. If sauce becomes too thick, add water, bring to a boil and stir until smooth. Makes about 1-1/4 cups sauce.

Peach Melba

You deserve this easy and delicious dessert.

1 (8-oz.) can sliced peaches or 2 peach halves
    in syrup
1 teaspoon vanilla extract
2 large scoops vanilla ice cream

About 1/4 cup Melba Sauce, see above
Sweetened Whipped Cream, page 149,
    if desired

Combine peaches and peach syrup with vanilla. Cover and refrigerate 3 to 4 hours. Scoop ice cream into stemmed dessert dishes. Arrange peach slices around ice cream or press peach halves into tops of scoops. Drizzle Melba Sauce over and top with Sweetened Whipped Cream, if desired. Makes 2 servings.

Raspberry Fool

Serve this delicate dessert in stemmed glasses with slices of pound cake.

2/3 cup whipping cream
1/3 cup Melba Sauce, see above,
    more if desired

Chill whipping cream in a small bowl. Whip until stiff. Fold Melba Sauce into whipped cream until blended. Spoon into stemmed glasses. Refrigerate until serving time. If desired, drizzle additional Melba Sauce over. Makes 2 servings.

Basic Ingredients

Many of the recipes in this book call for one or another of the basic ingredients in this section. Instructions for making these useful items are included in case you don't already have your own method. You probably know how to make hard-cooked eggs, but the extra tips included here can give you better results. When you make recipes calling for chicken stock, you can use either the recipe here or make it quickly from chicken stock granules. Duxelles can add great convenience to your cooking. Roux isn't specifically called for in the recipes in this book, but you'll find it useful to have. Keep a supply of buttered breadcrumbs in your freezer so you can discover their versatility.

All of these recipes are easy to prepare ahead when you have a little extra time in the kitchen. Clean the bread scraps out of the freezer and make soft breadcrumbs or flavored croutons. Gather up the odds-and-ends of butter and turn them into clarified butter. Toast a few walnuts or almonds for an upcoming occasion. On another day you'll appreciate having these ready-to use ingredients. Master these recipes soon so you won't need to refer to them later.

Clarified Butter

A must in every kitchen as a sauce for vegetables or for frying in butter without burning.

Any quantity of butter, salted or unsalted

Melt butter in a heavy saucepan over medium-low heat. The butter will separate into 3 parts: a watery layer on the bottom, a large amount of butter oil in the middle, and a white protein layer on top. Boil the butter until the watery portion evaporates and the white fluffy portion becomes granulated. Do not brown the oil or protein portion. Using a fine mesh tea strainer or a sieve lined with 4 layers of cheesecloth, strain oil into a jar or crock that can be sealed. If any water remains in the bottom of the pan, boil it off before straining. Cool clarified butter. Cover and refrigerate. Store several weeks in the refrigerator or freeze for long storage. One-half pound butter (2 sticks) makes about 3/4 cup clarified butter.

Note:
If butter overheats and turns amber, store it as clarified butter, but use it to make Buttered Breadcrumbs, page 164, or Noodles Polonaise, page 104. It can be used in various vegetable and noodle dishes or whenever browned butter is used.

Roux

Here's a shortcut thickening for cream soups and all sorts of sauces!

1/2 cup butter (1 stick)
1/2 cup flour

Melt butter in a small saucepan over medium-low heat. Boil until most of the moisture evaporates. Do not brown. Stir flour into butter. Blend well. Cook and stir until flour becomes frothy. Cook over low heat about 1 minute without browning. If flour or butter browns, use only in brown sauces and gravies. Cool to room temperature. Stir to mix evenly. Put equal amounts in 8 small containers, such as ice cube molds or plastic cups with lids. Chill until firm. Store individual portions in a plastic bag and freeze. Makes 8 portions.

ROUX makes:
White Sauce: Heat 1/2 cup stock, milk or half-and-half in a small saucepan. Add 1 portion Roux. Cook and stir over low heat until thickened and smooth. Add 1/8 teaspoon salt, dash ground red pepper and a few drops Worcestershire sauce. Use as base for creamed eggs, tuna, chicken, chipped beef, turkey, peas and potatoes and other creamed dishes. Makes sauce for 1 main dish serving.
Cheese Sauce: Prepare White Sauce, see above. Add 1/4 cup shredded, aged sharp Cheddar cheese. Cook and stir over low heat until thickened and smooth.
Cream Soups: Heat 1/2 cup milk or half-and-half in a small saucepan over low heat. Add 1 portion Roux. Cook and stir until thickened and smooth. Blend in about 1/2 cup finely chopped cooked vegetables such as celery, carrots, cauliflower, broccoli, asparagus or peas. Blend in 1/4 to 1/2 cup chicken stock or liquid from cooked vegetables. Season to taste with salt, pepper, herbs and spices.

Hard-Cooked Eggs

If you think hard-cooking an egg is as easy as boiling water—read on!

Eggs   **1 teaspoon salt, if desired**
Water   **Ice**

With a push-pin, puncture large end of each egg. Place eggs in a saucepan. Add water to cover by 1/2 to 1 inch. Add salt, if desired; it may make eggs easier to peel. Bring to a boil. Cover and reduce heat. Cook just below a simmer 15 minutes. Immediately drain hot water from pan. Fill pan with cold water and ice to retard discoloration of yolk. Refrigerate eggs in the shell, or peeled and covered with cold water. To peel a hard-cooked egg, crack shell all over. Start peeling from large end, letting cold water run under shell to release it. To stop discoloration of cooked yolk, store yolks and whites separately. Use within 1 week.

Variation

Soft-Cooked Eggs: Bring water to a boil. Add punctured eggs and immediately reduce heat to maintain a bare simmer. Cook eggs 3 to 5 minutes depending on softness desired.

Duxelles

A little time spent now will give you fresh cooked mushroom flavor for months to come.

1 lb. raw whole mushrooms or stems
1/4 cup butter (1/2 stick)
2 tablespoons oil
1/4 cup minced shallots or green onions

Salt and pepper to taste
1/4 cup dry sherry
1/4 cup beef stock, if desired

Wash mushrooms by rolling between palms under running water. Dry on paper towels. Finely chop. Squeeze juice from mushrooms by placing a handful at a time in the center of a tea towel or a square of muslin and wringing out into a bowl. Freeze juice for use in sauces and soups, if desired. Heat butter and oil in a large stainless steel, enamel or nonstick skillet over medium-high heat. Add mushrooms and shallots or green onions. Sauté 6 to 8 minutes, stirring frequently, until the mixture looks crumbly. Season mildly with salt and pepper. Add sherry and beef stock, if desired. Cook until liquid is boiled off. The mushroom pieces should be crumbly. Cool. Pack into several small tightly sealed jars or crocks. Store several weeks in the refrigerator or several months in the freezer. Makes about 1-1/2 cups.

DUXELLES MAKE: Flavoring for crepe fillings, omelet fillings, creamed vegetables, spinach, rice, dressing, hot appetizers or quiche; substitute for other forms of mushrooms as shown on page 7.

How To Make Duxelles

Misshapen and less than fresh mushrooms are a good buy and perfect for duxelles. Use a square of muslin cloth or a sturdy kitchen towel to wring the juice from each handful of chopped mushrooms.

Either shallots, in background, or green onions can be used in duxelles. Store duxelles in several small air-tight containers in the refrigerator or freezer.

Plain Croutons

Add a crisp touch to a meal.

Yeast bread slices or rolls

Preheat oven to 250°F (120°C) for unbrowned croutons or 350°F (175°C) for golden brown croutons. Cut bread or rolls into uniform 1/2- to 1-inch cubes. Spread in a single layer on a shallow baking sheet. Place in oven. Stir once or twice during baking. Baking times vary with different breads. Generally, bake 1-inch bread cubes about 30 minutes at 250°F (120°C) for unbrowned croutons, or 15 minutes at 350°F (175°C) for golden brown croutons. Croutons should be crisp and dry throughout. Test doneness by cutting a crouton in half. One bread slice makes about 3/4 cup croutons.

Chicken Stock

Don't miss the chance to have homemade chicken stock or chicken soup.

1 lb. chicken bones, skin and meat, not including liver	1 (1/2-inch) slice turnip, if desired
About 1 quart cold water	1/4 teaspoon mixed herbs such as chervil, tarragon and thyme
1 small onion, chopped	1/2 bay leaf
1 small carrot, peeled and sliced	2 whole cloves
3 leafy top sections of celery stalks, chopped	4 peppercorns
3 or 4 parsley stems	1/2 teaspoon salt, more as needed

Weigh chicken bones, skin and meat; increase other ingredients proportionately. Break up chicken bones as much as possible. Place in a large pot or Dutch oven. Add cold water to cover. Bring to a boil over medium heat. Reduce to a slow simmer. Skim off white protein froth. Add onion, carrot, celery, parsley stems and turnip, if desired. Return to a boil. Skim again. Add remaining ingredients. Cover and reduce to a slow simmer. Cook at least 2 hours, or longer if very low heat can be maintained. Skim off protein froth occasionally. Add water as necessary to keep bones and meat covered. After cooking, ladle stock through a fine strainer or colander into a bowl or pan. Pick meat from bones for use in soup, crepes, omelets, salads, sandwiches or creamed chicken. To freeze meat, pack in freezer containers and cover with stock. Discard bones, skin and vegetables. Return stock to pot. Simmer uncovered until chicken flavors concentrate to desired taste. Add salt as needed. Refrigerate stock to solidify fat on top. Remove fat layer; discard or save for use in chicken soups and sauces. Warm stock to liquefy. Pour into wide-mouth 1- to 2-cup freezer containers or plastic ice cube trays and freeze. Store frozen cubes in a plastic bag. Makes 2 to 3 cups stock.

Variation

Substitute turkey or beef for chicken.

Flavored Croutons

These are especially good in salads or as a garnish for savory casseroles.

1 slice yeast bread or 1 small roll
1 tablespoon oil
1 to 2 teaspoons grated Parmesan cheese

Seasoned salt, ground herbs, curry powder,
   chili powder, onion salt, garlic salt
   or other seasoning blends to taste

Preheat oven to 350°F (175°C). Cut bread or roll into uniform 1/2- to 3/4-inch cubes. In a small bowl, toss cubes with oil. Spread cubes in a single layer on a shallow baking sheet. Place in oven; stir once or twice during baking. Baking times vary with different breads. Generally, bake croutons about 10 minutes until golden brown and crisp throughout. Cut a crouton in half to check doneness. Combine Parmesan cheese and seasonings in a small bowl or small paper bag. Toss with hot croutons. Makes about 3/4 cup croutons, enough for 2 servings tossed salad.

Variation

Pan-Fried Buttered Croutons. Substitute 1 tablespoon butter for oil. Melt butter in a medium skillet over medium heat until frothy. Add bread cubes. Sauté and stir until golden brown and crisp.

How To Make Chicken Stock

Pull skin from chicken breast halves and use your thumb to separate meat from ribs and breast bone. Wrap breast halves separately in foil for freezing. Use bones, skin and other parts to make chicken stock.

Protein from the meat juices forms a froth on the simmering stock. For clearer stock, skim it off as it appears.

Soft Breadcrumbs

A great way to turn unwanted bread scraps into a useful ingredient.

**Yeast bread slices or rolls,
  without added flavorings**

Tear 1 small roll or 1 slice of bread at a time into a blender. Cover. Turn blender on and off repeatedly until bread is torn into light, uniform crumbs. Or put bread on a cutting board and use fork tines to tear off crumbs. Put into a plastic bag and toss to mix. Press air from bag, close with a twist tie and freeze. One (1-oz.) bread slice makes about 1/2 cup lightly packed crumbs.

Variation

Dry Breadcrumbs: Preheat oven to 250°F (120°C). Spread soft breadcrumbs in a thin layer on a shallow baking sheet. Dry in oven 30 minutes. Cool. Spread out in an open plastic bag and crush with a rolling pin. One-half cup lightly packed soft breadcrumbs makes about 3 tablespoons fine dry breadcrumbs.

SOFT BREADCRUMBS make: Buttered Breadcrumbs, see below; filler for ground meat mixtures such as Basic Ground Beef Mix, page 72; Bread stuffings, pages 107 to 108; and other recipes in this book.

Buttered Breadcrumbs

For extra-rich buttered breadcrumbs, double the amount of butter.

1 tablespoon butter
**1/2 cup Soft Breadcrumbs, see above,
  lightly packed**

Melt butter in a small skillet over medium-low heat. As soon as butter is melted and frothy, stir in breadcrumbs. Continue stirring until crumbs are evenly crisp and golden brown. Makes about 6 tablespoons.

Variation

Seasoned Buttered Breadcrumbs: Add to finished Buttered Breadcrumbs to taste, grated Parmesan cheese, minced parsley, minced Toasted Walnuts, Toasted Almonds or Toasted Sesame Seeds, page 165, chili powder or curry powder, herbs, salt and pepper.

BUTTERED BREADCRUMBS make: Toppings for casseroles and au gratin dishes; garnish for meats, vegetables, hors d'oeuvres; and other recipes in this book.

Toasted Walnuts

A delectable tender-crisp ingredient for salads, hors d'oeuvres and baked goods.

2 cups water
1/2 cup walnut pieces

Preheat oven to 325°F (165°C). Bring 2 cups water to a full boil in a small saucepan. Add walnuts. Boil 3 minutes. Drain; dry on paper towels. Spread evenly on a shallow baking sheet. Bake about 15 minutes, stirring 1 or 2 times, until crisp and golden. Cool. Refrigerate in an airtight container. Makes 1/2 cup.

Toasted Almonds

You'll be putting these on almost everything!

1/2 cup sliced, slivered or chopped almonds

Preheat oven to 325°F (165°C). Spread almonds on a shallow baking sheet. Bake 8 to 12 minutes, stirring 1 or 2 times, until almonds begin to turn color. Almonds will continue to brown after removing from oven. Cool. Refrigerate or freeze in an airtight container or plastic bag. Makes 1/2 cup.

Toasted Coconut

A great garnish to have in the freezer.

Shredded or flaked coconut

Preheat oven to 350°F (175°C). Spread a thin layer of coconut on a shallow baking sheet. Bake about 8 minutes, stirring 1 or 2 times, until golden brown. Coconut will darken slightly after removing from oven. Cool. Refrigerate or freeze in an airtight container.

Toasted Sesame Seeds: *Preheat oven to 350°F (175°C). Spread sesame seeds evenly on a shallow baking sheet. Bake about 10 minutes, stirring 1 or 2 times, until golden brown. Cool. Store in an airtight container.*

Equipping Your Kitchen

You can spend a small fortune equipping a kitchen, even if you cook for only 1 or 2 people. Stores are full of exciting and beautiful kitchenware that promises to produce romantic gourmet dinners. The temptation to buy is high, but restrain yourself. Here are some guidelines to help you select the best equipment for a kitchen you'll use and love:

Buy only what you need and will use. This means fewer things to clean, repair and move, and you'll use less storage space.

Buy good quality equipment. Unless you're in a temporary situation, don't handicap yourself with equipment that will get out of shape, is difficult to clean, or has poor heat distribution. Buy a few good things and enjoy them longer.

Buy small-capacity equipment. Small saucepans and skillets will eliminate a lot of burning. Small baking pans will give better results for small batches. Small mixing bowls cut down mixing time.

Buy basic equipment first. The basic pans, bowls and tools you'll use over and over should be the foundation to which you can add special items. It's really nice to have a copper bowl for beating egg whites and a wooden bowl with years of garlic rubbed into it for salads. But you'll find a set of all-purpose glass, crockery or stainless steel mixing bowls are ideal for years of daily use.

Buy multipurpose equipment. Look for appliances, pans and tools you can use several ways. A small enameled iron pot in a color that coordinates with your dinnerware can be used on the range top, in the oven or under the broiler, or even placed on a trivet at the table as a serving dish.

LARGE APPLIANCES

I assume most singles and couples have a range with oven and broiler. Choose the largest refrigerator you can accommodate, with the largest proportion of freezer space.

A microwave oven is a marvelous appliance for small and busy households. It not only cooks many foods from scratch, but it's at its best reheating refrigerated or frozen foods. As you buy equipment, keep the requirements of a microwave in mind. Choose glass and ceramic utensils and dinnerware without metal trim.

SMALL APPLIANCES

Housewares departments are full of small electric appliances tailored to the needs and lifestyles of singles and couples. Choose just the ones that will earn their space in your kitchen.

A blender is my favorite multipurpose appliance. It chops, crumbs, purees and even makes exotic drinks. A toaster-oven can do most of the baking for 1 or 2 more economically than a full oven. Because of the top heat it produces, some foods come out looking better than from a big oven.

Many small families can use a full-size electric skillet. If you buy one, select a versatile style that will look good on your table so you can prepare Steak Diane or other dishes at the table. If you love deep-fried foods, get a small deep-fryer. Don't overlook slow cookers, broilers, grills and other miniature appliances.

You may want to add a 24-hour timer to your collection. It can switch on the coffeepot or start your dinner when you're not there.

STORING EQUIPMENT AND SUPPLIES

Stacks of small kitchen items next to stacks of other little items can make it nearly impossible to find what you want, much less get to it. Portable slide-out shelves, plastic turntables, portable half shelves, spice racks and cup hooks are a great help in making kitchen equipment more accessible.

As much as possible, store together those things that are used together. Keep flour, sugar and similar staples with the baking pans, mixing bowls, measuring equipment and mixing tools. Keep the potholders, broiler pan, skillet, pancake turners and other range-cooking tools near the range. Saucepans, cleaning equipment, beverage-making equipment, knives and cutting boards are most convenient near the sink. Dinnerware should be stored near the serving table or next to the dishwashing area. The items you use most often should be stored in the most convenient spots.

The variety of equipment available for your kitchen seems almost endless. The pieces shown here and elsewhere in this book have been chosen because they are especially useful for small-quantity cooking. Several types and sizes of many items, such as mortars and pestles, are shown for your information. You really won't need two. The basic equipment list includes what you will need to start. Add other items to suit your tastes and needs. For measuring, I recommend glass liquid measures and stainless steel cups and spoons with both standard and metric measures. A coffee measure or a pony measure from the bar are ideal for making 1 ounce, 2 tablespoon or 1/8 cup measurements. Your baking and cooking equipment should include custard cups, soufflé pots and au gratin dishes in any of the sizes shown here. A French chef's knife, wire whisk and an adjustable manual slicer are also useful. The hot water dispenser here isn't a necessity, but it is handy any time you need a small amount of boiling water.

Equipping Your Kitchen

ESSENTIAL	USEFUL
TO MEASURE:	
Measuring spoons, nested measuring cups, 1-cup glass measure, 60-minute timer, oven thermometer, 12-inch ruler, coffee measure.	1-quart glass measure, 1-lb. (450 gram) scale, refrigerator-freezer thermometer.
Buy utensils with both metric and standard measures. Include 1/8 teaspoon and 1/2 tablespoon measures for halving recipes. Metal measuring cups with long handles are handy for melting butter. Use a straight-edge spatula or knife for leveling dry ingredients in measuring cups and spoons. A glass measuring cup can also be a mix-and-pour container. A coffee measure equals 1 ounce, 2 tablespoons or 1/8 cup.	
FOOD PREPARATION:	
Thin utility knife; serrated slicing knife, shredder-grater, vegetable peeler, juicer, large and small strainers, cutting board, can opener, pepper grinder, kitchen shears, electric blender, knife sharpener, vegetable brush.	Mortar & pestle, garlic press, ice cream scoop, salad spinner, grapefruit knife, ice crusher, French chef's knife, adjustable manual slicer.
A 4-sided shredder-grater with 2 shredding sizes and 2 grating sizes is the most useful. A plastic cutting board also works as a pastry board and does not retain flavors. A large strainer can double as a colander and a flour sifter. Crush leaf herbs, seeds and whole spices with a mortar and pestle. Salad greens dry quickly in a salad spinner. Manual slicer makes fast, uniform slices from potatoes, zucchini, cucumber and similar vegetables.	
MIXING & HANDLING:	
Rubber spatula, wire whip, stainless steel spoons and forks, tongs, wooden spoons, nested mixing bowls, electric hand mixer, pastry brush, pancake turner, ladle, cooking fork, slotted cooking spoon.	Funnel with wide and narrow spouts, flour sifter, 2-inch biscuit cutter, rolling pin.
Glass, crockery or stainless steel mixing bowls work best. A 6-oz. juice can with ends removed works as a 2-inch biscuit cutter.	
STOVE-TOP TOOLS:	
1-quart saucepan, 2- or 2-1/2-quart saucepan, 4- to 6-quart saucepan, 8-inch slope-sided skillet, 10- to 11-inch skillet, double boiler.	Heat insulator, single-serving nonstick egg poacher, vegetable steamer rack, spatter shield, electric hot water dispenser.
All saucepans and skillets should have their own covers. Use a glass or stainless steel double boiler; aluminum discolors milk, egg and acid mixtures. You can use an egg poacher to melt butter and to warm sauces or small amounts of fillings. A heat insulator between pan and burner slows cooking and keeps small pans from tipping.	
OVEN TOOLS:	
2 (10-oz.) soufflé pots, custard cups or casseroles, 4 (5- or 6-oz.) custard cups or soufflé pots, 1-quart casserole, 9" x 5" loaf pan, 7" x 3" loaf pan, 8-inch glass pie plate, cooling rack, small baking sheet, pot holders.	2 individual au gratin dishes, 2 (2-cup) soufflé pots or casseroles, 8- or 9-inch round cake pan, 8-inch square baking pan, 2 tart pans, small broiler pan.
Use 10-oz. soufflé pots for individual main dishes, desserts or vegetables. The 5- or 6-oz. custard cups are perfect for individual desserts or warming small amounts of food.	
BEVERAGE PREPARATION:	
1- or 2-cup coffeemaker, individual teapots, bottle opener, corkscrew.	Covered pitcher, large coffeemaker, tea ball.
A coffeemaker is worth the cost; even if you don't drink coffee, your guests will.	
ITEMS TO CHECK FREQUENTLY:	
Paper towels, wax paper, plastic wrap, foil trays, string and cheesecloth.	

Setting The Scene

When it's just the two of you for dinner, or you alone, the table and the surroundings become an important part of a meal's chemistry. Interesting new tablesettings in unexpected locations can pleasantly affect the mood, stretch out the dinner hour and even improve the taste of your food.

A special table can express the desire to make this time enjoyable and leisurely. It's an easy way to tell yourself and another person how important you both are and how much you deserve this special attention. Here are a few pointers:

Watch for innovative tablesettings. The best place to get great table setting ideas for singles and couples is a good department store, particularly if it is just opening or has a storewide event going on. The furniture and china departments are filled with long lasting settings created by professional interior designers and decorators. Other ideas can be found in the food pages of magazines and newspapers, or in books on the subject.

Choose moods, colors and textures to fit your decor. Whether your surroundings are French provincial or hand-me-down, you should be able to work up several possible color schemes that will work on your table. Try something bright and informal, soft and elegant, warm and wintery, or cool and summery. Select a range of textures that will work, somewhere between satin and burlap and cut crystal and clay. Consider the size and scale of your furnishings and develop images of tablesettings for candlelight dinners, indoor picnics, patio suppers and Sunday brunches.

Search your home for pleasant dining spots. Floor plans with rooms labeled *dining room* or *breakfast room* tend to confine our thinking about where we can eat. It doesn't take a lot of space to set up 2 people for dinner. A small table and two chairs, or matching trays with a couple of pillows to sit on, are equally appropriate. Smallness makes for a more personal, warmer mood.

Each season and time of day may attract you to different places around the house. Just keep looking. Here are a few possibilities:

By the fireplace.

By any window with an interesting view.

At a coffee table, sitting on pillows.

On the patio, no matter how small.

In bed, from bed trays.

On the floor, picnic-style, surrounded by plants.

On your lawn, picnic-style.

At the breakfast bar.

In the bedroom at a small table.

On your front porch.

Once you've decided where to eat, spend some time creating a little atmosphere. Shut out harsh noises, turn on some music or hang a wind chime. Soften any glaring lights and light candles.

Don't be tied to conventional tablesetting rules. When seating two people at a small or oddly shaped table, there may not be enough room to spread out with a conventional setting. There's nothing wrong with setting the silverware above or on the plate, or with putting the napkin in the glass. If it works and it looks good, do it!

Expand your collection of dinnerware. It's much easier to afford 1 or 2 place settings of china and crystal than 8. It's also easier to find 2 place settings! Beside the regular stock in department and housewares stores, check out year-end sales, swap meets and thrift stores. You could be the natural recipient of extra pieces of family dinnerware when everyone else has children and needs 6 of everything.

If limited storage is a problem, look for multipurpose tableware. A wine or champagne cooler can double as an ice bucket for a larger party or as a vase for long-stemmed flowers. Choose cocktail icers with sections that can be used independently.

Your collection of tableware might include:

Dinnerware—2 dinner plates, 2 salad plates, 2

butter plates, 2 soup or cereal bowls, 2 sauce dishes and 2 cups and saucers or mugs.

Glassware—2 tall cold drink glasses, 2 short juice or bar glasses, 2 all-purpose wine glasses, 2 stemmed sherbet or champagne glasses and 2 after-dinner drink glasses, if desired.

Flatware—4 dinner knives, 4 dinner forks, 4 salad or dessert forks, 4 teaspoons, 4 cereal or soup spoons, 2 steak knives, 2 cocktail forks, 2 iced tea spoons, 1 meat fork, 1 tablespoon and 1 ladle.

Use napkins to add color and softness to the table. Flowers are usually used to soften the hard textures of the glass, china and metal in table settings. When fresh flowers are not practical, let cloth napkins give some of that softness. Collect pairs of napkins in a variety of colors and prints to coordinate with your table coverings and general decor. They should also coordinate with each other so you can use them together when you're entertaining a crowd. Interesting effects can be achieved by folding harmonizing napkins together.

If you are presented with a beautifully folded napkin, don't put it in your lap until you have visually mastered the fold. A standard napkin is about 17-inches square. Find 20-inch squares if you want to do any of the more complex folds.

Collect a variety of colorful easy-care table linens. A beautiful wood, marble or glass tabletop really needs no covering. But if you're improvising places to eat around your home, you'll probably want to do something special with tablecloths. A card table or round pedestal table covered to the floor looks more important. Measure the height and diameter of your table carefully before buying the cloth. A king-size sheet can be cut and hemmed to make a full-length cloth for a card table. Use placemats, runners and small round or square tablecloths over your long cloths to protect them, or use the placemats and runners by themselves.

Use your imagination in finding centerpieces. A centerpiece is not an absolute requirement on the dining table. Often just the necessities of the table provide the dominance, beauty and center of interest a centerpiece is expected to give. A wine cooler, cheese or pastry under a glass dome, a bowl of fruit or even oversized salt and pepper grinders can stand in for centerpieces.

Whether two people sit opposite each other or at adjacent sides at the table, there is always a corner or side that can display the centerpiece wihout it being in the way. The size is limited only by the size of the table and general scale. When one side of the table is against a wall, the centerpiece can tie in with a picture or wall hanging.

A shallow glass bowl is a good basic centerpiece holder. It can be used to float flowers or candles, to hold a fruit arrangement or to make a sophisticated arrangement of long-stemmed flowers. But containers for centerpieces can be found in many places in and around the house. Possibilities include interesting bottles, baskets, shells, copper or enamel cooking pans, teapots, soufflé pots, stemmed glasses, clay pots, wooden bowls and pitchers.

Many items can be used as centerpieces. Besides lovely and perishable fresh flowers, look for some more durable possibilities to pull out at a moment's notice. How about dried, paper or cloth flowers, potted plants, dried weeds and seeds, real or artificial fruits and vegetables, leaves, candles, sea shells, rocks or sculptures? Use your imagination.

Keep your eyes open to the possibilities for beautiful or amusing or charming scenes for eating alone or alone together. Ideas may pop into your mind when you're in the last-minute panic trying to pull a dinner together or when you're taking a shower. Be constantly open for inspiration!

In Appreciation

There are many who warrant my appreciation for their contribution to the creation of this book. My friends, relatives and students shared their ideas, tried my recipes, and encouraged, supported and sympathized with me throughout. I have relied on the expertise of food companies, advisory boards and government agencies for the information necessary to make this book as useful as I can. My thanks go to Elizabeth Pierce and Judy Masters for their invaluable editorial assistance, and to Carol Taylor and Nora Baer for their capable hands, both in front of and behind the camera. For his ability to spot a misused or misspelled word, I am grateful to my friend Gordy Weir. And special commendation must go to Diana Rattan for her typing, and to Debbie Broach for her cooking. My thanks to all!!

Barbara Swain

How To Enjoy Eating Alone

For those of us who deal with the masses all day, dinner alone can be a treasured time of relaxation. But for some of us, it is a lonely time spent devouring too much of too many wrong foods. Here are ways to help make those mealtimes a joy.

When you shop, pick out some special foods to ration out to yourself during the week. Include an exotic fruit, hors d'oeuvres you've always wanted to try, and a goodie or two.

Keep some healthful snacks on hand such as cheese, fruit, wheat crackers and fresh vegetables, to nibble on while you prepare your dinner. Satisfying your immediate hunger will help you finish cooking dinner before you start picking at it. It is important to sit down to your complete meal.

Hold a dress rehearsal for a dinner you plan to give a friend later. Set up your dinner table in a new location, test out your menu, including a new recipe or two, plan your garnishes and plan the table setting and centerpiece.

Use your cooking-alone time to develop your cooking skills and try risky new recipes.

Once in a while, prepare those healthful foods you probably wouldn't serve to company, like liver and kale.

THINGS TO DO WHILE YOU'RE EATING

Use your eating-alone time to develop your sense of taste and awareness of food. Savor every bite! You'll be eating less and enjoying it more.

Make plans for the future. In particular, make plans for things you want to do after you eat, even if it is just to go shopping, work on a project, attend a lecture or see a movie. Brainstorm a problem, plan your vacation or just work out tomorrow's schedule.

Watch television. Plan your cooking and eating time to coincide with favorite shows.

Read the paper, a book, the mail, a catalog or the latest magazine. Do the crossword puzzle.

Telephone a single friend for a little mutual dinnertime conversation.

Listen to language records or favorite music.

PLAN SOME SPECIAL TIMES

If there is one day or evening of the week that seems too quiet, always have something planned for that time such as:

Join a club or take a class and get together with some of the others for dinner before or after.

Buy season tickets with a friend to a musical, theatrical or sports event for that evening. Or get two series tickets and invite different friends.

Start a bridge or poker group.

Plan some self-improvement nights—fix up your wardrobe or do some personal grooming projects.

If you're bothered by loneliness during a particular time of the year, pick that time to take a cruise, go to a spa or take a tour with a group. Or use the time to catch up on all your entertaining. Have dinner guests or invite friends from out-of-town for the weekend.

ANOTHER SOLUTION: DON'T EAT ALONE

Invite another single person to dinner. Maybe you can work out a regular exchange.

Allow some couple an evening alone together by inviting their children or live-in relative for dinner.

Join a club that has an eating facility and eat there occasionally.

Find a good local coffeeshop and eat there enough to get to know the people.

Develop a list of restaurants you'd like to try. Know what dishes you would like to order before you go. Go to dinner alone and learn all you can.

Index

Index

Index

8.47892103